A WORLD BANK COUNTRY STUDY

Egypt
Alleviating Poverty during Structural Adjustment

The World Bank
Washington, D.C.

Copyright © 1991
The International Bank for Reconstruction
and Development/THE WORLD BANK
1818 H Street, N.W.
Washington, D.C. 20433, U.S.A.

All rights reserved
Manufactured in the United States of America
First printing July 1991

World Bank Country Studies are among the many reports originally prepared for internal use as part of the continuing analysis by the Bank of the economic and related conditions of its developing member countries and of its dialogues with the governments. Some of the reports are published in this series with the least possible delay for the use of governments and the academic, business and financial, and development communities. The typescript of this paper therefore has not been prepared in accordance with the procedures appropriate to formal printed texts, and the World Bank accepts no responsibility for errors.

The World Bank does not guarantee the accuracy of the data included in this publication and accepts no responsibility whatsoever for any consequence of their use. Any maps that accompany the text have been prepared solely for the convenience of readers; the designations and presentation of material in them do not imply the expression of any opinion whatsoever on the part of the World Bank, its affiliates, or its Board or member countries concerning the legal status of any country, territory, city, or area or of the authorities thereof or concerning the delimitation of its boundaries or its national affiliation.

The material in this publication is copyrighted. Requests for permission to reproduce portions of it should be sent to Director, Publications Department, at the address shown in the copyright notice above. The World Bank encourages dissemination of its work and will normally give permission promptly and, when the reproduction is for noncommercial purposes, without asking a fee. Permission to photocopy portions for classroom use is not required, though notification of such use having been made will be appreciated.

The complete backlist of publications from the World Bank is shown in the annual *Index of Publications*, which contains an alphabetical title list (with full ordering information) and indexes of subjects, authors, and countries and regions. The latest edition is available free of charge from the Publications Sales Unit, Department F, The World Bank, 1818 H Street, N.W., Washington, D.C. 20433, U.S.A., or from Publications, The World Bank, 66, avenue d'Iéna, 75116 Paris, France.

ISSN: 0253-2123

Library of Congress Cataloging-in-Publication Data

Egypt : alleviating poverty during structural adjustment.
    p. cm. — (A World Bank country study)
  Includes bibliographical references.
  ISBN 0-8213-1873-X
  1. Poor—Egypt. 2. Public welfare—Egypt. 3. Egypt—Economic conditions—1952- 4. Economic assistance—Egypt. 5. World Bank.
I. International Bank for Reconstruction and Development.
II. Series.
HC830.Z9P64 1991
362.5'8'0962—dc20
                                                    91-14785
                                                      CIP

CURRENCY EQUIVALENTS

Currency Unit = Egyptian Pounds (LE)
US$1.00 = LE 2.61

Abbreviations and Acronyms

CAPMAS	:	Central Authority for Public Mobilization and Statistics (Central Government's Bureau of Statistics)
CDA	:	Community Development Association
CPI	:	Consumer Price Index
GASC	:	General Agency for the Supply of Commodities
HBS	:	Household Budget Survey
LE	:	Egyptian Pound
MOE	:	Ministry of Education
MOF	:	Ministry of Finance
MOH	:	Ministry of Health
MOHE	:	Ministry of Higher Education
MOL	:	Ministry of Labor
MOSA	:	Ministry of Social Affairs
NGO	:	Non Governmental Organizations
PFP	:	Productive Families Program
SME	:	Small and Medium-Sized Enterprises

FOREWORD

The World Bank has placed high priority on the alleviation of poverty. Indeed, through the years, this concern has permeated the Bank's analysis and lending. In order to reaffirm this priority and complement the poverty alleviation initiatives which the Bank has supported in different parts of the globe, the Bank's 1990 <u>World Development Report</u> was devoted to the issue of poverty. It sought to identify the poor: their numbers and location. It then explored means of addressing the problem, through policy and programs. Its themes included increasing the participation of the poor in economic growth by increasing their access to productive employment and enhancing their human capital, principally through social investment in health and education.

At the same time that the Bank was reaffirming its global commitment to the alleviation of poverty, the Government of Egypt began to develop a comprehensive macroeconomic reform program. The Bank in consultation with the Egyptian Government noted the need to carefully monitor this program, not only to mitigate its adverse short-term social impacts on the poor, but as important, to ensure that the poor would benefit most once the reforms took hold and the country resumed a path of sustained economic growth. There is a need to institute processes that would enhance the poor's human capital and facilitate their increased participation in productive economic activities. In order to understand the dimensions of poverty problems in Egypt as a first step towards their resolution, the Bank undertook this study. The study uses the format of the 1990 <u>World Development Report</u> as its guide, and addresses similar questions. It presents analytical work on the social dimensions of adjustment and possible poverty reduction measures in keeping with the priorities of the macroeconomic reform program. Its intention is to shed light on poverty issues in the context of structural adjustment, and to contribute to the discussion of poverty and its reduction in Egypt. As such, the study exemplifies the World Bank commitment to reducing poverty as an integral part of its overall development strategy.

W. A. Wapenhans
Vice President, EMENA Region

Acknowledgements

This report is based on the findings of a mission that visited Egypt in October-November 1989. The study was carried out under the direction of Mr. Jamil Salmi, who has prepared this report with Messrs./Mmes. Van Adams (Labor Market and Employment), Susan Joekes (Social Programs), Eileen Kennedy (Food Policy), Jorge Martinez (Transfers and Taxation) and Jean Puyet (Health). The final text and graphs were prepared by Ms. Conchita Castillo.

TABLE OF CONTENT

	Page Number
Executive Summary	xiii
I. Introduction	1
Background	1
Objectives and Scope of the Study	2
Conceptual and Methodological Framework	3
Data Availability	4
Organization of the Report	4
II. The Dimensions of Poverty	5
Introduction: Economic Growth and Persistence of Poverty	5
Incidence of Poverty	6
Characteristics of the Poor	9
Demographic Characteristics	9
Spatial Distribution	11
Employment Characteristics	13
Poverty and Basic Needs Satisfaction	19
Malnutrition	19
Health	24
Access to Safe Water and Sanitation	28
Shelter	30
Education	33
Conclusion: Poverty Matrix for Egypt	37
III. The Roots of Poverty	38
Introduction: Evolution of Income Distribution	38
Assets and Poverty	40
Employment and Poverty	43
The Employment Challenge	43
Trends in Wages	46
Government Labor Market Policies	48
Income Transfers	54
Food Subsidies	54
Other Subsidies	58
Direct Transfers	61
Social Security	66

Table of Contents (cont'd)   **Page Number**

III. The Roots of Poverty (cont'd)

    Social Services for Human Capital Formation 71
        Health 71
        Education 75
        Population Pressure 79
    Taxation 80
        The Distribution of Income Before Taxes 81
        Tax Sources in Egypt 84
        The Incidence of Indirect Taxes 85
        The Incidence of Direct Taxes 87
        Summary of Findings 89
    Conclusion: The Limits of the Egyptian Welfare State 89

IV. From Economic Crisis to Reform:
    Assessing the Social Costs of Adjustment 91
        Introduction: From Recession to Adjustment 91
        Impacts on Producers 94
            Employment Effects 94
            Agricultural Prices and Farmers 102
        Impacts on Consumers 103
            Food Products 103
            Other Goods and Services 108
        Incidence of New Tax Measures 109
        Social Security Benefits 110
        Provision of Social Services 111
        Conclusion: Adequacy of the Existing Safety Net? 118

V. Toward a Poverty Alleviation Strategy 121
        Introduction: Presentation of the Overall Strategy . . . 121
        Income Generation Policies 125
            Employment Promotion Policies 125
            Access to Productive Assets 132
        Human Capital Maintenance 134
            Health 135
            Education 138
            Retraining Assistance 139
        Income Transfers and Price Subsidies 140
            Food Subsidies 140
            Utilities, Transport, Energy and Housing. 143
            Social Welfare 145
            Unemployment Benefits 147
            Early Retirement Options 149
            Social Security 149
    Protecting the Poor during Adjustment:
    The Emergency Social Fund 150
    Budgetary Implications of the Poverty Strategy 151
    Role of the Bank 151

Table of Contents (cont'd)

Page Number

Annexes 153

Annex A: General Data on Egypt 153
    Table A1 - Economic and Social Development Indicators for Egypt. 155
    Table A2 - Incidence of Poverty in Selected Countries. 156
    Table A3 - Degree of Income Inequality in Selected Countries . . 157
    Table A4 - The Need for Adjustment in Egypt 158
    Table A5 - Consumer Price Index in Cairo During 1989 158

Annex B: Statistical Tables on Poverty and Income Distribution . . . 159
    Table B1 - Expenditure Levels of the Poor and the Non-Poor . . . 161
    Table B2 - Age Structure of the Rural Poor in 1977 161
    Table B3 - Income Differentials Between Rural and Urban Areas. . 162
    Table B4 - Incidence of Poverty by Governorates 163
    Table B5 - Distribution of the Poor by Occupational Activity
           of Households Head 164
    Table B6 - Distribution of the Poor by Economic Activity 164
    Table B7 - Relative Incidence of Poverty by Economic
           Activity of Household Head 165
    Table B8 - Average Household Income by Occupation Rural
           Household Head 165
    Table B9 - Distribution of Household Expenditures 166
    Table B10 - Distribution of Assets in Rural Areas in 1977 . . . 166
    Table B11 - Distribution of Expenditures by Socioeconomic Origin. 167

Annex C: Demographic Data 169
    Table C1 - Social Composition of Households, Cairo, 1980 170
    Table C2 - Population and Labor Force Activity: 1976-1986 . . . 171
    Table C3 - Population and Labor Force Activity by Sex for
           Rural and Urban Areas: Egypt 1976-1986. 172

Annex D: Data on Employment and Wages 173
    Table D1 - Distribution of the Labor Force by Occupation
           of Household Head 175
    Table D2 - Size of the Total Labor Force Age 6 and Older 175
    Table D3 - Employment by Sector of Economic Activity:
           1976 and 1986 176
    Table D4 - Employment by Type of Employer: 1976 and 1986 176
    Table D5 - Real Wage Trends by Sector (1973-100) 177

Table of Contents (cont'd)

Page Number

Table D6 - Real Wage Trends by Economic Sector	178
Table D7 - Unemployment by Education Level (1986)	178
Table D8 - Open Unemployment Rates for Men and Women in Urban and Rural Areas: 1976-1986	179

Annex E: Nutrition Data ... 181

Table E1 - Average Per Capita Food Supply of Egypt	182
Table E2 - Daily Calorie Supply Per Capita For Selected Countries of the Region	182
Table E3 - Mean HB Values and Prevalence of Anaemia Among Mothers of Different Physiological Status	183
Table E4 - The Quantity and Value for the Rationed Supplies for Individual in Ration Card (1984-1989)	184
Table E5 - Income Transfers from Food Subsidies and Distorted Prices by Employment Groups	185
Table E6 - Ratio of Area Planned by Crop to Total Area (By Farm Size, 1976)	186
Table E7 - Source of Cereals for Households of Varying Farm Sizes	187

Annex F: Data on Health ... 189

Table F1 - Evolution of Infant and Child Mortality (No. of Deaths per Thousand)	190
Table F2 - Infant and Child Mortality Rates by Governorates	191
Table F3 - Bilharzia Control Program	192
Table F4 - The Rural Primary Health Care Network (1989)	193
Table F5 - The Urban Primary Health Care Network (1989)	194
Table F6 - Expanded Program of Immunization	195
Table F7 - The Hospital Network	196
Table F8 - Other Providers of Secondary Level Medical Care	197
Table F9 - Degree of Utilization of Health Services	198
Table F10 - Functional Distribution of MOH Personnel	199
Table F11 - Infant and Child Mortality by Cause of Death (1982)	200

Annex G: Data on Housing and Water Supply ... 201

Table G1 - Dwellings by Source of Water in 1986	203
Table G2 - Distribution of Housing Units by Type	203
Table G3 - Distribution of Housing Units by Type	204
Table G4 - Housing Deficit	204

Annex H: Statistics on Education ... 205

Table H1 - Growth of Education Enrollments	207
Table H2 - Illiteracy in Egypt (% of Population Age 10 and Above)	207
Table H3 - Sex Disparities in Primary Schooling	208
Table H4 - Evolution of the Non-Schooled Population (Age 6-11)	209

Table of Contents (cont'd)

	Page Number
Annex I: Data on Social Security and Taxation	211
Table I1 - Organization of the Egyptian Social Security System	212
Table I2 - Numbers of Health Insurance Beneficiaries 1977-1987	214
Table I3 - Total Number of Insured in Social Insurance Schemes	214
Table I4 - Total Social Insurance Earnings and Expenditures (1984-1989)	215
Table I5 - Earnings by Social Insurance System	216
Table I6 - Expenditures by Social Insurance System	216
Table I7 - Composition of Egyptian Tax Revenue (1980/81 to 1986/87)	217
Annex J: Social Sectors Budget Data	219
Table J1 - Functional Distribution	220
Table J2 - Distribution of Expenditures by Level of Education	220
Table J3 - Proportional Distribution of Resources Between Level and Types of Education (1987/88)	221
Table J4 - Expenditures on Subsidies and Supplies	222
Table J5 - Share of Expenditures in GDP	222
Table J6 - Social Expenditures in Government Budget	223
Table J7 - Total Expenditures per Capita/per Student in 1980	223
Table J8 - Social Expenditures: Health	224
Table J9 - Social Expenditures: Social Affairs	224
Table J10 - Social Expenditures: Education	225
Table J11 - Social Expenditures: Higher Education	225
Table J12 - Recurrent Budget Expenditures (Education)	226
Table J13 - Recurrent Budget Expenditures (Health)	227
Table J14 - Recurrent Budget Expenditures (Higher Education and Science)	228
Table J15 - Recurrent Budget Expenditures (Social Affairs and Insurance)	229
Table J16 - Functional Distribution of MOH Investment Budget	230
Annex K - Calculation of an Ultra-Poverty Line	231
Annex L - Methodological Note on the Calculation of Educational Expenditures Among Various Groups	235
Bibliographical References	238

EXECUTIVE SUMMARY

Introduction

1. After almost a decade of rapid economic growth following the start of President Sadat's open door policy in 1974, Egypt is now experiencing a recession which has had adverse social consequences in terms of employment and standards of living. The growing budget deficit and the rising cost of external debts have placed new pressures on government expenditures in an economy characterized by a predominant public sector. The outcome has been a marked decline in the level of job creation in the public sector, a pattern of wage compression for civil service employees, diminishing public resources for the social sectors, and cutbacks in the food ration and subsidy system. The slowdown of investment and output in the private sector has had similar negative employment and income effects. Since the beginning of the recession in 1986, open unemployment, largely among youths, has risen rapidly, real wages have fallen in most economic sectors, and there are indications that the poorest groups in the population have been badly hurt.

2. The potential for significant further extension and deepening of poverty poses a major challenge to the Egyptian government in the light of its longstanding commitment on behalf of social progress and equity. Confronted with a growing resource gap, the government has undertaken a series of corrective policy measures since 1986 and is now considering a comprehensive macroeconomic reform program to reduce external and internal imbalances, eliminate distortions in the economy, and promote sustainable growth in the productive sectors. Many of the measures included in the macroeconomic adjustment program will put further pressure on the government budget while, at the same time, raising the risk of spreading and aggravating deprivation among poorer groups. Therefore, the success of this program will be conditional upon the government's ability to protect the most vulnerable segments of Egyptian society.

3. The main objectives of this report are to (i) analyze the importance and causes of poverty in Egypt in the context of the present economic crisis, (ii) assess the distributional impacts of the macroeconomic reforms envisaged under the structural adjustment program, and (iii) outline a strategy for policy interventions to alleviate the aggravation of poverty which might otherwise result.

Who are the Poor?

4. The most recent figures available reveal that poor households still represent between 20 and 25% of the Egyptian population:

- women and children are among the most vulnerable groups; poor children, in particular, are exposed to difficult living conditions (lack of protection from malnutrition and preventible diseases), have no or limited access to school, and are put to work at a young age;

- Upper Egypt is the poorest region in the country, together with Kalyubia, Gharbia and Munufia governorates in the Delta region;

- in the rural areas, the poor are either farmers with no land or little land or agricultural laborers; in the cities, poverty is associated with industrial employment and services, including a significant number of government employees; for the urban self-employed, poverty is concentrated among low-skilled and marginal activities; and

- there is a smaller group of ultrapoor (10 to 13% of the population), including widows, older, sick and disabled people, heavily dependent on direct income transfers.

How Do the Poor Live?

5. Several outcome indicators can be used to describe how the poor are able to meet their most fundamental needs and the kinds of material hardship they are confronted with in their daily lives, notably in terms of protection from malnutrition, protection from preventible diseases and death, access to safe water and sanitation, access to adequate shelter, and protection from ignorance.

6. **Nutrition**. Egypt has done well in safeguarding the food security of the population and average food availability is comparable to levels in industrialized countries. However, this has been achieved at high costs, both absolutely and in terms of market distortions. Even from a distributional viewpoint, there remain significant groups in the population with inadequate consumption levels (35% of the population consumes less than 2,000 calories a day) and malnutrition appears to have increased between 1978 and 1986, particularly among preschool age children.

7. **Health**. As measured in terms of mortality and morbidity, the general health of the entire population has steadily improved during the last two decades, with progress in child survival being more accentuated since 1980. However, the beneficial effects are unevenly distributed, with urban areas being more favored than villages, and with the health conditions of the high and middle income groups improving faster than those with lower incomes, some of the very poor remaining totally untouched. Infant mortality remains still high at 60 per thousand. With a child mortality rate (1-4 age group) of 7.4 per thousand and a survival ratio of 87.1, the situation in Egypt is relatively worse than in most other Middle East and North African countries. Regional inequalities in infant

and child mortality are considerable. The risk of death at birth is five times higher in rural areas than in urban and 4.7 times greater in Upper Egypt than in the rest of the country. Infant and child mortality rates are also significantly higher for girls than for boys. Finally, there is clear evidence of a close link between socio-economic origin and child mortality.

8. <u>Access to Safe Water and Sanitation</u>. Although access to water services has improved significantly over the last decade, the lack of access to safe water for many households, especially in rural areas, and the poor quality of the service at times pose a considerable, if not the most important, threat to the welfare of Egypt's population. In rural areas, 44% of the population is not connected to public water systems and the coverage of sewage systems is very small. Even in urban areas, one third of households have no access to flush waste disposal. The lack of access to safe water and adequate sanitation constitute the main reason behind the large incidence of water-borne diseases such as infectious diseases, parasites and related illnesses in Egypt. Rural areas with the most acute water problems, such as Upper Egypt, also exhibit the highest morbidity and mortality rates.

9. <u>Access to Adequate Shelter</u>. Housing has been among the most neglected sectors in Egypt and the present situation is characterized by serious problems of shortage and overcrowding. The shortage of low cost housing due to the stagnation of the stock of rental housing units and the high cost of newly built units. For over three-fourths of the population, the price of a standard new dwelling in an urban area exceeds one hundred times their annual income. As a result of rent control, a black market for new rental units has developed, in which tenants pay large up-front sums in the form of "key money". At the same time, there is an excessively high vacancy rate of housing units in the face of the severe housing shortage. To cope with the housing shortage, many poor income households have built substandard units, "squatting" on public land in areas lacking water, sewage, garbage collection and basic social services.

10. <u>Access to Education</u>. Despite tremendous progress in enrollments at all levels, education expansion has not entirely kept pace with population growth. As a result, illiteracy remains high and a non-negligible proportion of school-age children have been essentially left out of the education process. In 1986, 17.3 million people representing about half of the population age 10 or above were classified by the Census as not able to read and write. The female illiteracy rate is even higher: 62% versus 38% for men. As with other dimensions of poverty, the incidence of illiteracy varies considerably across Governorates, with a strong correlation between poverty incidence and low levels of educational development.

What Are the Roots of Poverty in Egypt?

11. Since the 1952 revolution, the Egyptian leadership has placed much emphasis on social development to foster greater equality and increased wealth. The implementation of successive land reforms and business nationalization measures, the establishment of an egalitarian wage structure and the pursuit of generous employment policies in the public sector which dominates the economy, the operation of a moderately progressive taxation system, the construction of

a national public health network and a comprehensive education and training system, and the introduction of direct and implicit subsidies in a wide range of economic and social sectors have all contributed to the marked improvements in standards of living and welfare enjoyed by the bulk of the population.

12. At the same time, however, these policies have had a high economic cost in terms of expansionary budget and increased market distortions. Furthermore, the government has failed in its attempt to eliminate poverty and absolute poverty has remained at a high level. The lack of access to productive assets, notably land in rural areas, and the unavailability of alternative sources of steady income through regular wage employment explain the persistence of chronic poverty among potentially productive groups. In the light of the failure of the welfare system built over the last decades to serve as an adequate safety net to protect the most vulnerable groups in the population, there is concern that the present economic crisis could bring about increased hardship for many households.

13. Assets and Poverty. Information about the distribution of and remuneration from assets is very scarce. With respect to the rural areas, the data on land ownership reveal that, despite the overall increase in equality due to the successive land reforms, the richest 20% landowners still control 70% of the agricultural land, versus only 5% for the poorest 20% farmers. The pattern of maldistribution is even stronger for other assets.

14. The Employment Challenge. During the 1970s and early 1980s, the informal and public sectors were the principal sources of employment for Egypt's rapidly expanding population and labor force. The public sector, representing government and public enterprises, was a major source of employment for new labor force entrants. It accounted for nearly 53% of nonagricultural employment in 1986, up from 51% in 1976. The informal sector offered the only source of expanding productive employment.

15. On the surface, Egypt responded to the challenge of its growing population and labor force. But full employment was achieved by the over-staffing of government and public enterprises and the economy was heavily dependent on migration to the Gulf as a safety valve. Government labor policies and regulations discouraged employment creation in the modern private sector. As government economic policies slowed the pace of economic growth and employment creation in the mid-1980s, open unemployment started to rise.

16. Income Transfers. The introduction, by the government, of direct transfer schemes and subsidies programs in a wide range of economic and social sectors has had a positive impact on the standards of living and welfare of the bulk of the population. Of particular importance is the extensive food subsidy system which covers 93% of the population and has been relatively effective in protecting the food security of the majority of the population. Education, health, potable water, electricity, fuel, transportation and housing have also been heavily subsidized.

17. However, the various existing social programs and transfer mechanisms have been very costly in terms of burden on the budget, market distortions and misallocation of resources, and have failed to reach the most vulnerable members of Egyptian society. Some of the poorest households are not among the

beneficiaries of the food ration program. Opportunities to gain access to self-sustaining income-earning opportunities and to raise individual productivity through human capital formation have not been available for the most needy. The housing market does not serve the poor. Even the direct welfare programs administered by the Ministry of Social Affairs, such as the Sadat Pension Fund, have not effectively reached the ultrapoor in terms of coverage of the target population and adequacy of the level of financial assistance offered.

18.   _Population Pressure._ The poverty problem faced by Egypt is compounded by rapid population growth which translates into increased pressure on the economy: pressure for jobs, pressure for social services, and pressure for an increase in consumer subsidies. The labor force is growing at an even faster rate than the population. Its growth at an average rate of 5% per annum reflects the rising number of youths and women entering the labor force. The economy has not been able to keep up with the need for jobs. Nor has it been able to meet the demand for building additional schools and health facilities. The financial pressures created by this growth have prevented any significant improvement in the quality of social services. There is even concern that the continuation of these pressures will lead to further deterioration in the quality of education at all levels and in health services. At the same time, demographic pressures are making it increasingly difficult to sustain existing consumer subsidies, especially food subsidies.

Assessing the Social Costs of Adjustment

19.   In the case of Egypt, there are three types of potential social costs associated with the effects of the current economic crisis and the likely impacts of the macroeconomic adjustment program: growing unemployment; price increases for food commodities and other goods and services; and deterioration in the provision of social services. The magnitude of the negative effects of the economic crisis is likely to increase in the absence of a strong macroeconomic reform program.

20.   _Employment Effects_. The deterioration of the economic situation has made it increasingly difficult for the government to sustain a full employment policy. The failure of the economy to stimulate private investment and employment has compounded the problem. Thus, as the 1980s progressed, labor force growth outpaced employment. Open unemployment, largely among new labor force entrants, has been rising and real wages have been falling significantly.

21.   In 1986, the government began to introduce a series of economic reforms to reduce the budget deficit. The gradual introduction of these reforms avoided significant labor displacement. The government is now contemplating broader and more aggressive reforms. With labor displacement concentrated in government and public enterprises, the impact of both programs will fall most heavily on urban areas. Significant numbers of the urban poor are employed in both sectors.

22.   _Price Increases_. As far as food prices are concerned, there is accumulating evidence that some of the changes in the ration and subsidy system that have already taken place have hurt the poor. It is estimated that the cost of the government "minimum cost diet" increased 216% in urban areas and 242% in rural areas between 1982 and 1987. Wages have not kept pace with the increases

in food prices. Very recent food price increases have created new pressures for the poor. Between May and August 1989 prices of foods consumed by the lowest income urban consumers increased 40%. Approximately 80% of this price increase for food is due to the higher price of bread. There is concern that the recent increases in food prices might have precipitated cut-backs in the quantities of food consumed by households, especially in the lowest income category of households who were already spending 75% of their incomes on food.

23. Not all households are likely to be adversely affected by reductions in the ration system and removal of other price subsidies. Those households for which there would be a negative food security impact include:

- the low income urban consumer for whom a disproportionate share of food intake is provided by the ration system;

- landless rural households, who have benefited from the cheap food policy pursued up to date by the government; and

- small farm households with less than 2 feddans of land. Although producer prices for many commodities will be increased, this will most likely be offset by higher food prices faced by these households who are net purchasers of wheat, rice and maize.

24. With regard to the prices of other goods and services, the urban poor are likely to suffer from the removal of existing subsidies and the resulting increases in the prices of utilities (water and electricity), transport (buses and railways) and energy products (especially kerosene used for cooking purposes). The overall distributional impact will depend on the possibility to introduce cross-subsidies in the price increases. In the rural areas, the small farmers who had been benefitting from the present agricultural policy combination of subsidized inputs (seeds, fertilizers and pesticides, energy, irrigation, credit) and controlled crop prices might be worse off after the removal of existing subsidies on input prices, depending on the net effect of the changes in input and output prices.

25. <u>Delivery of Social Services</u>. In the social sectors, the rapid demographic expansion against a background of tighter budgets has made it increasingly difficult for the government to sustain the present level of expenditures. While the Ministries of Health and Education have struggled to keep up with the quantitative needs of expansion of their facilities, the quality of the services provided has been decreasing. One of the manifestations of the crisis has been the growing share of salaries in total spending at the detriment of other categories of expenditures. This has meant less resources for drugs and other medical supplies in the health sector, and for textbooks and other educational materials in education. There has also been a steady deterioration of the physical infrastructure (hospitals, health centers, schools and universities) due to the lack of funding for maintenance and repairs.

26. There is concern that additional reductions in budgetary resources might compromise further the coverage and quality of programs in health and education, especially in the rural areas. This would undermine the prospects for reducing existing regional inequalities in the provision of medical and

educational services and would adversely affect the bulk of the rural poor whose degree of protection from preventible diseases and ignorance is already much lower than for the rest of the population.

27. **Adequacy of the Existing Safety Net**. Despite the government's commitment on behalf of social justice and welfare, the various existing social programs and transfer mechanisms do not constitute a sufficiently adequate safety net to protect the most vulnerable members of Egyptian society from the negative social effects of adjustment. The government has no targeting mechanisms to cushion the negative effects of food prices increases and reductions in the ration program. In terms of employment policy, there are no employment adjustment services to provide unemployment benefits, special re-training and re-skilling programs, and job-seeking and relocation assistance.

Toward A Poverty Alleviation Strategy

28. The 1990 World Development Report on poverty emphasizes the fact that, historically, social progress has been achieved only when there is a satisfactory combination of substantial economic growth and an appropriate pattern of growth. Economic recovery is therefore the first condition of success for any poverty alleviation strategy in Egypt. The second condition is an adequate pattern of growth from the viewpoint both of the efficiency of the growth process and of the distribution of the benefits of economic growth. The history of the last two decades in Egypt shows that economic growth alone is not sufficient to eradicate poverty, even when the State is as committed to the promotion of social justice and welfare as the Egyptian government has been. The design of a poverty alleviation strategy for Egypt needs therefore to reflect this dual preoccupation of increased economic growth and appropriate pattern of growth.

29. Given the heterogeneity of the groups in poverty in Egypt, a diversified approach to poverty alleviation needs to be adopted. It is important to recognize that, before the poor can respond to policy incentives provided by the macroeconomic reform program, they may require initial help for the satisfaction of their basic needs, notably in terms of food, health, and access to productive employment. Similarly, in the case of the ultrapoor, a welfare approach is likely to remain predominant considering the difficulties involved in attempting to integrate older people, widows with young children, and handicapped or sick people in mainstream economic activities. For the chronic poor, on the other hand, an economic approach should prevail as this group is made of people who are already engaged in economic activities but whose incomes are too low. Human capital formation operations are crucial for all vulnerable members of society, but their impact is dependent on the success of reforms on the economic side as improvements in the human capital of the poor can be translated into productivity gains only if there is an economic demand to use the labor force effectively. Ideally, the strategy adopted should combine these various forms of intervention, **economic**, **human capital formation** and **welfare**, with a different emphasis depending on the degree and type of poverty of each target group.

30. Both the short term and the long term requirements of a poverty alleviation strategy must be considered. Short of rapid and massive income

transfers which would not be desirable per se and would be impossible to consider under the prevailing economic conditions, there is no short term answer to the kind of chronic poverty which has persisted in Egypt for at least three decades. Effective as they may be, measures to provide better income-earning opportunities for the poor have a long maturation span. Similarly, interventions to improve access for the poor to public services in health or education take a long time to bear their fruits. At the same time, however, it is impossible to ignore the immediate adverse effects of the economic crisis, notably the growing unemployment, falling wages, and higher prices, and the need to protect the human resources of the poor as early as possible. Therefore, the goals of the poverty alleviation strategy should be not only to suppress chronic poverty in the long run, but also to ease the burden of the economic crisis and reduce the social costs of structural adjustment on the economically vulnerable members of the population.

31. Taking these dimensions into consideration, the poor should not be seen as a burden, but as a potential resource. A comprehensive Poverty Alleviation Strategy should include the following elements:

- structural measures to increase income-earning opportunities for the poor through improved access to productive employment and assets;

- structural measures to improve the equity and cost-effectiveness of public expenditures in health and education to increase opportunities for human capital formation for the poor;

- structural measures to achieve a more equitable and efficient targeting of all secondary income transfers, including consumer subsidies, producer subsidies and direct welfare transfers; and

- an Emergency Social Fund to protect the low-income population groups directly affected during implementation of macroeconomic reforms.

32. While all these measures are equally important to achieve the overall goal of poverty alleviation, their implementation schedules would vary significantly. In the short term, the government's priority is obviously to set up the Social Fund and to initiate emergency measures to protect the poor during the adjustment period. The next priority would be to work on the targeting aspects in order to establish mechanisms which are both more efficient and more equitable. Introducing reforms in public expenditures allocation and utilization in the social sectors and improving access of the poor to productive employment and assets are measures with a longer term horizon.

33. Effective targeting is a fundamental determinant of success and cost-effectiveness of government intervention under each of the four components. Moving toward selective targeting would represent a significant departure from past practices based on the belief that generous equal opportunity policies would automatically benefit the whole population. Both the persistence of poverty and the financial unsustainability of present social policies of generalized

subsidies, access to free health and education, government employment guarantee and egalitarian salary scales regardless of actual need, ability, performance or merit underline the urgency of designing appropriate targeting mechanisms. This would make it possible to ensure that subsidized resources reach the most needy groups, increase the benefits to the targeted population and, at the same time, lower the cost of the programs to the government.

34. The availability of timely and accurate information is sine qua non for any attempt to improve targeting. At the present time, the possibility to reach the poor is constrained by the ability to identify them and to monitor the evolution of their living conditions. Among other agencies, the Ministries of Social Affairs (Sadat pension), Education (scholarships and fees), Health (cost-recovery), Supply (food subsidies), Energy (electricity and fuel subsidies), Housing (water tariffs) and Labor (employment and retraining) would benefit from the capacity to target their programs to protect the most vulnerable groups. The establishment of monitoring mechanisms will therefore be an integral part of the poverty alleviation strategy.

35. In deciding which targeting mechanisms would be appropriate, the Egyptian authorities will face the challenge of finding the right balance between the degree of precision sought in identifying the target population, the administrative cost of targeting and the level of acceptable leakage. This implies looking at alternatives based either on direct targeting mechanisms or on indirect targeting using characteristics of the poor as proxies, depending on data availability and the cost of information collection in each specific case. Flexibility should also be a feature of the targeting system because of the need to provide the capacity to admit new households or remove old households as their income situations change over time.

36. <u>Income Generation Policies</u>. Strategies for income generation will need to focus on employment promotion and measures to improve access of the poor to productive assets. Employment promotion is a key element in any strategy to reduce the social costs of economic reforms and their impacts on the poor. The availability of productive jobs for displaced workers will reduce their loss of income and resistance to structural adjustment. Without this, displaced workers will need protection from economic hardship. If this protection is not offered, worker resistance to adjustment can be expected. This protection is justified on equity grounds. It represents society's transfer of a share of the benefits of adjustment to those who bear its cost. These benefits come to consumers in the form of lower prices for goods and services and in expanding employment, although not necessarily in the same communities where workers are displaced.

37. Employment promotion can be encouraged by (i) financial market reforms, (ii) labor market reforms, (iii) emphasis on technology and productivity in the enterprise, (iv) support for small and medium-sized enterprises, and (v) direct expenditures on transitional employment. Financial market reforms are essential to reducing the capital bias of the modern sector. Laws, policies and practices (negative real interest rates, rationing of capital) which have stifled capital market activity and distorted the allocation of scarce capital resources in favor of large public enterprises should be changed. Financial reforms would improve the mobilization of capital resources and increase the level of private investment. This would have an important impact on incentives for employment creation in both sectors.

38. An efficient labor market will facilitate change in the economy and reduce the social cost of adjustment. It will permit faster rates of economic growth and employment creation without accelerating inflationary pressures. An efficient labor market requires flexible wages linked to productivity and low barriers to labor mobility. Six types of reforms can be identified:

- phasing out the guarantee of employment for graduates of secondary schools and universities and freezing new hires in the government;

- introducing a civil service reform to improve the link between wages and productivity. This would require a plan for the organizational and personnel structure of government, policies for merit selection and determination of the redundant workforce, programs for the integration of redundant workers into the private sector, and procedures for implementation of the reform;

- implementing, in public enterprises, wage and employment policies which are consistent with market conditions, in order to encourage a closer connection between wages and productivity. This would involve uncoupling wage and employment policies in these enterprises from those of government under Public Law 48;

- improving the functioning of labor markets and avoiding interventions that distort the operation and efficiency of these markets. In this context, the government monopoly on job placements through the Ministry of Labor and its employment service should be eliminated;

- improving access to labor market information which is important for macroeconomic planning, monitoring the impact of structural adjustment, planning for education and training, career counselling, and job placement. A special government taskforce should be created to make recommendations for improving the labor market information provided by CAPMAS and the Ministry of Labor; and

- amending the government's regulations of dismissals in Public Law 137-1981 to reduce barriers to labor mobility. By making it difficult to displace redundant labor, enterprises are forced to treat labor as a fixed resource, which discourages employment creation. In the case of layoffs, prior notice should be required to give public officials adequate time to organize services to meet the needs of displaced workers, including job search assistance, career counselling, training grants, and assistance with unemployment benefits.

39. Support for small and medium-sized enterprises can be an important means for employment creation. To support small and medium enterprises, the government can: (i) allow the capitalization of job separation benefits giving displaced workers a source of capital for private investment; (ii) assist the

banking system in establishing credit mechanisms for small enterprises; (iii) create a division within the productivity centers offering entrepreneurs technical assistance involving technology choices, productivity and marketing, plus access to management training; and (iv) provide an infrastructure of services and facilities to launch new small and medium enterprises.

40. Provision of small scale credit, technical assistance and training, especially to women, has a great potential for income generation. Plenty of examples of successful pilot project schemes exist in Egypt, in both urban and rural settings, some in the public sector, others administered by NGOs. The objective should be to ensure that every person in the country has access to credit even for the smallest undertaking. The poorest, especially women, are the group which has had least access to credit up to now.

41. The government should commission the preparation of a review of such schemes to evaluate best practice methods and decide on the appropriate implementing agency in different cases. Government effectiveness in the field of small scale credit could be increased in any of three ways:

- first, consideration should be given to extending the scope of existing financial institutions (e.g., the Village Banks). This might be done through village and neighborhood Community Development Associations.

- second, the Productive Families Program might be modified so as better to serve the poorest groups, not by reducing the cost of credit to borrowers -- studies show that borrowers see a good return on their activities and in NGO projects accept higher charges without difficulty -- but by lowering the size of loans.

- third, consideration should be given to concentrating the activities of the Productive Families Program entirely on the training and loans side and delegating the direct employment and production aspect to the private sector. It is far less risky and costly for the state to disburse a given fund in credit than in direct production: credit schemes can benefit from the diversity of activities among borrowers and from coopting the interests of borrowers in achieving high returns.

42. <u>Human Capital Maintenance</u>. It is crucial that human capital formation programs be protected during the transition period of economic reforms despite the planned reductions in government expenditures. This can be achieved through improvements in the pattern of allocation and utilization of available resources. Measures taken to improve the targeting of health and education programs to persons with the greatest need and to increase the efficiency with which services are delivered can lead to the simultaneous improvement of equity and efficiency in these sectors. With this type of measures, the most economically vulnerable members of the population can be sheltered from the social and economic costs of the structural adjustment program without increasing the government's budget for the social sectors, though it should be maintained at its current level in real terms.

43. The following options would need to be considered in the health sector:

> (i) downscaling of the investment program with respect to the construction of new secondary or tertiary curative facilities in urban areas;
>
> (ii) rationalization of the existing network of curative facilities on the basis of effective utilization rates and reallocation of recurrent resources to the primary health care facilities and programs;
>
> (iii) introduction of differential user fees to promote cost-recovery in curative services in conjunction with an extension of medical insurance coverage;
>
> (iv) strengthening of the infectious and parasitic diseases control programs, and of maternal and child health programs; and
>
> (v) complementary measures to improve the quality of care at all levels.

44. In the education sector, given the need to achieve universal basic education, particularly for girls, and to improve the qualitative aspects of the educational process, the present level of government expenditures devoted to basic education should be at least maintained in real terms. At the same time, it is equally important to rationalize the pattern of allocation and utilization of resources within the education system, considering that the present policy of unlimited expansion at all levels is neither sustainable from an economic viewpoint nor equitable from a social perspective. Greater emphasis should be given to basic education in recognition of the higher social rates of return at that level and the necessity to offer better opportunities to those who are not able to go beyond that level of education.

45. The following options could be implemented to increase equity and cost-effectiveness in the delivery of education programs:

> (i) elimination of fees in basic education;
>
> (ii) generalization of cost-recovery measures in higher education;
>
> (iii) improvement in the quality of basic education financed through transfers of budgetary resources from higher education to basic education; and
>
> (iv) introduction of more restrictive procedures for access to post-secondary education.

46. _Transfers_. Despite the political and social difficulties involved in implementing major changes in the ration/subsidy system, there is an urgent need to take effective measures to reduce the burden on the government budget while at the same time improving the targeting of the nutritionally at-risk segments of the population. While it is wise to experiment first with new approaches on a pilot basis before recommending adoption of the changes on a larger scale, the government should move rapidly on this issue as there is no

income or nutritional justification for subsidizing 93% of the population. The following measures could be considered:

- scaling down of the number of ration cards, limiting participation in the ration system to the lower income groups;

- undertaking pilot operations to experiment with geographical targeting of food subsidies; and

- eliminating subsidization through the distribution cooperatives which have been found to benefit mainly middle and upper income groups.

47. To achieve a more equitable and efficient targeting of direct welfare transfers and other subsidies, the following measures could be implemented:

- restoration of the public basic safety net schemes administered by the Ministry of Social Affairs (social pension and Sadat pension) to a more appropriate level of benefit (approximately four times the current value) and redefinition of the target population to include all vulnerable groups defined as ultrapoor;

- introducing progressive rate schedules to protect the poorest households from price increases for public transportation and utilities; and

- introducing a kerosene coupons program rigorously targeted on the very poor.

48. _Social Fund_. Within the overall strategy defined above, the Social Fund would function as a transitory institution, set up primarily to support income-generation and human capital formation projects targeted to protect the most vulnerable groups. The Social Fund would focus on:

- integrated employment and training operations to reduce unemployment and improve access to human capital and productivity (retraining, reskilling, job search and relocation assistance); and

- nutrition, health, literacy, education and environmental projects to improve the well-being of the most needy.

49. The Social Fund's principal functions would be:

- to mobilize international and local financial resources;

- to solicit, and promote and identify sub-projects addressing the needs of the most vulnerable households selected as target groups;

- to provide technical assistance for the preparation of sub-projects;

- to appraise and select sub-projects for funding; and

- to assist in the contracting and procurement for these sub-projects and supervise their implementation.

50. Another important mission of the Social Fund would be to finance studies along the Living Standards Measurement Survey (LSMS) format, designed to identify with precision who are the poor and what are their characteristics. The results of this operation would be used to define a more appropriate targeting system for subsidies and social welfare payments and to establish permanent monitoring mechanisms to provide the government with the capability to evaluate, on a regular basis, the impacts of macroeconomic and sectoral policy measures on vulnerable groups.

51. The poverty alleviation interventions supported by the Social Fund would be financed by additional resources mobilized specifically for this purpose. No extra budgetary cost would result from this operation.

Role of the Bank

52. The World Bank could support the proposed poverty alleviation strategy with the following:

- participation in funding the transition costs borne by the most vulnerable members of society during the adjustment period within the framework of the Social Fund.

- assistance to design and implement the restructuring measures associated with the setting up of a new macroeconomic and regulatory framework (labor market reform, retraining programs, food subsidy targeting, reallocation of resources in Ministries of Education and Health, etc); and

- assistance in the establishment of evaluation mechanisms to monitor, on a continuing basis, progress in the social sectors (poverty, income distribution, nutrition, health, literacy, employment, living conditions).

I. Introduction

"Government sensitivity toward the possible impact of particular adjustment measures on lower-income groups and on income distribution in general should be fully appreciated."

Foreign Minister Esmat Abdel Meguid
Presentation to the American Chamber of Commerce, November 1, 1989

Background

1.01 After almost a decade of rapid economic growth following the start of President Sadat's open door policy in 1974, Egypt is now experiencing a recession precipitated by the collapse of world oil prices in 1986 and the levelling off of worker remittances and foreign aid. The growth of the late 1970s, under the thrust of rising oil production and prices, increased remittances and expanding foreign aid, obscured distortions in the economy and weaknesses in the balance of payments. As the economy slowed down in the 1980s, Egypt's ability to sustain a pattern characterized by an over-reliance on oil exports, stagnating non-oil exports against a background of rapidly growing imports, inefficiencies in resource allocation and use, and a balance of sectoral growth favoring the service sectors, diminished dramatically. Since 1986, real GDP growth has been less than 3% a year, investment has dropped sharply, inflation has been running at 25% a year, per capita consumption has declined in real terms, and external indebtedness has grown to 47 US$ billion.

1.02 The deterioration of the economic situation has had adverse social consequences in terms of employment and standards of living. The growing budget deficit and the rising cost of external debts have placed new pressures on government expenditures in an economy characterized by a predominant public sector. The outcome has been a marked decline in the level of job creation in the public sector, a pattern of wage compression for civil service employees, diminishing public resources for the social sectors, and cutbacks in the food ration and subsidy system. The slowdown of investment and output in the private sector has had similar negative employment and income effects. Since the beginning of the recession in 1986, open unemployment, largely among youths, has risen rapidly, real wages have fallen in most economic sectors, and there are indications that the poorest groups in the population have been badly hurt. The potential rise of poverty poses a major challenge to the Egyptian government in the light of its longstanding commitment on behalf of social progress and equity.

1.03 Confronted with a growing resource gap, the government has undertaken a series of corrective policy measures since 1986 and is now considering a comprehensive macroeconomic reform program to reduce external and internal imbalances, eliminate distortions in the economy, and promote sustainable growth in the productive sectors. Many of the measures included in the macroeconomic adjustment program will put further pressure on the government budget while, at the same time, raising the risk of deprivation among poorer groups. Therefore, the success of this program will be conditional upon the government's ability to protect the most vulnerable segments of Egyptian society. Furthermore, concern over growing poverty and disinvestment in human resources is justified on grounds beyond the social and political costs involved. Nutrition, health, education and training programs are needed not only on humanitarian grounds, but also as an investment in human resources required to foster higher productivity in the economy. Similarly, improving the efficiency of labor markets to facilitate the flow of human resources to more productive sectors is central to the objective of alleviating poverty through employment.

Objectives and Scope of the Study

1.04   The main objectives of the study are to analyze the importance and causes of poverty in Egypt in the context of the present economic crisis, to assess the distributional impacts of the macroeconomic reforms envisaged under the structural adjustment program, and to outline a strategy for policy interventions to alleviate poverty, and promote broad-based growth.

1.05   The study addresses three major issues which critically affect the government's ability to design and implement an effective poverty alleviation strategy:

(a)   Identification of the Poor. Most social programs and services offered by the government are available at no cost to all members of Egyptian society, regardless of their socio-economic status. In addition, the government makes large income transfers through an extensive subsidy and price control system from which the vast majority of the population benefits in an indiscriminate manner. The pressure to reduce public expenditures makes it imperative to consider ways of containing the overall cost of the various social services and transfer programs while ensuring that the neediest people are not adversely affected. In seeking to achieve this objective, the government is constrained by the difficulty in identifying the poor with precision. The report reviews the available data and indicators on this issue and explores the feasibility of setting up effective targeting mechanisms to streamline the subsidy system (food, transport, utilities, energy). The report also investigates improvements in the patterns of resource mobilization and allocation in the education and health sectors. The overriding concern is to ensure that responses to the tightening budgetary situation do not have negative impacts on the quantity and quality of services offered and on the degree of equity of public expenditures for human capital formation.

(b)   Compensatory Measures. To assist the most needy in the Egyptian population, the government has put in place a safety net of welfare programs administered by the Ministry of Social Affairs. The study examines the coverage and performance of the existing programs and explores alternative institutional mechanisms to provide short term compensatory measures aimed at protecting the low income population groups likely to be directly affected during the transition period of implementation of macroeconomic reforms.

(c) **Employment Promotion**. The deteriorating employment situation and the prospect that unemployment may rise even further if public enterprise reforms are undertaken is one of the major challenges confronting the government. Measures to provide incentives for investment and job creation and to improve the efficiency of labor markets are an important component of any poverty alleviation strategy while, at the same time, being a necessary adjunct to structural adjustment programs that seek to remove barriers to economic growth. However, such measures produce transitional costs associated with the shifting of labor to more productive uses. The size and distribution of these costs is an equity issue which requires careful attention. The report reviews policy options to promote employment and improve the efficiency of Egyptian labor markets and proposes strategies to reduce and redistribute the resulting social and economic costs of these reforms.

Conceptual and Methodological Framework

1.06   While there is unanimity in recognizing the pressing need to address the poverty issue in the context of adjustment programs, there are wide differences of views on how to define and measure poverty. This report does not purpose to contribute to the on-going debate. But this conceptual issue cannot be ignored as it affects the analytical approach followed in the study.

1.07   Defining poverty requires the selection of welfare indicators to draw a line, the poverty line, which divides the population into the poor and the non poor. Welfare economics makes a distinction between absolute and relative poverty. Absolute poverty corresponds to the situation of households whose level of income or expenditure is insufficient to ensure a minimum level of welfare. Relative poverty refers to the situation of the lowest income groups in relation to the national income. For instance, the European Community measures the level of poverty as the share of population receiving an income lower than half of their country's average income. Relative poverty, which exists irrespective of the level of wealth in a given economy, is a useful concept to analyze inequality in any type of society, but is not as meaningful for an assessment of the plight of the most vulnerable groups in times of economic recession. Therefore, the main focus of the present report is on absolute poverty.

1.08   A variety of indices, such as per capita food consumption or per capita income, are commonly used to define and measure absolute poverty (Glewwe, 1988). But reference to these apparently neutral and objective aggregate measures should not obscure the fact that **poverty is essentially a normative concept.** Any statistical definition of poverty reflects a set of values regarding a minimum standard of living to meet basic needs in a specific social and cultural context at a given moment in time (Altimir, 1980). For the purpose of this study, poverty is defined as a level of income or standard of living that is insufficient to meet minimal life-sustenance needs including adequate nutrition, decent shelter, access to safe water, protection from unnecessary disease and death, and protection from ignorance.

1.09   This definition reflects a basic needs approach inspired by a universalist notion of human dignity involving the right to be protected from economic deprivation and insecurity. While this approach does not lend itself easily to the use of aggregate indices, it provides a more flexible framework to apprehend the multidimensional and dynamic nature of poverty. The main concern is not to propose a statistically exact measure of poverty in Egypt, but to make a realistic assessment of the magnitude and causes of the problem on which operational recommendations can be based.

1.10   In terms of time horizon, the report addresses both short term and long term poverty. The poverty alleviation strategy proposed takes into consideration not only the temporary setbacks from the current economic recession and the transition costs likely to result from the implementation of an adjustment program, but also the chronic and structural aspects of poverty and the mechanisms that should ensure an equitable distribution of the benefits of economic growth in the long run.

Data Availability

1.11   The lack of reliable and relevant data on poverty in Egypt is a serious constraint. There are no official surveys or statistics designed specifically to permit the analysis of income, inequality, or living standards issues. The only sources providing data of a comprehensive nature are the Household Budget Survey and the Census. For lack of a more appropriate database, this report relies heavily on the results of Household Surveys which were conducted in 1974/75 and 1981/82 and on those of the 1976 and 1986 Censuses. The Household Budget Surveys (HBS) offer the only desegregated household data on expenditures which can be used, with extreme caution, to make assumptions about the evolution and distribution of incomes. The results of the last two Censuses give some information on the demographic, education, employment and housing characteristics of the population. To complement these two sources, the report draws upon data collected from various ministries and government agencies (Finance, Labor, Education, Health, Social Affairs and CAPMAS).

Organization of the Report

1.12   The next chapter presents a profile of the poverty problem in Egypt and examines the characteristics of the poor. Chapter III analyzes the causes and determinants of their condition. Chapter IV assesses the social costs of the present economic crisis and attempts to map the likely impacts of the proposed macroeconomic adjustment program on the most vulnerable groups in Egyptian society. The fifth and final chapter proposes a poverty alleviation strategy and outlines the role that the Bank could play to assist the Egyptian Government in the implementation of this strategy.

II. The Dimensions of Poverty

Introduction: Economic Growth and Persistence of Poverty

2.01   Since the 1952 revolution, the successive governments of Egypt have sought to promote social equity and progress among the population. Over time, various configurations of income distribution and social development policies have been used to achieve these goals. After an initial emphasis on land reform (1952 and 1961) and nationalization measures (1956-66), the government has relied increasingly on taxation and subsidies as transfer mechanisms (Abdel-Khalek, 1982). To promote human resource development and raise standards of living, priority has been given to the establishment of a comprehensive social infrastructure. The commitment on behalf of social justice and welfare is still very strong today, as evidenced by the Second Five-Year Plan (1987/88 - 1991-92) which reasserts in its introduction the government's "responsibility for meeting the basic needs of the population". The Plan's social objectives are to make social services available to everyone and to improve income distribution.

2.02   Egypt's economy expanded rapidly in the 1970s after the launching of the Open Door policy (Infitah). The annual rate of growth of GDP was 7.5% in real terms between 1975 and 1982, and 5.0% between 1982 and 1986 (World Bank, 1989). The favorable economic situation and the resulting high revenues for the public sector facilitated a smooth financing and implementation of the government's social policies and programs. Investment in social infrastructure reached an unprecedented level during the First Five-Year Plan (1981/82 - 1986/87): 22% of the total public investment program went to projects in education, health, water supply, or housing. An even larger share of investment is expected during the current plan period as 28% of total public expenditures have been targeted for the social sectors.

2.03   Incomes and living standards rose steadily under the joint influence of rapid economic growth and active social policies.

Graph 2.1 Economic and Social Development Indicators

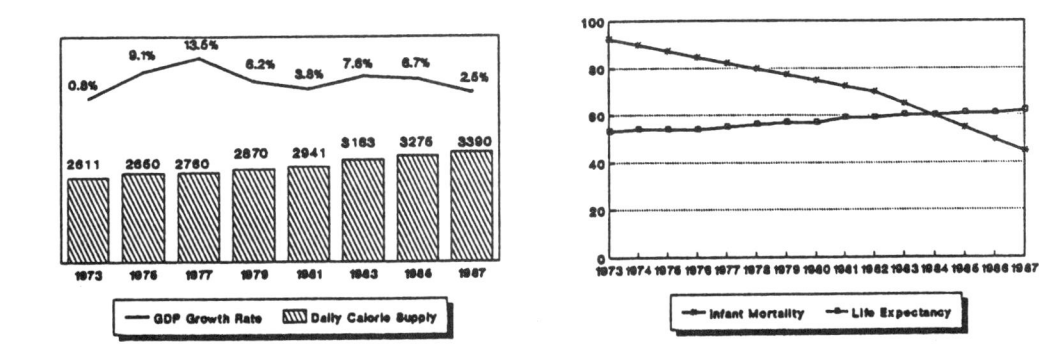

Source: World Development Report, World Bank

Per capita income grew by 7% a year in real terms between 1973 and 1982 and the per capita daily calorie supply increased from 2,400 to 3,300. The health status of the population improved drastically. During the 1970-87 period, crude death rates fell from 20 to 10 per thousand, infant and child mortality rates declined from 179 to 60 per thousand and from 16 to 7 per thousand respectively, and life expectancy grew from 46 to 62 years.

2.04   Nevertheless, despite the overall rise in incomes and the significant social progress during this period, **poverty has not been eliminated**. While the incidence of both urban and rural poverty has declined between 1975 and 1982, many studies have documented the persistence of a serious poverty problem (Radwan, 1982; Abdel-Khalek et al, 1982; Korayem, 1987; Hansen, 1989). Analyzing the magnitude of this problem requires to ask how many poor people there are, what is the degree of severity of their poverty, who they are and what are their individual characteristics, and how they live, i.e. what is the extent to which they are able to satisfy basic life-sustenance needs.

Incidence of Poverty

2.05   A number of estimates of the poverty line have been calculated for Egypt. Despite their methodological and data limitations (Box 2.1), they can be used an approximate measure of the overall incidence of poverty. The most recent figures reveal that, in 1982, poor households still represented between 22 and 30% of the total number of households.

Table 2.1   Incidence of Poverty in Egypt

	Proportion of Poor Households (%)	Number of Poor Households ('000)
1958/59 [1]		
Rural	35.0	1,161
Urban	30.0	597
1974/75 [1]		
Rural	44.0	1,833
Urban	34.5	1,076
1981/82 [2]		
Rural	24.2 - 29.7	1,023 - 1,240
Urban	22.5 - 30.4	756 - 1,196

Sources: [1] Hansen and Radwan
         [2] The source for the lower figures is World Bank, 1989. The larger figures are from Korayem, 1987.

BOX 2.1

Calculating Poverty Lines for Egypt: Methodological and Data Constraints

Calculating a poverty line requires the definition of the minimum income which allows a household to buy enough food to meet biological needs plus a minimum level of non-subsistence goods and services indispensable to satisfy non material needs. There are serious constraints attached to this operation. First, while the notion of being able to measure with objectivity the cost of the minimum food ration on the basis of international nutrition standards has a certain inherent logic, there is an important element of arbitrariness involved in the determination of "minimum non-subsistence" expenditures. Second, in countries like Egypt where almost half of the population still lives in the countryside, the subsistence consumption of rural households needs to be taken into consideration. Estimating the exact monetary value of this element is not a straightforward task.

In the absence of data on household income for Egypt, the only way to derive poverty lines is to use the results of the various household budget surveys. A number of researchers have proposed estimates of the poverty line in Egypt following that methodology. The most recent ones, relying on data from the 1974/75 and 1981/82 HBS, are those of Ibrahim (1982), Korayem (1987) and Ghattas (World Bank, 1989). However, the use of data from expenditure surveys presents several drawbacks. First, there is a tendency to leave out the most extreme cases at both ends of the distribution, i.e. the poorest and the richest households. Second, consumption expenditures do not reflect the differences in prices experienced in real life, for similar commodities and services, by different income groups or different age groups and people in different areas. Third, the value of goods and services which are provided free or at nominal rates by the government are not taken into account in the surveys. In the case of Egypt, education and health are two examples of social services offered free of charge; a wide range of goods (food stuffs, housing, energy products, agricultural inputs, utilities, transportation) are also heavily subsidized. Fourth, comparing expenditures across income groups does not allow for consideration of the present and future impact of past and current savings. Finally, the aggregate level of expenditure that can be extrapolated from the Egypt HBS falls 25% short of the national accounts figures. This significant discrepancy may be symptomatic of a high degree of inaccuracy and lack of reliability of the HBS data.

In addition to these generic constraints, the poverty line estimates used in the report, those of Korayem and Ghattas, suffer each from a particular methodological limitation. Korayem's figures, which are built upon an estimate of income distribution derived from the HBS, are higher than other estimates due to a different definition of minimum nutrition requirements and non material needs. Ghattas's figures, on the other hand, represent an attempt to update Ibrahim's estimates by applying the official CPI. They are likely to be on the low side considering that the CPI is biased toward expenditures of middle income groups and does not reflect adequately the real cost of living increase for the poorest groups. For example, the official CPI for the first nine months of 1989 is 15% in urban areas while the mission's estimate for population groups with a yearly income below 500 Egyptian Pounds is 43%.

2.06   In the urban areas, the incidence of poverty decreased slightly between 1975 and 1982, but was still as high in 1982 as in the late 1950s. Improvements in the rural areas have been more sustained as indicated by the long term decline and the sharp drop between 1975 and 1982.

2.07   Data on per capita consumption indicate that the consumption level of the poorest 10% of the rural population represents 23% of expenditures for the average rural Egyptian, while the richest 10% consume about 227% of the national average. In urban areas, the figures are 26% and 255% respectively.

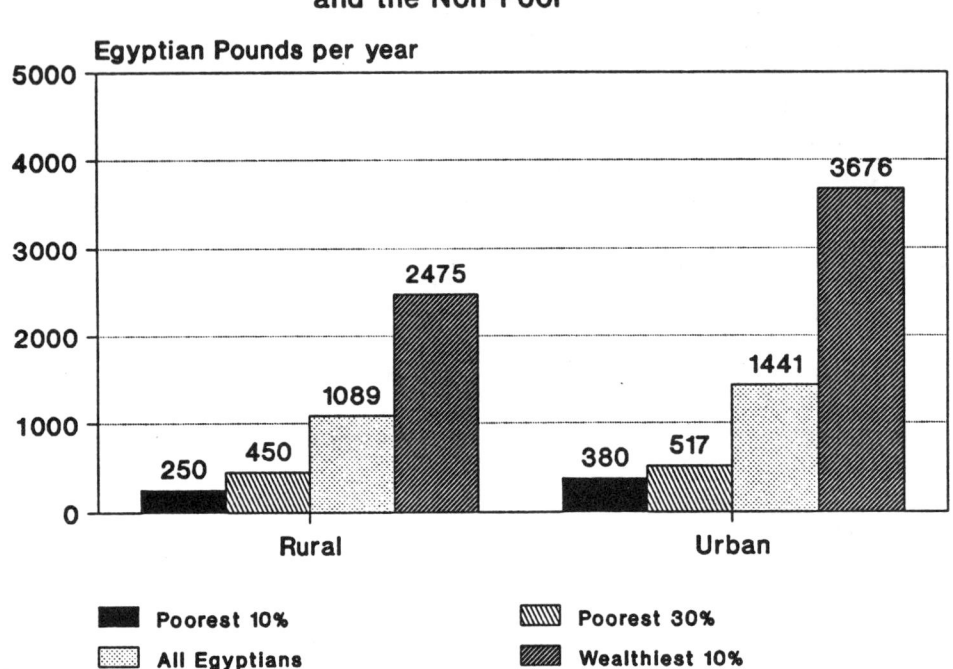

Graph 2.2 Expenditure Levels of the Poor and the Non-Poor

Egyptian Pounds per year

	Poorest 10%	Poorest 30%	All Egyptians	Wealthiest 10%
Rural	250	450	1089	2475
Urban	380	517	1441	3676

Source: 1981/82 HBS, CAPMAS

2.08   From an international perspective, the level of poverty in Egypt is about average compared with other developing countries. Out of 44 countries for which data on the proportion of the population living in absolute poverty are available, Egypt's place in the ranking from highest to lowest poverty incidence is 7th for urban poverty and 6th for rural poverty (Table 2, Annex A).

2.09   The concept of poverty line used here to describe the aggregate level of poverty rests on the assumption that poverty is a discrete characteristic which can be summed up with a single measure. This is equivalent to saying that people are either poor or not poor depending on their position relative to the line. In real life, however, poverty is a multidimensional and continuous variable and there is no clear cut position.

2.10   This discrepancy has two consequences. First, households with an income only marginally larger than the poverty line are not classified as poor even though they may be poor in reality. There is regrettably no satisfactory solution to this problem as the cut off point is, by definition, somewhat arbitrary. Second, the proportion of households below the poverty line hides differences in individual characteristics among the poor, thereby not measuring the real degree of poverty of the population groups classified as poor. Studies have revealed that the poor are not a homogeneous category (Lipton, 1988) and that there is a need to distinguish between the "poor" and the "ultrapoor", the latter category corresponding to people living in near destitution and unable to take advantage of income-earning opportunities and available social services.

2.11   There are three ways of addressing this issue of potential heterogeneity among the poorer segments of society. One possibility would be to calculate one of the various statistical indices developed by researchers to measure the severity of poverty (Sen, 1981; Foster et al., 1984). Unfortunately, the data needed to calculate this type of index and make meaningful comparisons over time are not available in the case of Egypt.

2.12   An alternative way would be to draw a second poverty line to separate the "poorest of the poor" from the other poor, using the methodology proposed by Lipton (Box 1). Based on the results of the 1981/82 HBS and bearing in mind all the methodological limitations involved in the calculation of any poverty line, it is estimated that approximately 12.8% of the rural households and 10.8% of urban households could be classified as "ultrapoor" (Annex K).

2.13   The third and perhaps most meaningful way of approaching the question of severity and heterogeneity of poverty would be to attempt to identify key characteristics of the poor and assess the degree of hardship concretely associated with their state of poverty.

Characteristics of the Poor

Demographic Characteristics

2.14   The only data that give some information on the demographic characteristics of the poor in Egypt come from an ILO survey undertaken in 1977 in 18 villages (Radwan and Lee, 1986). The results of this survey show that there is a significant difference in age structure between various income groups.

Graph 2.3 Age Structure of the Rural Poor
1977

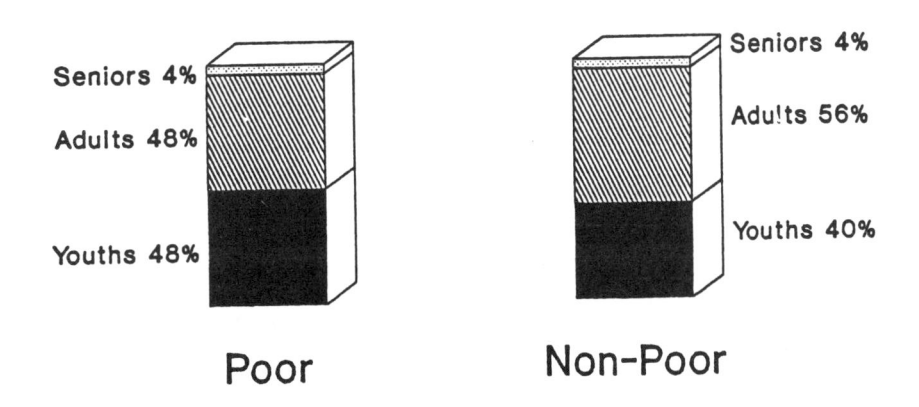

Poor: Seniors 4%, Adults 48%, Youths 48%

Non-Poor: Seniors 4%, Adults 56%, Youths 40%

Source: Radwan and Lee, 1986

2.15   On the average, poor households have to support a relatively larger number of youths under 15 years than the non-poor (48 versus 40%). As a corollary of this situation, the proportion of working age members is smaller in poor families than in non-poor households (48 versus 56%). According to the 1977 survey, the incidence of disability is much higher among the poorest groups. Between 19 and 30% of the people belonging to the three income groups which make up the 10% poorest group were disabled, as compared to a proportion of 3% among the rest of the rural population.

2.16   In many countries, the poor are characterized by a larger household size. The 1977 survey revealed an average household size of 6.4 for the poor population as compared to 5.3 for the non-poor. But the 1982/82 HBS data support this observation only for the urban areas where poor households had 5.5 persons on the average while the national figure was 5.2. In the rural areas, there was no significant difference. In any event, it would be erroneous to assume an inverse relationship between per capita expenditures and household size. While in some cases, it is true that poor families have to divide the family income among a larger number of people their overall income is on the average lower than non-poor households. Table 2.2 reveals that the low income of the poor is reflected in both household and per capita expenditures account. One group stands out, though: among the 10% poorest of the poor, household size is much smaller, this group including a high proportion of single member households headed by old persons.

Table 2.2   Relationship between Household Size and Expenditures
(1981/82)

	Poor Households	National Average
Household Size		
Rural	5.8	5.8
Urban	5.5	5.2
Household Expenditures (LE)		
Rural	450	1,059
Urban	517	1,441
Per Capita Expenditures (LE)		
Rural	78	188
Urban	94	277

Source: 1981/82 HBS, CAPMAS

2.17   One disturbing implication of these demographic features is that **children are the country's poorest age group**. Depending on the poverty line estimate selected, between one in four and one in three Egyptian youths live in poverty. The equivalent proportion for the USA is 20%.

2.18   Finally, even though the 1977 study indicated that the female/male distribution of the poor population is normal, it would be useful to be able to carry out a more detailed analysis of the sex ratio in the poorest households and to look at the male/female distribution and the marital status of heads of households. The experience in other middle income countries and in high income countries has been that the poorest households tend to have lower male/female ratios than less poor families (Lipton, 1988). Furthermore, even when the probability of being among the poorest is the same for women and men, the effect is usually worse for women who usually face more constraints in terms of work load (at home and outside), access to education and employment. As a result, they generally need to put in a larger effort to improve the standard of living of the family. Similar comments apply to divorced or widowed women who are heads of households.

2.19   Although their focus was not directly on poverty, two recent studies (Zurayk et al., 1988; Shorter, 1989) indicate that certain groups of women in urban areas fell clearly in high risk categories in terms of economic vulnerability. First, many elderly widows seem to be left outside the system. Most single person households are elderly widows, with a few women who have divorced and not remarried. Among women aged 65 years or more living in Cairo, 10% live alone. Even the youngest widows have no realistic prospect of making any but the most casual and intermittent earnings, and the more elderly none whatsoever. Despite the traditional custom of support for widows through transfers from family members, even if they do not live in the same household, many widows in practice are not adequately supported by members of their family. They are destitute and depend on casual charity from neighbors to survive. Field reports from charity organizations operating in Cairo reveal that elderly widows form the single most important client group. Non Governmental Organizations recognize them as a group prone to poverty and in need of special assistance.

2.20   Members of multiple-person female-headed households constitute a second group of highly vulnerable persons. According to the official statistics, around 10% of multiple person households living in Cairo have a female head (Table 1, Annex C). Between 2 and 4% of married women of different ages live alone with their children. In addition, many de facto female headed households are not included in official statistics, for example, women married to men whom they still declare as the head, but who have abandoned them economically in favor of a second marital household. Another case is when women's earnings support the household because the husband is unemployed or unemployable through old age, sickness or disability. In a low income neighborhood in Cairo 9.4% of households had a woman as the principal earner (Shorter, 1989); almost half these women had husbands.

Spatial Distribution

2.21   Incomes have always been lower in the rural areas than in the cities, although the gap has been slowly decreasing. At present, urban incomes are about 46% higher than rural incomes on the average.

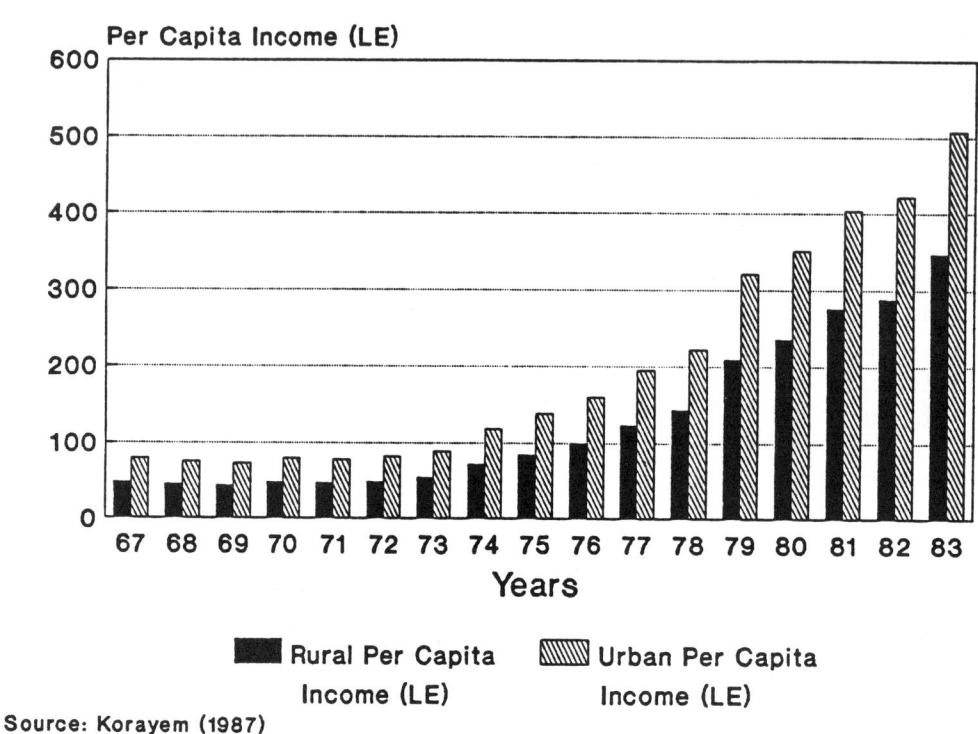

Graph 2.4 Income Differentials Between Urban and Rural

[Bar chart showing Per Capita Income (LE) from 1967 to 1983, comparing Rural Per Capita Income (LE) and Urban Per Capita Income (LE)]

Source: Korayem (1987)

2.22   Despite this difference in standards of living, the poor are evenly distributed between rural and urban areas: 56 to 59% of the poor live in the countryside whereas the share of the rural population in the overall population is 56%. Moreover, in the Egyptian case, the distinction between rural and urban areas is less meaningful than elsewhere because of the high degree of concentration of the population in the Nile valley and delta. As a result, most of the rural population lives close to urban areas. Analyzing differences among regions is therefore more significant.

2.23   The largest concentration of poor people is found in Upper Egypt: 41% of all poor live in the southern part of the country which accounts for only 29% of Egypt's population. The second largest group lives in the Delta, although there the poor are proportionally less represented: 38% for a 45% share of the Delta in the overall Egyptian population.

Table 2.3 Geographical Distribution of the Poor
(%)

	Rural Population		Urban Population		Total Population	
	Poor	Total	Poor	Total	Poor	Total
Cairo/Giza	2.5	5.1	30.6	31.8	11.9	16.2
Alexandria	-	-	14.6	15.4	6.5	6.4
Delta	42.7	56.7	25.4	29.1	37.8	45.2
Upper Egypt	54.1	38.1	23.0	17.3	41.6	29.5
Canal and Sinai	0.7	0.1	6.4	6.4	2.4	2.7
TOTAL	100.0	100.0	100.0	100.0	100.0	100.0

Source: 1981/82 HBS

2.24   The incidence of poverty varies considerably across governorates. (Table 4, Annex B) illustrates the wide range prevailing in both urban and rural areas as well as within regions. In some rural governorates, the incidence of poverty can reach as much as 114% above the national average, versus 87% in urban governorates. Most of the governorates with a relatively high degree of poverty are found in Upper Egypt, as expected. But even within the Delta region, the governorates of Munufia and Kalyubia show a poverty incidence much higher than the national average, even though the overall poverty problem is relatively smaller in that region.

Employment Characteristics

2.25   Any attempt to analyze the employment characteristics of the poor is constrained by the lack of appropriate data. The population's ability to meet basic economic needs is defined in terms of the household unit. Income derived from employment is an important means to meet these needs in most households. However, in Egypt, like many countries, employment and labor force activities are reported for individuals and not for households.

2.26   The fact that an individual is unemployed or out of the labor force does not necessarily mean that his or her household is incurring economic hardship. Youths, for example, may be engaged in the search for employment or in schooling as members of households where income is provided by the employment of a father or a mother. A spouse may elect to care for the home while the partner is employed in business. Even when an individual is reported as employed this does not automatically translate into the household being able to maintain a minimum standard of living. This depends on the earnings and the hours of employment, plus the possibility of other earners in the household.

2.27   Thus, to fully link an individual's employment status with the poverty status of the household requires the reporting of labor force and earnings activities for the individual as a member of a household. The failure of the census or annual labor force surveys to report information in this manner in Egypt, and in other countries as well, makes it difficult to assess the ability of households to meet their basic economic needs through employment.[1]

2.28   Several special surveys related to consumer expenditures and rural poverty, however, shed some light on this issue in Egypt. The Bank's study of poverty using the 1981/82 Household Budget Survey (HBS) provides information on the employment characteristics of heads of households by poverty status (World Bank, 1989). This information is limited to occupation and economic sector of activity. The 1977 ILO survey of rural households in 6 Governorates mentioned earlier provides additional information on rural poverty and employment (Radwan and Lee, 1986). The ILO survey includes information on the occupational structure of households and income from employment.

2.29   The choice of a poverty line in the HBS changes the number of households in poverty, but the profile of employment characteristics is relatively insensitive to the poverty line used. Employing the lower of two alternative poverty lines, the incidence of poverty in urban households is similar to that in rural households, 22% and 24% respectively. In both urban and rural areas, employment plays an important role in a household's ability to escape poverty. As shown in Graph 2.5, over one-third of the urban and rural poor heads of households are out of the labor force with no declared occupation. There are differences in the occupations and economic activities of the poor in urban and rural areas.

Graph 2.5 Distribution of the Poor by Occupation of Household Head (%)

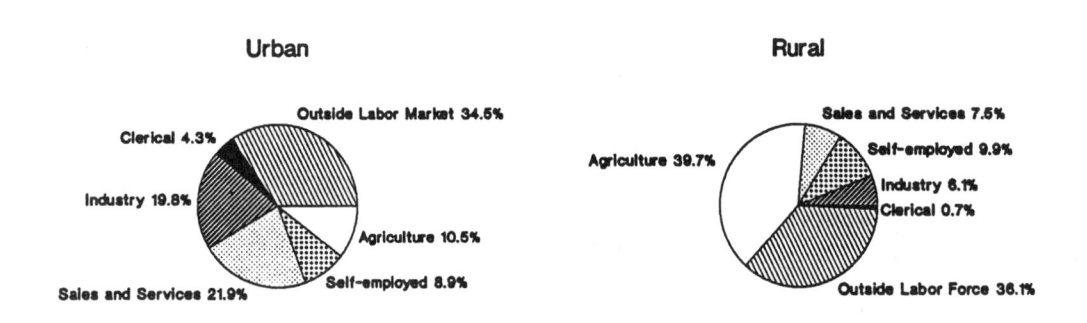

Urban
- Outside Labor Market 34.5%
- Clerical 4.3%
- Industry 19.8%
- Sales and Services 21.9%
- Self-employed 8.9%
- Agriculture 10.5%

Rural
- Sales and Services 7.5%
- Self-employed 9.9%
- Industry 6.1%
- Clerical 0.7%
- Outside Labor Force 36.1%
- Agriculture 39.7%

Source: 1981/82 HBS, CAPMAS

---

[1] For a discussion of labor market-related economic hardship and methods for measuring its incidence see <u>Counting the Labor Force</u>, report of the National Commission on Employment and Unemployment Statistics, Washington, D.C.: U.S. Government Printing Office, 1979.

2.30   In urban areas, poverty is associated with industrial employment and services. Both include large numbers of public enterprise and government employees. One-third of the urban poor work in production, transport, and communications and service occupations. Agricultural workers account for only 10% of the urban poor. The importance of industrial and service employment is reflected in the profile of the urban poor by sector of economic activity. In Graph 2.6, manufacturing industries employ nearly 13% of the urban poor. The majority are public enterprises. In the service sector, public and private social services account for more than 17% of the urban poor. This is mostly government employment. Another 11% are employed in food establishments and hotels in the tourism sector.

Graph 2.6 Distribution of the Poor by Economic Activity

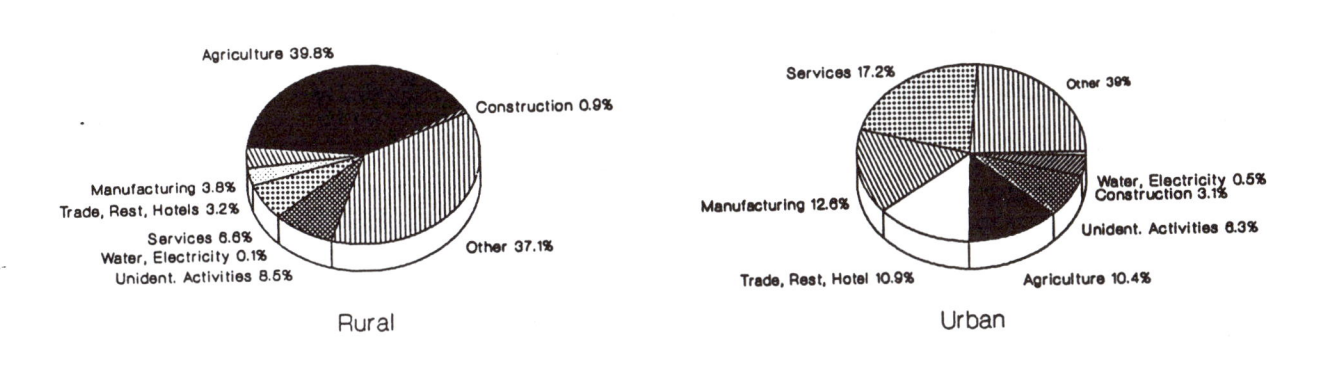

Rural
- Agriculture 39.8%
- Construction 0.9%
- Manufacturing 3.8%
- Trade, Rest, Hotels 3.2%
- Services 6.6%
- Water, Electricity 0.1%
- Unident. Activities 8.5%
- Other 37.1%

Urban
- Services 17.2%
- Other 39%
- Water, Electricity 0.5%
- Construction 3.1%
- Manufacturing 12.6%
- Unident. Activities 6.3%
- Trade, Rest, Hotel 10.9%
- Agriculture 10.4%

Source: 1981/82 HBS, CAPMAS

2.31   Not surprisingly, poverty in rural areas is linked closely to agriculture. Among the rural poor, nearly 40% are agricultural workers, and another 10% are self-employed which includes farm owners. The self-employed in rural areas have a much higher relative incidence of poverty than the self-employed in urban areas. In rural areas, the self-employed represent slightly over 6% of households, but 10% of the rural poor. By comparison, in urban areas the self-employed comprise over 12% of households, but slightly less than 9% of the urban poor. The problems of the self-employed in rural areas are evident in the sizeable share of the rural poor employed in unclassified activities, 8.5%, many of which are doubtless small enterprises in the informal sector.

2.32   The relative incidence of poverty described for the urban and rural self-employed is shown in Table 2.4 along with ratios for other occupations.

Table 2.4 - Relative Incidence of Poverty by Occupation of Household*

Occupation	Urban	Rural
Self-employed	0.7	1.6
Administrators and Directors	0.1	0.1
Clerical	0.5	0.3
Sales	0.9	0.6
Service	1.3	0.7
Agriculture	1.3	0.8
Production, Transport, and Communications	0.7	0.6
Unclassified	2.4	1.1
Outside Labor Force	1.6	1.9

* Occupational share of total household poverty divided by occupational share of total households.

Source: 1981/82 HBS, CAPMAS

Poverty is concentrated among low-skilled and marginal activities. Occupations with an above average share of urban household heads in poverty include service, agriculture, and unclassified workers. Household heads who are out of the labor force with no declared occupation are also over-represented among the urban poor. A similar picture emerges for household heads out of the labor force in rural areas along with unclassified workers and the self-employed. Unclassified and other sector activities have more than their proportionate share of household heads in poverty in both urban and rural areas (Table 7, Annex B).

2.33   The ILO survey provides a more extensive look at the employment characteristics of the rural poor. Even though this profile is over a decade old, it is consistent with the picture of employment provided by the HBS four years later which shows that non-agricultural activity is an important feature of the Egyptian rural economy and that agricultural employment is a major source of rural poverty.

2.34   One of the main findings of the survey is the existence of two significantly different sub-groups within the poor: the chronic poor, representing the poorest 10% of the rural population, and the poor who are economically active. The first group, corresponding to the earlier definition of the ultrapoor, stands out as a hard-core poverty group of households with a high level of dependence on transfer payments: 48% of their income is from remittances, the proportion being as high as 80% for the poorest 2%.

2.35   With regard to the bulk of the poor, the distribution of the rural labor force by occupation of household head in Graph 2.7 reveals that farmers and farm laborers accounted for 59% of the rural poor. This percentage is higher than that found for the rural poor in the HBS. However, the HBS included persons not in the labor force in calculating this percentage. If the HBS occupational profile were limited to those in the labor force, agricultural workers would account for nearly 63% of the rural poor, a figure reasonably close to that above for farmers and farm laborers considering possible differences in occupational classification.

Graph 2.7 Distribution of Rural Labor Force by Occupation of Household Head

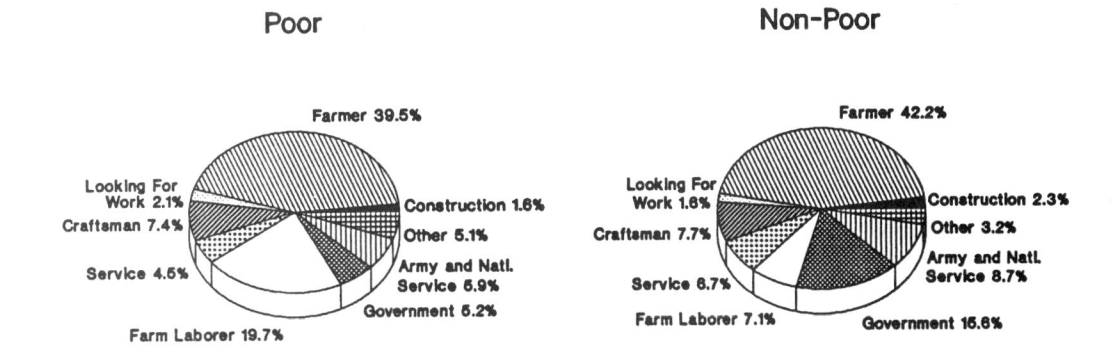

Poor

- Farmer 39.5%
- Looking For Work 2.1%
- Craftsman 7.4%
- Service 4.5%
- Farm Laborer 19.7%
- Government 5.2%
- Army and Natl. Service 5.9%
- Other 5.1%
- Construction 1.6%

Non-Poor

- Farmer 42.2%
- Looking For Work 1.6%
- Craftsman 7.7%
- Service 5.7%
- Farm Laborer 7.1%
- Government 15.6%
- Army and Natl. Service 8.7%
- Other 3.2%
- Construction 2.3%

Source: Radwan and Lee, 1986

2.36   Household heads in poor and non-poor households in rural areas display similar labor force participation patterns. This suggests that differences in incomes do not flow from the failure of the poor to engage in employment or search for work. Refined activity rates for both groups were calculated by dividing the rural labor force, excluding wives, by the population 6 years of age and over. The results show an activity rate for poor households of 40% and for non-poor households of 39%. These rates are low by international standards, but they reflect the presence of large numbers of youths in the Egyptian population.

2.37   Since both groups participate in the labor force at roughly the same rate, the difference in their incomes is attributable to skill levels, the utilization of these skills, and the compensation earned. Some evidence of these differences is found in a comparison of the occupational distribution of household heads and average household income by occupation of both groups. Differences in the skill mix are reflected in relatively more of the rural poor holding low-skill employment as farm laborers, while a larger share of the non-poor are government employees. With employment guarantees, the latter tend to be secondary or post-secondary graduates.

2.38   The importance of the observed differences in average household incomes is enlarged when the age structure of the two populations is considered. The poor in rural areas support a proportionately larger number of youths than the non-poor. Youths under 15 years of age represent 48% of the population in poverty households and only 40% of the population in non-poverty households. This is reflected in a dependency ratio that expresses the number of dependents (youths under 15 years of age, adults over 65 years, students, disabled, and the unemployed) in the household as a ratio of the total rural labor force, excluding wives. For poor households this ratio is 2.8 compared with 2.4 in non-poor households. The ratio varies randomly across occupations of household heads.

2.39   Both surveys while providing information on the employment activities of household heads fail to describe the activities of other household members. This precludes answering the question how many households require a second earner's income to escape poverty. In a partial response, the presence of child labor is frequently seen as an indicator of household poverty. Compulsory schooling in Egypt extends to 15 years of age, although it is legal to work at 12 years of age and older. The full extent of child labor is difficult to assess. Under 12 years of age it is illegal to work which discourages accurate reporting. Also, much of the work of children is intermittent which is difficult to capture in surveys. Children who work and attend school, moreover, are excluded from the labor force by the census.

2.40   The census estimate of child labor, as a result, is nearly 1 million less than that of the annual labor force survey. The 1984 annual labor force survey, the most recent available, counted as employed or looking for work nearly 1.5 million youths between 6 and 15 years of age. Slightly over 1 million were under 12 years of age. Two years later, in 1986, the census measured a half million youths between 6 and 15 years of age in the labor force with half this number under 12 years of age. By excluding those in school, the census estimate is probably a good measure of the core number of children facing economic hardship. Children under 12, as measured by the annual labor force survey, have been increasing as a percentage of the total labor force, rising to 7% in 1984. Seventy percent were in rural areas. This pattern reflects demographic trends in the context of household poverty.

2.41   Two main conclusions emerge from this profile of the employment characteristics of the poor. First, with the exception of the ultrapoor who are heavily dependent on income transfers, the poor and the non-poor have an equal commitment to employment as a means to meet their basic economic needs. It is the outcome of this experience in earnings that separates the two. Second, there are important differences in the employment profiles of urban and rural areas. Poverty alleviation strategies will need to consider these differences.

Poverty and Basic Needs Satisfaction

> "Everyone has the right to a standard of living adequate for the health and well-being of himself and his family, including food, clothing, housing and medical care and necessary social services, and the right to security in the event of unemployment, sickness, disability, widowhood, old age, or other lack of livelihood in circumstances beyond his control".
>
> Universal Declaration of Human Rights, Article 25

2.42   Another way of measuring poverty is to look at outcome indicators describing how the poor live, i.e. what kind of material hardship they are confronted with and how they are able to meet their most fundamental needs. Five key aspects need to be explored in this perspective: protection from malnutrition; protection from death and diseases; access to adequate shelter; access to safe water and sanitation; and protection from ignorance.

Malnutrition

2.43   Ensuring the food security of the population has historically been a major priority of the Government of Egypt. This concern for the nutritional welfare of the population is reflected in the food consumption profile of the country. From 1970 onward, the food availability per capita has increased steadily in Egypt with caloric availability reaching 3390 calories per capita in 1980 (Table 1, Annex E). Per capita food availability has remained at that level since the early 1980s.

2.44   The food availability in Egypt is comparable to levels in developed countries and far exceeds the average availability for developing countries (2150 calories/capita) as a whole. Even comparing the food availability to only other countries in the region, the levels of consumption in Egypt are superior to Morocco, Tunisia and Turkey.

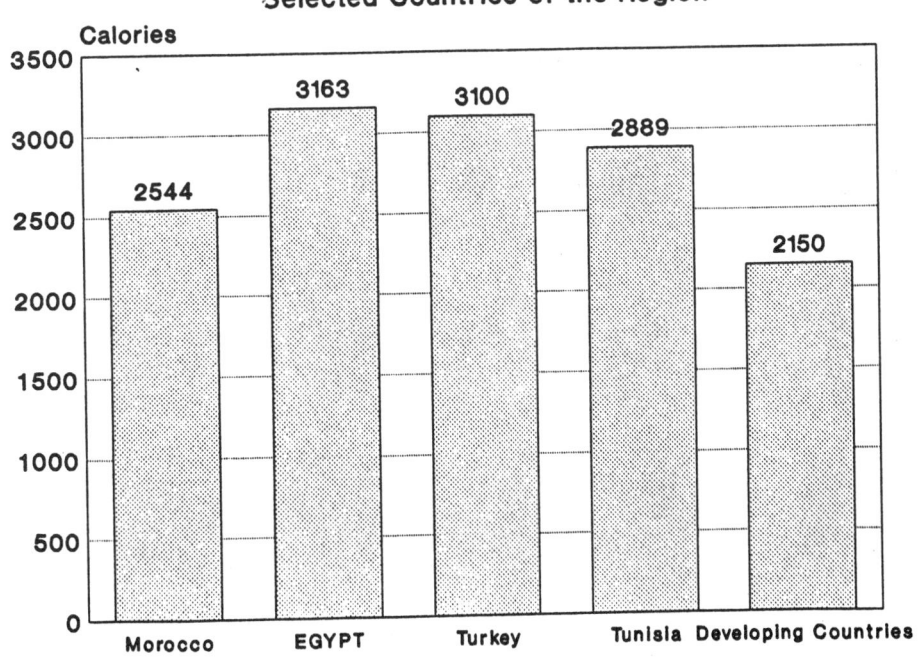

**Graph 2.8 Daily Calorie Supply Per Capita
Selected Countries of the Region**

Country	Calories
Morocco	2544
EGYPT	3163
Turkey	3100
Tunisia	2889
Developing Countries	2150

Source: World Development Report, 1986

2.45   Food availability per capita can overestimate actual consumption since no account is taken of waste, non-human consumption of food, etc. However a 1981 survey of actual food intake of the population also showed levels of consumption in excess of requirements; on average, caloric intake per capita was 2843 and protein intake 96 grams per capita. This represents 103% and 117% of energy and protein requirement respectively.

2.46   However, while these per capita levels of food intake seem high for the population as a whole, the data by themselves are misleading since there are significant portions of the population with inadequate energy intakes. Approximately 35% of the population consumes less than 2,000 calories per capita. The problem of inadequate consumption is slightly worse in the rural compared to the urban areas of the country.

Table 2.5   **Average Percentage Distribution of Families According to Levels of Caloric Intake**
(%)

	No. of Families	<1500	1500-	2000-	2500-	3000-	3500-
Urban	3780	14.8	18.3	20.4	17.2	11.7	17.6
Rural	2520	19.7	18.8	18.0	16.7	10.4	16.4
Total	6300	16.8	18.5	19.4	17.0	11.2	17.1

Calories (Cal/Head/Day)

Source: Galal and Amine, 1984.

2.47   On average Egypt has done well in safeguarding the food security and making gains in the health profile of the population. However, the decreases in infant and child mortality over recent years have not been paralleled by an equivalent improvement in nutritional status (CAPMAS and UNICEF, 1988). Data from a 1978 National Nutrition Survey were compared to a follow-up survey conducted nine years later in 1986. The original 1978 survey data are presented in two ways, first for the 1978 sample as a whole and secondly only for the 34 sites that were surveyed again in the 1986 study.

Table 2.6   Prevalence of Malnutrition[2]
(%)

	National Survey 1978	34 Sites 1978	34 Sites 1986
Acute undernutrition	2.3	2.9	7.0
Chronic undernutrition	21.2	26.5	24.1
Gomez classification (1st, 2nd and 3rd degree)	47.0	52.0	47.0

Source: CAPMAS and UNICEF, 1988

The data indicate that between 1978 and 1986 the levels of chronic undernutrition stayed about the same. However the prevalence of acute undernutrition appears to have increased. One note of caution in interpreting the information from the two periods is warranted; some of the difference in prevalence of acute undernutrition may be due to a seasonality effect. The 1986 survey was conducted in the summer months when acute undernutrition tends to be higher in Upper Egypt but not in Lower Egypt (Galal and Amine, 1984). A conservative interpretation of the 1978/1986 comparison is that nutritional status has not improved between the two time periods. Alternatively, the data might also indicate that the nutritional status of preschool age children has deteriorated. In either case there is room for substantial improvement in the nutrition situation.

2.48   The pattern of growth retardation varies by age of the child. Table 2.7 presents anthropometric data from the 1978 National Nutrition Survey desegregated by age groupings.

Table 2.7 Malnutrition in Preschoolers by Age Category
(Based on weight-for-age)

Months	Weight-for-Age % of Median Severe	Moderate
6 - 11	2.5	8.4
12 - 23	1.8	16.7
24 - 35	0.5	7.9

---

[2] Acute undernutrition equals weight for height less than 85% of standard. Chronic undernutrition equals height less than 90% of standard. Gomez: 1st degree equals weight/age 75 to 89%; 2nd degree equals weight/age 60 to 74%; 3rd degree equals weight/age less than 60%.

Table 2.7 (Cont'd)

	Weight-for-Age % of Median	
Months	Severe	Moderate
36 - 47	--	4.5
48 - 59	--	3.5
60 - 71	--	3.5
Total	0.8	8.0

Source: CAPMAS and UNICEF, 1988.

Moderate and severe malnutrition, as evidenced by low weight for age, is most pronounced in the 12 to 23 month old child. Extensive data (Capmas and Unicef, 1988) indicate that much of the documented malnutrition is due to a combination of poor weaning and breastfeeding practices, and high rates of morbidity including diarrhea. Poor health and sanitation practices are linked to poverty.

2.49 Breastfeeding remains the norm in Egypt with over 90% of mothers initiating breastfeeding. By six months of age, however, 25% of the mothers have stopped breastfeeding their infant (Galal and Amine, 1984). Infant mortality in Egypt is significantly higher in infants who are not breastfed (CAPMAS and UNICEF, 1988); infants who are breastfed are also less likely to be malnourished.

2.50 Malnutrition rates in preschoolers also vary by geographic area in Egypt. Both wasting (low weight-for-height) and stunting (low height-for-age) are more prevalent in rural than in urban areas. In addition, preschooler malnutrition is significantly worse in rural Upper Egypt compared to rural Lower Egypt. For example, 12.9% of preschoolers are moderately and severely malnourished in rural Upper Egypt compared to 8.4% in rural Lower Egypt. Cairo and Alexandria have higher rates of malnutrition than other urban areas in the country.

2.51 Despite the fact that household food availability is, on average, greater than 100% of needs, childrens' energy intakes are low. Food linked malnutrition in children has been related to maldistribution of food within the household rather than an absolute deficit in household food supplies; 65% of preschoolers consumed less than 90% of their caloric requirements. Similarly, 79% of school-aged children consumed less than 90% of their energy requirements (Hussein et al, 1978). These apparently low caloric intakes in school age children exist in tandem with a growing problem of obesity of school age children, particularly girls.

2.52   One nutrition related problem which often receives less attention than protein-energy malnutrition is anemia. The anemia rates in Egypt for women and children are alarmingly high. The data from Table 2.8 indicate that 38.4% of preschoolers are anemic with 11.2% severely anemic. Anemia is most prevalent in the 12 to 23 month old child, the same age group that is also most likely to be growth retarded.

Table 2.8 Prevalence of Anaemia among Preschool Children by Age Group
(%)

	National Survey 1978	34 Sites 1978	1986
6 - 11	57.3	77.8	74.4
12 - 23	59.4	57.8	60.4
24 - 35	41.1	44.8	56.0
36 - 47	31.9	40.7	48.3
48 - 59	16.6	27.2	38.5
60 - 71	12.8	33.3	35.1
Total	38.4	48.0	51.6

Source: Capmas and Unicef, 1988

2.53   The profile of anemia in women is equally serious. Graph 2.9 shows that 22.1% of pregnant women and 25.3% of lactating women are anemic. Not surprisingly, infants born to anemic women are more likely to also be anemic (CAPMAS and UNICEF, 1988) and thus start off life already nutritionally disadvantaged.

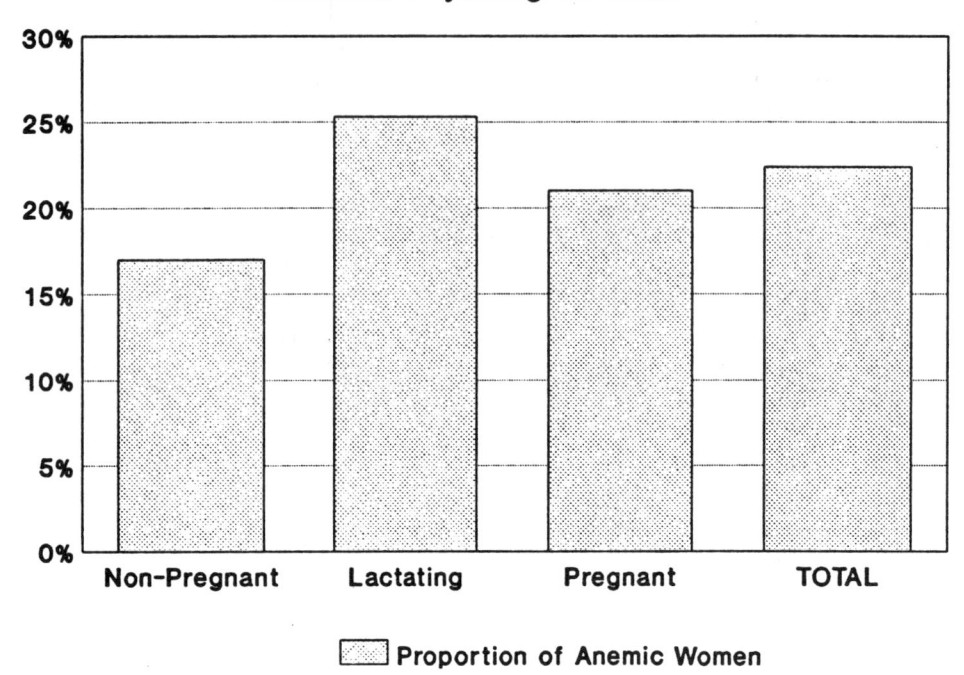

Graph 2.9 Prevalence of Anemia Among Mothers of Different Physiological Status

Source: CAPMAS and UNICEF, 1988

2.54   For young children anemia is caused by a combination of poor diet, parasitic infections and, in some cases, a genetic predisposition. In addition to the obvious health consequences, anemia also influences the cognitive development of the child and dampens the impact of educational investments on the child.

Health

2.55   As measured in terms of mortality and morbidity, the general health of the entire population has steadily improved during the last two decades, with progress in child survival being more accentuated since 1980. However, the beneficial effects are unevenly distributed, with urban areas being more favored than villages, and with the health conditions of the high and middle income group improving faster than those of lower income, some of the very poor remaining totally untouched.

2.56   Notwithstanding the great improvements in child survival achieved so far, infant mortality (first year of life) remains still high at 60 per thousand (adjusted rate)[3]. Similarly, with a child mortality rate (1-4 age group) of 7.4 per thousand and a survival ratio of 87.1, the situation in Egypt is relatively worse than in most other Middle East and North African countries. (Table 1, Annex F) presents the evolution of the infant and child mortality rates between 1970 and 1987.

2.57   Many of the deaths of Egyptian babies and children could be prevented, as evidenced by the pattern of infant and children deaths which is characterized by the predominance of the three following causes: complications of pregnancy, acute respiratory infections and diarrheal diseases (Graph 2.11). The leading cause of neonatal deaths (50%) is complication of pregnancy such as neonatal tetanus, birth trauma and low birth weight. Diarrheal diseases and acute respiratory infections account for more than half the total infant deaths and two-thirds of child deaths.

2.58   Considerable inequalities exist in infant and child mortality by region. The risk of death at birth is five times higher in rural areas than in urban and 4.7 times greater in Upper Egypt than in other parts of the country. In terms of child mortality, the urban governorates measure the most favorable rates (3.5) while rates are more than three times higher (11.1) in Upper Egypt.

Table 2.9   Infant and Child Deaths by Regions

Region	Infant Mortality (per thousand)	Child Mortality (per thousand)
Urban Governorates	44	3.5
Delta	43	5.6
Upper Egypt	91	11.1
Frontier	42	4.3
National	60	7.5

Source: Ministry of Health

The differences in infant and child mortality across individual governorates are even more striking (Table 2, Annex F).

---

[3]   Delays in birth registration result in some inaccuracy, because deaths occurring before registration often remain unreported. While under-registration is minimal in Cairo and moderate in urban areas, it is fairly substantial in rural areas (Rashad, 1988). Official rates therefore tend to underestimate the degree of infant mortality and have to be adjusted accordingly.

Graph 2.10 Infant and Child Mortality by Cause of Death

Neo-Natal Deaths

- Complications Due Mainly To Pregnancy 49.6%
- Diarrhea and Other Intestinal Diseases 11.6%
- Acute Respiratory Diseases 12.0%
- Communicable Diseases 0.03%
- Others 19.1%
- Congenital Anomalies 7.6%

Infant Mortality

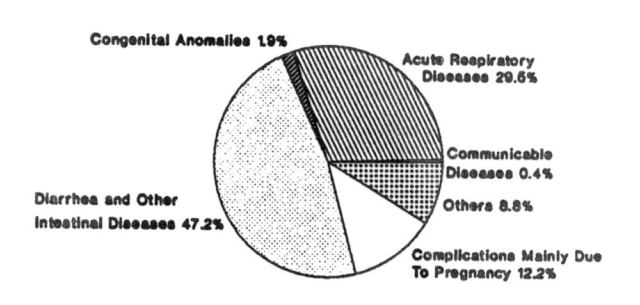

- Congenital Anomalies 1.9%
- Acute Respiratory Diseases 29.5%
- Communicable Diseases 0.4%
- Others 8.8%
- Complications Mainly Due To Pregnancy 12.2%
- Diarrhea and Other Intestinal Diseases 47.2%

Child Mortality

- Complications Due Mainly To Pregnancy 8.5%
- Acute Respiratory Diseases 35.4%
- Communicable Diseases 0.3%
- Others 7.4%
- Congenital Anomalies 2.4%
- Diarrhea and Other Intestinal Diseases 46.8%

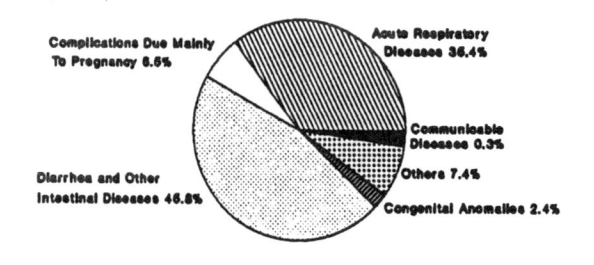

Source: CAPMAS, Births and Deaths Statistics 1970-1982

2.59   There is clear evidence of a close link between socio-economic status and child mortality. Data from the Egypt Fertility Survey demonstrate the strong effect of household income on childhood mortality (Ismail et al, 1988). Households living in crowded conditions (3 or more persons per room) have higher child mortality rates (Capmas, 1988). The highest mortality rates are found in those governorates which present the largest concentration of low income families.

2.60   Infant and child mortality rates are significantly higher for girls than for boys (Makinson, 1986). This pattern holds true for the various causes of death. Data from nutritional surveys, observations on medical practices and the reduction in birth intervals after the birth of a girl all indicate a clear differential treatment of children based on sex within households.

2.61   In the adult population, maternal mortality related to complications of pregnancy remains the leading cause of death among women of reproductive age. The Ministry of Health reports a constant rate of 0.8 deaths per thousand live births during the period 1981-1985.

2.62   Morbidity in Egypt is characterized by the predominance of chronic infectious and parasitic diseases. The poorest section of the population is usually the group most exposed to these highly debilitating disorders. Bilharzia (Schistosomiasis) remains one of the most serious public health problems. Carried by blood flukes and transmitted by fresh water mollusks which thrive in polluted water, the disease is acquired by wading, bathing, or washing clothes in the Nile River and its tributaries--or by drinking the infested water. Two clinical types coexist in Egypt: the urinary (S. Haematobia) with a prevalence rate of 7.3% in Upper Egypt and the intestinal (S. Mansoni), with a very high prevalence rate in the Delta: from 20 to 53% depending on the governorate (Table 3, Annex F). Bilharzia has grave clinical manifestations involving tract diseases, bladder cancer, liver failure and dysfunction of the portal circulatory system.

2.63   Leprosy, with an estimated overall prevalence of 4.1 per thousand remains of high endemicity in Upper Egypt and of moderate endemicity in Lower Egypt. Prevalence in the slums of Cairo and Alexandria remains unknown.

2.64   Pulmonary tuberculosis is still a serious problem. Persistent government efforts have succeeded in reducing the incidence of open cases but overcrowding, poor sanitary conditions and inadequate nutrition are responsible for maintaining a low endemicity among the underprivileged groups, estimated at 20 new cases per 100,000 inhabitants.

2.65   Unsafe water supplies in the rural areas and in urban slums favor the occurrence of acute enteric infections such as typhoid, paratyphoid and infectious hepatitis. These remain endemic with limited occurrence of sporadic outbreaks. Similarly, improper disposal of human excreta is responsible for the widespread problem of various intestinal parasites, the most serious being amoebiases which remains endemic throughout the country. Hookworm infestation is reported to be present in about half of the preschool and school children. It contributes to severe anemia commonly found among children, pregnant women and lactating mothers.

2.66   To conclude this analysis of the impact of poverty on health, it should be emphasized that, even though most data available are related to mortality aspects, the primary concern in terms of health of the poor should be the crippling effects of disability on the _living_ poor. The majority of the poor who survived childhood are condemned to drift through life in a state of chronic ill-health and debility which sets them apart from other groups and limits their participation in normal social and economic life.

2.67   Disability syndromes prevalent in the Egyptian context include difficulties in working and productivity, seeing, speaking, hearing, writing, walking, learning, and many other functions. Malnutrition among children has compounded effects on the physical well-being and productive capacities of adults. Schistosomiasis is a disabilitating disease due to the extensive involvement of the intestine, liver and bladder. In urinary schistosomiasis, which is prevalent in Upper Egypt, urination becomes painful and there is progressive damage to the bladder, ureters and kidneys. In intestinal schistosomiasis, there is progressive enlargement of the liver and spleen as well as damage to the intestine. Work performance is constrained by diarrhea and abdominal pains. Trachoma affects millions and causes varying degrees of sight impairment and blindness. Even a simple problem like the lack of spectacles for children in school can turn a remediable impairment into permanent disability.

Access to Safe Water and Sanitation

2.68   Population access to water services has improved significantly over the last decade. However, the lack of access to safe water for many households, especially in rural areas, and the poor quality of the service at times pose a considerable, if not the most important, threat to the welfare of Egypt's population.

2.69   The 1986 Census offers information on the type of water source available in dwellings in both urban and rural areas. In urban areas, the vast majority of households (92.4%) has access to piped public water systems. In rural areas, however, only a little over half the total number of dwellings (55.9%) are connected to public water systems. In Upper Egypt, only 42% are connected. Furthermore, other Census data show that only 29% of rural buildings are connected to piped systems. In view of these statistical inconsistencies and based on complementary information obtained through field visits and interviews, there is reason to believe that the 55.9% is a very optimistic figure.

Graph 2.11 Dwellings by Source of Water

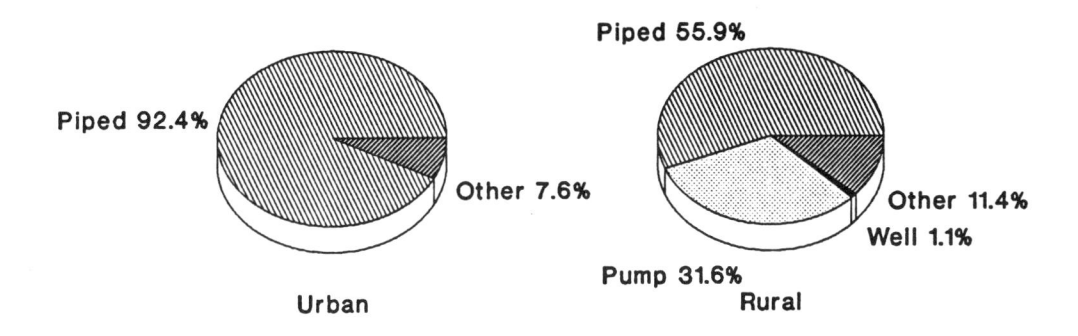

Urban: Piped 92.4%, Other 7.6%

Rural: Piped 55.9%, Pump 31.6%, Well 1.1%, Other 11.4%

Source: PHE Census, CAPMAS, 1986

2.70   Rural households who are not connected to public water systems get their water from deep and shallow wells or surface waters, including the Nile and irrigation canals. The use of shallow wells, most common in Upper Egypt, and surface waters, most common in the Delta region, pose the gravest health hazards because these water sources are easily contaminated or are already polluted. The lack of maintenance equipment, the existence of broken pipelines, and shortages of chlorine have meant that many water systems, especially small ones outside large urban areas, are frequently supplying contaminated water. In some instances, public water systems have pumped water directly from the Nile.

2.71   The situation is even worse for sewage systems. In Egypt as in many other developing countries, the coverage of sewage services lags considerably behind that of water services. The Census does not report household access to sewer lines. It appears that sewage systems are non existent in rural Egypt, and that only a small proportion of rural households have access to latrines. Stables and open fields are used for personal relief. In urban areas, around one third of households have no access to flush waste disposal (sewer lines or septic tanks), and most sewage lines and treatment plants are in a poor state of repair and working to over capacity. Thus, a substantial fraction of the Egyptian population, which is likely to include most of the poor, live without access to hygienic waste disposal systems.

2.72   **The lack of access to safe water and adequate sanitation constitute the main reason behind the large incidence of water-borne diseases** such as infectious diseases, parasites and related illnesses in Egypt (Par. 2.65). Rural areas with the most acute water problems, such as Upper Egypt, also exhibit the highest morbidity and mortality rates.

> "Provision of piped water to the dwelling is associated with
> higher survival probabilities during early childhood.
> In contrast, children in households relying on water from
> public faucets experience lower survival probabilities
> at this age."
>
> (Hallouda et al, 1988, p. 308)

Shelter

2.73   Housing is among the most neglected socio-economic sectors in Egypt. Widespread rent controls have practically frozen official rental prices since the mid-1960s. After a quarter of century of such government policy, the housing situation has become serious, characterized by the four following problems. First, there is a serious shortage of rental housing combined with poor maintenance or no maintenance at all of existing units. Second, new housing units are being built almost exclusively to be sold so that the stock of rental housing units is not growing. Furthermore, most new housing units are sold at a prohibitive price. For over three-fourths of the population, the price of a standard new dwelling in an urban area exceeds one hundred times their annual income. Third, a black market for new rental units has developed, in which tenants pay large up-front sums in the form of "key money". Fourth, there is an excessively high vacancy rate of housing units in the face of a severe housing shortage.

2.74   The 1986 Census reports a total stock of 11.3 million housing units in Egypt. Approximately 52% of these units are located in urban areas and 48% in rural areas. **The Census data on housing units by type indicate that an important share of dwellings are substandard.** "Separate rooms" are defined as rooms used for habitation and not provided with special facilities, typically found on roofs or in courtyards. "Rural houses" are usually built of clay and equipped with an animal shed. The "marginal residential places" are generally considered as units not intended for habitation. These units include tents, cemetery yards or fixed vehicles. It should be noted that the figure for marginal residential places in urban areas (61,000 units) seem to be grossly underestimated in the light of numerous press reports on the growing squatter population of the City of the Dead in Cairo (Waterbury, 1982).

2.75   Census data on the average number of people per housing unit and per room reveal a situation of overcrowding. In 1986 the average number of people per housing unit was 4.9 and the average number of persons per room was 1.5. Unofficial estimates show significantly higher levels for these two indicators, owing to the fact that many of the housing units included in the Census computation of the averages are substandard or entirely inadequate for human habitation. Also, many of the units and/or rooms have been subdivided at least once.

Graph 2.12 Distribution of Housing Units by Type (%)

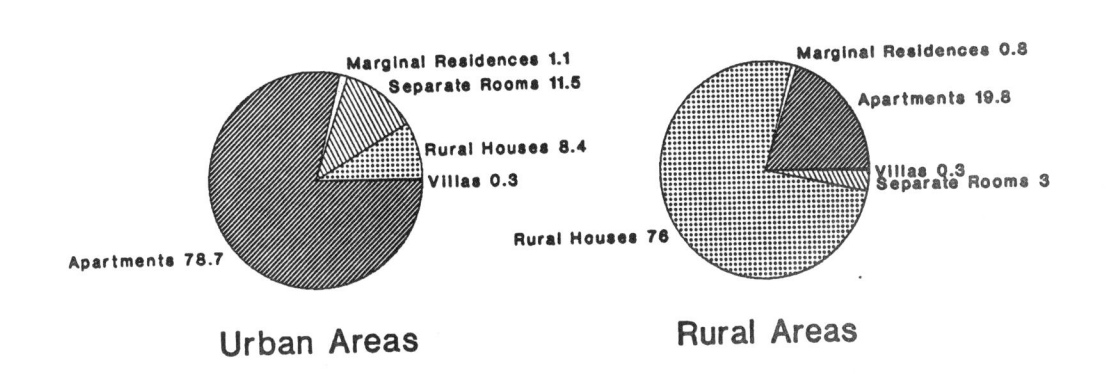

Urban Areas
- Marginal Residences 1.1
- Separate Rooms 11.5
- Rural Houses 8.4
- Villas 0.3
- Apartments 78.7

Rural Areas
- Marginal Residences 0.8
- Apartments 19.8
- Villas 0.3
- Separate Rooms 3
- Rural Houses 76

Source: 1986 Census, CAPMAS

2.76   The present situation of housing shortage, which explains the relatively high proportion of substandard housing units and the problem of overcrowding, is the result of many years of insufficient investment in the context of rapid demographic growth. Between 1960 and 1979, the supply of new housing units was only 700,000 while the population of Egypt almost doubled, from 26 to 40.8 million. During the first five-year plan (1982/83 - 1986/87), the rhythm of construction accelerated, with 812,000 new units built in that period. But this improved performance was barely enough to keep up with the additional population of 4.1 million, let alone to absorb part of the deficit.

Graph 2.13 Housing Deficit
(Figures in Thousands)

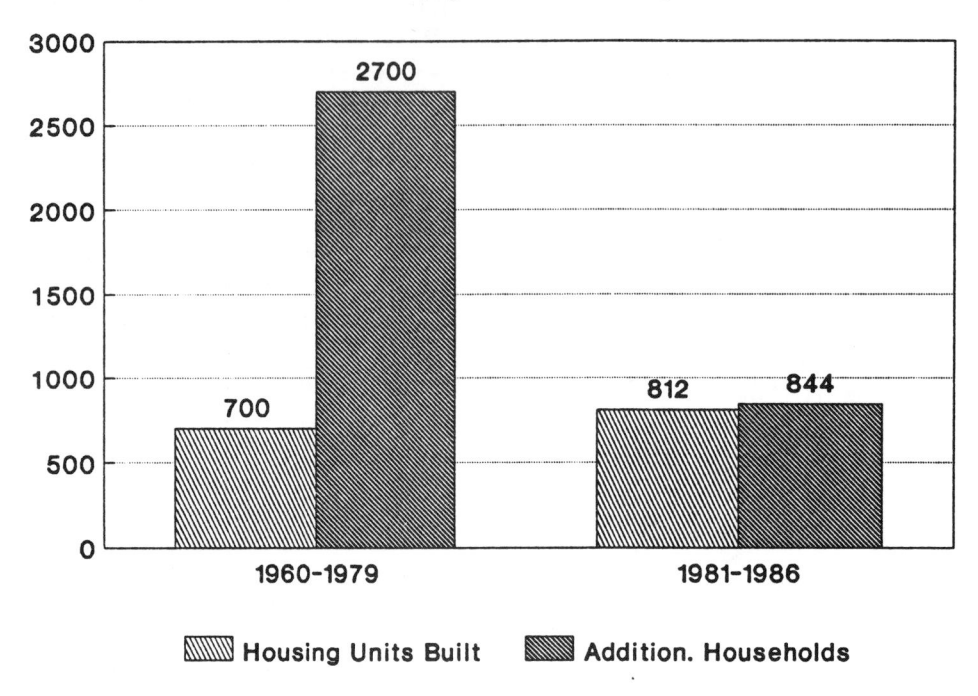

Period	Housing Units Built	Addition. Households
1960-1979	700	2700
1981-1986	812	844

Source: Ministry of Planning

2.77   At the same time, there are an estimated 1.8 million vacant housing units overall. This represents a vacancy rate of 17.3 percent in urban areas and 15.9 in rural areas. These vacancy rates are surprisingly high in the context of the housing shortages which have been reported almost throughout Egypt. They reflect the existence of a substantial inventory of unsold units due to the high price of land and to the fact that rent controls have led homeowners and landlords to hoard housing for future needs of family relatives.

2.78   The standard economic indicators used to measure living standards do not reflect the decrease in welfare linked to the housing situation. For example, the housing component of the consumer price index is essentially based on the official, frozen rental rates and does not incorporate either the "key money" cost or other forms of black market payments for rental units nor the high price of new dwellings for sale. Nevertheless, there is enough evidence that the housing shortage in Egypt has a significant negative impact on the welfare of low income households. In addition to hurting the poor, the unavailability of affordable housing has affected also many middle income households, specially younger households residing in urban areas. The housing shortage has been especially hard on young couples not fortunate enough to inherit a rent-controlled apartment.

2.79   To cope with the housing shortage, the poor and middle income households frequently have built their own substandard units in squatted public land, with the tacit or reluctant approval of the public authorities. In these situations, households do not have ownership of the land and only the structures are bought and sold. Shorter (1989) describes how poor households in Cairo have settled in areas lacking water, sewage, garbage collection and basic social services, and have to travel outside the settlements to buy subsidized food.

2.80   A second way of coping with the housing shortage has been to add to existing structures, converting one or two story buildings into high rises. Sometimes additions consist of simple rooms built in the yards or on the roof of the buildings. The additions typically violate building codes for safety, and hygienic conditions. A third method of coping with the housing shortage has been to subdivide existing units making two and sometimes three apartments out of one. The internal conditions of some of these units have been described as "inconceivable" (El Safy, 1987). In some instances, rooms were built below the staircase, kitchens had been partitioned to include toilets without separation from the kitchen, and the latrines were overflowing due to overcrowding and poor maintenance.

2.81   A consequence of the housing shortage has been to postpone marriage. In some instances, couples get married but continue to live separately with their respective parents. Many other couples start married life with parents or other relatives. In Cairo, one-third of all couples start married life with parents (Shorter, 1989). When children are born, this percentage declines, but 27% of couples with 3 children or more still live with parents. In rural Egypt, over 40 percent of couples start married life with parents. In the recent past, the only hope for many couples of moving into their own dwelling has been for the husband to migrate to the Gulf States for a number of years and to save enough.

2.82   Egypt's housing shortage has caused in urban areas a reversal in trend from the nuclear family back to the traditional extended family, although in a distorted way (El Safy, 1987). Many nuclear families have been forced to live together with little else in common than the place of residence, thus lacking the cohesiveness of the traditional extended family. Household activities such as cooking and eating are fragmented while the high level of crowding is a constant source of tensions.

Education

2.83   Soon after the 1952 revolution, the government embarked on a policy of education development which has never wavered since. Increasing resources have been devoted to build up the education network and enrollments have grown rapidly at all levels. The number of children in primary education increased from 1 million in 1952 to close to 7 million in 1989 at an average annual growth rate of 5.1% (Table 1, Annex H). Secondary education enrolments increased from 154,000 to 3.8 million, with a 9.1% growth rate. In higher education, enrolments by 7.1% a year, from 37,000 to about half a million today.

2.84   But despite this tremendous progress, education expansion has not entirely kept pace with population growth. As a result, **illiteracy remains high and a non-negligeable proportion of school-age children have been left out.** In 1986, 17.3 million people representing about half of the population age 10 or above were classified by the Census as not able to read and write. The absolute number of illiterate people has actually increased since 1976, when it was 15.1 million. The female illiteracy rate is even higher: 62% versus 38% for men.

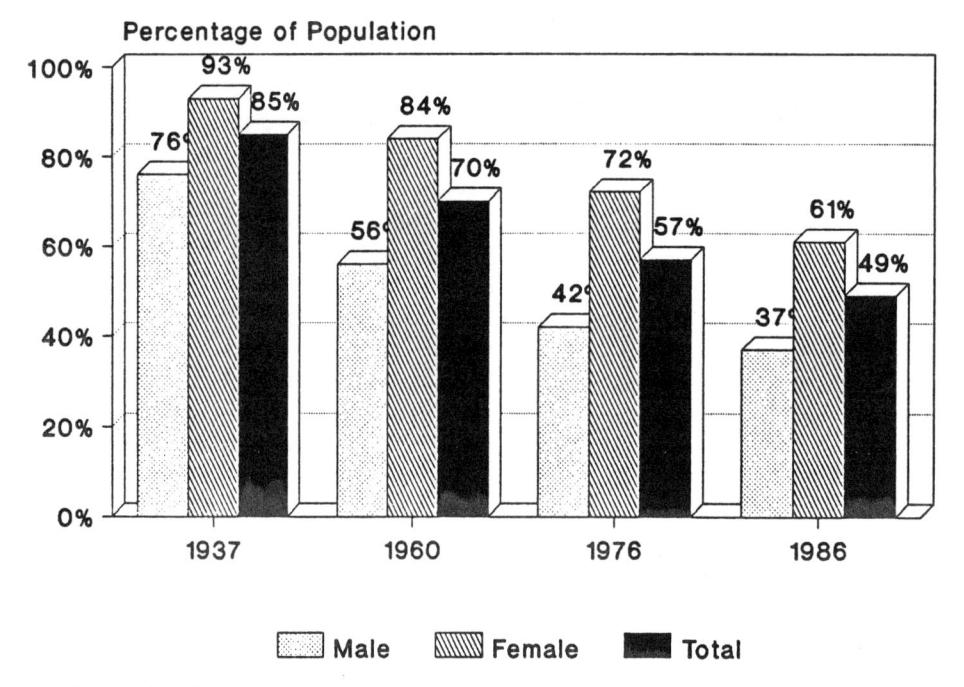

**Graph 2.14 Illiteracy in Egypt
(Age 10 and Above)**

Year	Male	Female	Total
1937	76%	93%	85%
1960	56%	84%	70%
1976	42%	72%	57%
1986	37%	61%	49%

Source: Population Census, CAPMAS
Hansen, 1989

2.85   Between 1966 and 1986, the primary school enrolment ratio at age 6 grew from 72 to 90% (Table, Annex). For the larger group of primary school age population (6-11), the enrolment ratio increased from 70 to 81%. However, this image of overall progress hides important variations in enrolments between girls and boys. For girls, the enrolment rates for the age 6 and age 6 to 11 groups were 82% and 74% respectively in 1986. Girls constitute only 45% of total enrolments in primary education, which is the same figure as in 1966. Graph 2.15 illustrates the evolution of the total number of out-of-school children distributed by sex, representing the sum of those who have never been schooled and of those who entered primary school but dropped out before finishing.

Graph 2.15 Children Out of School
(Age 6-11)

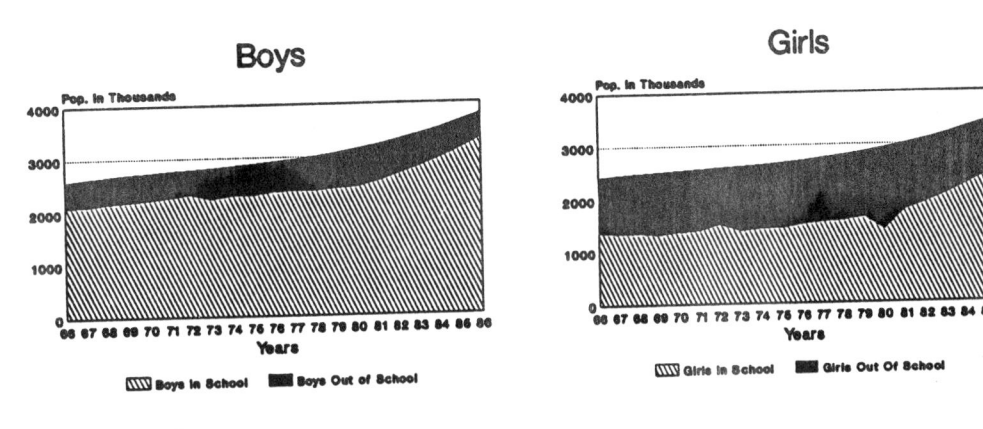

Boys

Girls

Source: MOE

2.86   As with other dimensions of poverty, the incidence of illiteracy varies considerably across governorates. Table 2.10, which looks at the regional differences in educational development in rural Egypt, exemplifies these differences. The most disadvantaged governorates are found in Upper Egypt (Fayoum, Beni-Suef, Sohag, Minya) and the Delta (Dakhaliya, Qualioubiya).

Table 2.10 Regional Differences in Educational Development
(1986)

Governorates	Incidence of Rural Poverty	Female Illiteracy (%)
Cairo	-	39.2
Alexandria	-	41.8
Port Said	-	39.1
Suez	-	44.4
Damietta	5.5	50.5
Dakhaliya	19.6	60.8
Sharkia	21.5	40.6

(Table 2.10 cont'd)

Governorates	Incidence of Rural Poverty	Female Illiteracy %
Qalioubiya	31.8	61.0
Kafr El Sheikh	15.6	73.1
Gharbiya	17.1	61.3
Menoufiya	25.6	63.9
Beheira	11.4	72.0
Ismalia	10.8	38.5
Giza	10.6	56.1
Beni Suef	51.8	78.4
Fayoum	34.0	79.0
Minya	41.3	79.2
Assiut	35.3	76.0
Sohag	25.1	79.7
Qena	21.4	78.7
Aswan	24.9	58.5
Red Sea	-	8.7
New Valley	-	50.7
Matrouh	-	76.4
Sinai	-	63.2

Source: 1986 Census, CAPMAS
MOE reports

2.87   These regional data on enrolments and illiteracy show a strong correlation between poverty incidence and low levels of educational development. This pattern is confirmed by a 1979 study prepared by the Joint Egyptian-American Team which documented the link between socio-economic level and access to primary education. It is safe to assume that a high proportion of children from poor communities have no access to school or leave school very early, with a likely relapse into illiteracy. Being illiterate has far-reaching and lasting negative consequences for the poor. Not only does it imply a denial of the right to be protected from ignorance, but it also involves a lack of access to productive skills and, as a corollary, income-earning opportunities.

Conclusion: Poverty Matrix for Egypt

2.88   The matrix below summarizes the most salient features of the poverty problem in Egypt.

POVERTY MATRIX

INDICATORS	RURAL POPULATION	URBAN POPULATION	NATIONAL
Proportion of Poor (%)	24.2	22.5	n.a
Proportion of Ultra Poor (%)	12.8	10.8	n.a
Malnutrition (%)	19.7	14.8	16.8
Infant Mortality (per thousand)	n.a.	n.a.	60.0
Child Mortality (per thousand)	n.a.	n.a.	7.4
Lack of Safe Water (%)	44.1	7.6	26.9
Poor Housing (%)	29.0	21.0	24.9
Illiteracy (%)	61.2	35.3	49.4

2.89   Beyond the picture depicted by these telling statistics, it is important to emphasize the following points to be taken into account in designing an appropriate poverty alleviation strategy:

- women and children are among the most vulnerable groups; poor children, in particular, are exposed to difficult living conditions (lack of protection from malnutrition and preventible diseases), have no or limited access to school, and are put to work at a young age;

- Upper Egypt is the poorest region in the country, together with Kalyubia, Gharbia and Munufia governorates in the Delta region;

- in the rural areas, the poor are either farmers with no land or little land or agricultural laborers; in the cities, poverty is associated with industrial employment and services, including a significant number of government employees and for the urban self-employed, poverty is concentrated among low-skilled and marginal activities; and

- there is a smaller group of ultrapoor (10 to 13%), including widows, older, sick and disabled people, heavily dependent on direct income transfers.

2.90   Analyzing the characteristics and the standards of living of the poor is a first step toward understanding poverty. But output indicators alone cannot explain why poverty has persisted. It is only by examining the determinants of income generation and distribution that the causes of poverty can be highlighted.

III. The Roots of Poverty

Introduction: Evolution of Income Distribution

3.01   In the absence of specific surveys and data on income distribution, measures of inequality in Egypt can only be based on information from the various household expenditure surveys. However, by definition, estimates of income distribution based on expenditures data are bound to understate the real degree of inequality as the share of savings in total income increases with the level of income.

3.02   The distribution of income that can be derived from the 1981/82 HBS reveals that, in rural areas, the richest 20% of households receive 44% of total income while the poorest 20% have only 6%. In urban areas, the proportions are 40% and 7.5% of total income respectively. Thus, the degree of inequality is relatively less in the cities than in the countryside.

Graph 3.1 Distribution of Household Expenditures in 1981/1982 (%)

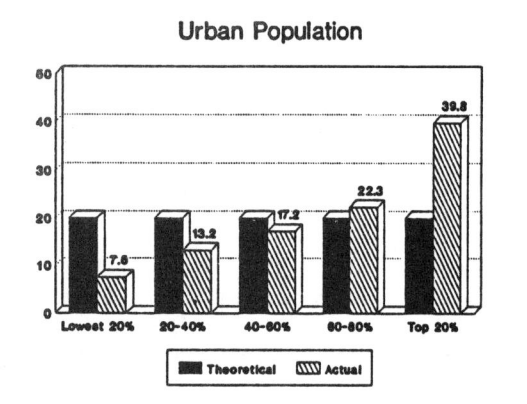

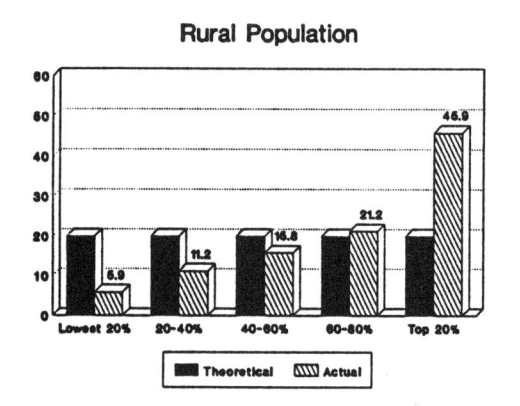

Source: Hansen, 1989
Hansen and Radwan, 1986

3.03   Despite small fluctuations during interim years, income distribution has remained fairly stable over the last thirty years. As indicated by both the Gini coefficient and the Theil measure, the degree of inequality decreased between 1958 and 1964, increased up to 1974, and declined again between 1974 and 1982 (Table 9, Annex B). The overall situation was marginally better in 1982 than in 1958. This is a substantial achievement in view of the external and internal difficulties and the important changes experienced by Egypt since the 1952 revolution.

3.04   Overall, Egypt has a more egalitarian income distribution pattern than many countries, both developing and industrialized. Out of 44 countries for which data on the degree of inequality are available, inequality being measured by the ratio between the share of income of the richest quintile over the share of the poorest quintile, Egypt's position is 14th. While the ratio is 7 to 1 in Egypt, it is for example, 18 to 1 in Zambia, 16 to 1 in Turkey, 11 to 1 in Argentina, 8 to 1 in Korea and in the United States, 6 to 1 in the UK and Finland, and 4 to 1 in Japan (Table 3, Annex A).

3.05   The relative improvement in income distribution over the last decade reflects the combined impact of overall economic growth and the government's distributive policies. Examining the patterns of creation and distribution of wealth should throw light on the respective contribution of these two elements and on the main causes of poverty in Egypt.

3.06   As Milton Friedman (1962) writes, income is given "to each according to what he and the instrument he owns produces". Indeed, income has two major sources: gains from ownership of physical means of production and the remuneration of labor. Understanding the determinants of inequality and poverty requires therefore data on the relative income share of each production factor and information on the relationship between the functional income distribution and the size-distribution of income. In the case of Egypt, the scarcity of data in general and of recent data in particular makes it difficult to draw definite conclusions. Thus, the following remarks on the evolution of the overall share of wages in national income are at best tentative.

3.07   Table 3.1 presents different measures of the relative evolution of property and labor income based on national account estimates. Though incomplete, the data give some indication of the share of wage income outside agriculture, as a proportion of GDP at factor costs, and as a percentage of total private income.

Table 3.1
Evolution of Share of Wages
(%)

Year	Non-Agricultural Sector	Total GDP At F.C.	Total Private Income Domestically generated	Including Remittances
1974		42.4	52.9	54.3
1975		43.2	55.1	57.5
1976		44.7	57.4	61.3
1977	) 45.0 (	44.1	57.1	61.3
1978	) (	43.0	56.5	63.1
1979	36.9	42.9	58.5	64.8
1981/82	42.1	44.6		
1986/85		39.0		
1986/87		42.3		

Source: World Bank Data, Hansen, 1980

Between 1974 and 1986, the share of wage income in total GDP remained fairly stable while, at the same time, the share in private income rose markedly, even excluding remittances. As noted by Hansen (1990), this difference is due to the rapid growth of oil revenues and revenues from shipping traffic in the reopened Suez Canal. In spite of the shift towards wage income observed in the distribution of private income, the overall distribution of income has not changed between the 1974 and 1981 HBS. One hypothesis put forward by Hansen (1990) is that the process of distribution within wage income and profits might have been stronger than the distribution between profits and wages.

3.08 To analyze the causes of poverty, this chapter examines the impact of the distribution of assets, the relationship between employment and poverty, and the effects of the government's direct and indirect transfer programs.

Assets and Poverty

3.09 Information about the distribution of assets and wealth in Egypt is very scarce. Besides data on land distribution that are available from the Ministry of Agriculture, the 1977 ILO survey (Radwan and Lee, 1986) is the only source with detailed data on the link between income distribution and poverty.

3.10 In the rural areas, the successive land reforms (1952, 1961, 1969) have resulted in a decrease in overall inequality as shown by the distribution of both holdings and land.

Table 3.2 Evolution of Land Distribution
(%)

	1950/52	1977/78
Land Ownership		
Lowest 20%	4	5
20-80%	18	25
Highest 20%	78	70
Gini Coefficient	.74	.66
Mean Size (feddan)	5.2	1.6
Land Holdings		
Lowest 20%	2	6
20-80%	25	41
Highest 20%	73	53
Gini Coefficient	.68	.48
Mean Size (feddan)	3.8	2.0

Source: Hansen and Radwan, 1982
Hansen, 1990

While land holdings are characterized by a stronger degree of equalization, land ownership remains highly unequal. There are even indications that inequalities in land ownership have been increasing since the early 1970s (Hansen and Radwan, 1982, Springborg, 1989). The rise in the share of middle size ownership appears to be due to wealth accumulation through land acquisition (Hansen, 1990).

3.11   Land is not the only asset that is unequally distributed in rural areas. The pattern of maldistribution is even stronger for other assets. Graph 3.2 presents the distribution of all assets (both productive and non productive) that can be derived from the data of the 1977 ILO survey. The poorest 20% of the rural households have almost no assets (0.6%) while the richest 20% possess 73% of all assets.

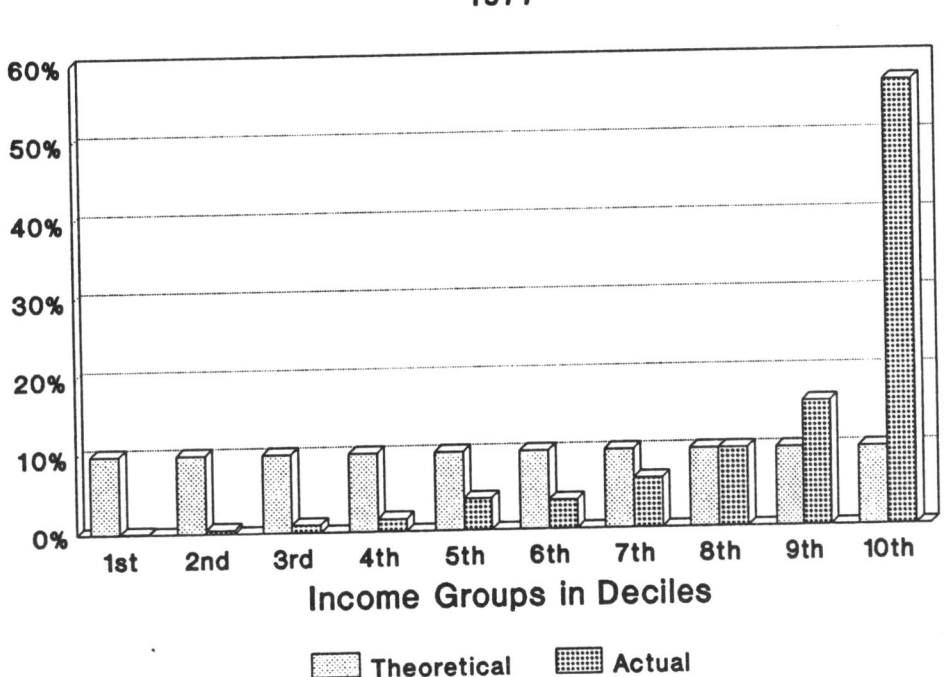

**Graph 3.2 Distribution of Assets in Rural Areas
1977**

Income Groups in Deciles

☐ Theoretical   ▨ Actual

Source: Radwan and Lee, 1986

3.12   Though dated, the data from the 1977 ILO survey provide relevant information on the effects of the distribution of land and other assets in rural areas on income distribution.

Table 3.3
Distribution of Income by Source in Rural Areas
(%)

Source of Income	Poorest 10%	Poorest 30%	Top 10%	Total
Family Farms	12.0	22.8	40.7	36.2
Agricultural Wages	21.7	31.0	2.7	12.3
Non-Agricultural Wages	12.2	21.5	31.5	33.8
Remittances	47.9	16.4	5.1	5.3
Rent from Land and Agriculture Assets	2.0	1.6	4.9	2.4
Non-Agricultural Production Assets	4.2	6.7	15.1	10.0
Average Income (EL)	65	126	1,082	383
Total	100.0	100.0	100.0	100.0

Source: Derived from detailed source-of-income matrix presented in Radwan and Lee, 1986.

Three general observations can be derived from these figures. The first striking feature is the multiplicity of income sources for all income groups, which complicates the income distribution picture. Overall, rural households receive 36.2% of their income from self-employment in farming, 51.4% from wage employment in agriculture as well as outside agriculture, and the rest (12.4%) from property income. Second, the lack of assets, especially agricultural land, is a key determinant in explaining poverty, as demonstrated by the very small share of income from family farms among the poorest population groups. Poverty, therefore, is the combined result of a lack of access to productive assets and very limited non-agricultural income-earning opportunities.

3.13   Data on the distribution of assets in urban areas are virtually non existent. But considering the rising share of wage earnings in non-agricultural sectors and the fact that a large proportion of enterprises are public, it would be safe to assume that the maldistribution of privately owned industrial and commercial assets is unlikely to be a significant factor of poverty. However, the increase in speculative investment in urban real estate, commodity trading, and import-export trade since the beginning of the Open Door policy has most probably contributed to increased inequality in urban income distribution.

Employment and Poverty

3.14   Egypt maintained a full employment policy in the 1970s and early 1980's. The availability of employment was an important element in the Government's strategy to meet the population's economic needs. The strategy fell short of its goal, however, as government economic policies and external events leading to the decline of oil prices slowed the pace of economic growth and the expansion of employment. Government labor policies and regulations were an impediment to the economy's ability to adjust quickly to changing economic conditions.

The Employment Challenge

3.15   The prosperity of the Egyptian economy in the 1970s was built on oil production in the Sinai, soaring oil prices, revenues from shipping traffic in the reopened Suez Canal, increased remittances from workers abroad, and expanding foreign aid. GDP growth averaged 9% per annum from 1974 to 1981. Government expenditures on social services expanded sharply with this growth leading to improvements in family welfare and education. Population growth, averaging 2.8% per annum, continued to expand the labor force. From 1980 to 1984, the labor force 12 to 64 years of age, measured by the annual labor force survey, grew 5.4% per annum reaching 12.6 million. Much of the growth took place in urban areas with numbers of youths and women entering the labor force.

3.16   The labor force 6 years of age and older stood at 13.4 million in 1986 as defined by the census (Table 2, Annex D). The percentage of those living in urban areas rose between 1976 and 1986, from 43% to 47%. The number of youths 15 to 24 years of age climbed sharply during this period from 1.4 to 3.4 million. As a share of the total labor force, this age cohort, shown in Graph 3.3,

Graph 3.3 Share of the Total Labor Force for Youths and Women (6 and Older)

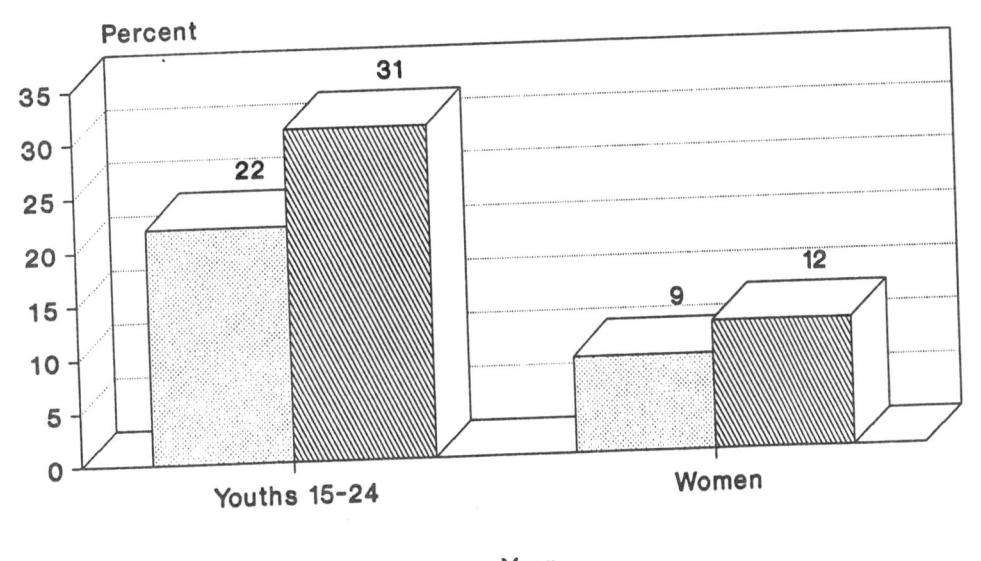

Group	1976	1986
Youths 15-24	22	31
Women	9	12

Source: Census, 1976 and 1986.

increased from 22% to 31%. Women were also entering the labor force in large numbers during this period. The number of female labor force participants increased from just under 1 million to over 1.5 million. Women's share of the total labor force, presented in Graph 3.3, grew from 9% to nearly 12%. This growth occurred in older as well as younger age cohorts. Over half of the increase came from women 25 to 39 years of age. Roughly 80% of the increase for women took place in urban areas.

3.17   Against a background of steady growth in the population and labor force, the structure of employment in the economy was changing. Agricultural employment declined from 4.9 million jobs in 1976 to 4.6 million in 1986. The share of total employment in agriculture, shown in Graph 3.4, fell from 48% to 38%. A combination of factors underpinned this decline. The expansion of employment in construction opened new opportunities to unskilled farm laborers as did the growth of employment opportunities in the Gulf States. The shift of farm labor to construction and migration to the Gulf helped contribute to scattered labor shortages and rising real wages in agriculture. The increase was larger than that in other sectors, doubling from 1974 to 1982 (Assaad and Commander, 1989). This contributed to the increasing capital intensity of agricultural production as the labor force declined (Richards, 1989).

Graph 3.4 Employment Share by Sector of Economic Activity

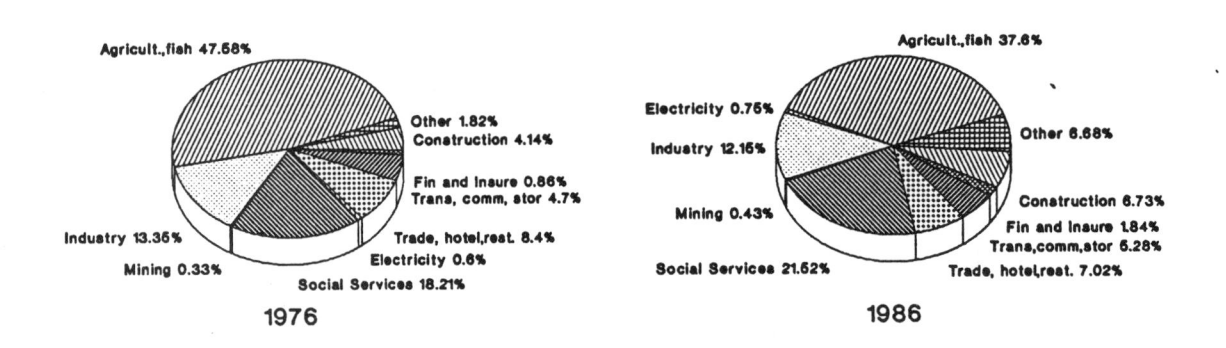

1976
- Agricult.,fish 47.58%
- Other 1.82%
- Construction 4.14%
- Fin and Insure 0.86%
- Trans, comm, stor 4.7%
- Trade, hotel,rest. 8.4%
- Electricity 0.6%
- Social Services 18.21%
- Mining 0.33%
- Industry 13.35%

1986
- Agricult.,fish 37.6%
- Electricity 0.75%
- Industry 12.15%
- Mining 0.43%
- Social Services 21.52%
- Other 6.68%
- Construction 6.73%
- Fin and Insure 1.84%
- Trans,comm,stor 5.28%
- Trade, hotel,rest. 7.02%

Source: Census, 1976 and 1986.

3.18   The decline of agricultural employment in this period produced a shift of employment from rural to urban areas. It also led to an increase of nonagricultural employment in rural communities. The share of nonagricultural employment in rural areas increased from 25% to 40% of total employment. Social services and manufacturing were the largest sectors of employment outside agriculture. Both were dominated by the public sector. Government employment in social services shown in Graph 3.5 swelled from 1.8 million in 1976 to nearly 2.6 million in 1986, an average increase of 4.4% per annum. This outpaced all other sectors with Government's share of total employment rising from 17% to near 22%.

Graph 3.5 Employment Growth Rates by Type of Employer (1976-1986)

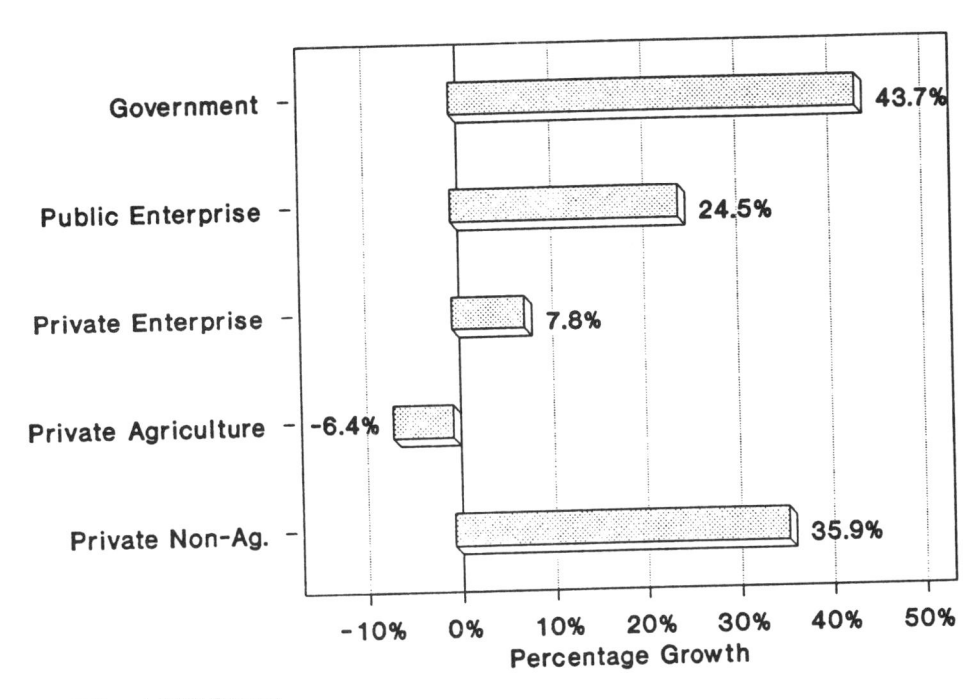

Type of Employer	Percentage Growth
Government	43.7%
Public Enterprise	24.5%
Private Enterprise	7.8%
Private Agriculture	-6.4%
Private Non-Ag.	35.9%

Source: 1976 and 1986 Census

3.19   In the 1960's, Egypt nationalized many of its industries. Public enterprises accounted for just under 1 million jobs in 1976. A majority were concentrated in manufacturing. This number grew in 1986 to 1.2 million. Employment in manufacturing, however, declined in this period as a percentage of the total from 13.4% to 12.2%. Excluding trade, hotels and restaurants, other sectors increased their share of total employment. The largest increase outside social services was in construction which provided nearly 400,000 jobs during this period. The public sector, comprised of government and public enterprises, accounted for nearly 53% of nonagricultural employment in 1986, up from 51% in 1976. The public sector led by Government was a major source of employment for new labor force entrants during the decade (Hansen, 1986).

3.20   The public sector was joined in this task by a surprisingly active informal sector. There is of course considerable controversy over the definition of the informal sector which is understood to consist of small, private enterprises hidden from the view of Government and regulation. Private nonagricultural employment in Egypt matched this definition in terms of employment. Well over 90% of private nonagricultural employment was located in establishments with less than 10 workers. Using this as a definition of the informal sector, nearly 2.5 million were employed in this sector in 1976. The number increased to 3.4 million in 1986. A special study of the informal sector during this period found large numbers employed in commerce, manufacturing, private services, and construction (Rizk, 1988).

3.21   Thus, the informal and public sectors, led by Government, were the principal sources of employment for Egypt's rapidly expanding population and labor force during the 1970s and early 1980s. The pressure of this growth on these sectors might have been even more intense had not external migration provided a safety valve throughout much of this period. Migration to the Gulf States continued to expand into the early 1980's. Remittances as an indicator of this growth reached a peak in 1984 of $3.9 million before sliding back in 1986 to $2.8 million. In 1986, the Central Agency for Public Mobilization and Statistics (CAPMAS) estimated that 2.2 million Egyptians were working abroad. Annual turnover was conservatively estimated at approximately 200,000.

3.22   On the surface, Egypt responded to the challenge of its growing population and labor force. Its response, however, obscured weaknesses in the economy. Full employment was achieved by the over-staffing of Government and public enterprises. Estimates of overstaffing in the 1970's were as high as 40% and increasing (Hansen and Radwan, 1983; Handoussa, 1983; Hansen, 1985). The economy was heavily dependent on migration to the Gulf as a safety valve. The informal sector offered the only source of productive employment. The success of the economy in maintaining full employment in the 1970's and early 1980's was therefore largely artificial. The economy began to show signs of deterioration. Open unemployment rose from 5.2% in 1980 to 6.0% in 1984.

Trends in Wages

3.23   The strength of the economy in the 1970s can be seen in the movement of real wages. Real wages rose as the economy expanded, reaching a peak in the mid-1980s (Assad et al., 1989). There were sharp differences, however, between industry sectors and occupations, and therein between public and private sectors (Table A, Annex A). These trends provide an indication of employment's contribution to the economic-well being of the population. The growth of the economy in the 1970's led to a construction boom and rising real wages. The growth of construction employment in urban and rural areas and rising real wages contributed to the shift of employment out of agriculture. This increase led to improvements in welfare. However, the construction boom slowed and real wages in this sector peaked early in 1979, and drifted downward afterwards.

3.24   Real wages in agriculture also rose sharply in the 1970s and continued to do so until 1985. The impact of mechanization, migration and urbanization, as discussed above, contributed to this increase. The growth in this sector of real wages far outpaced that in other sectors. By contrast, real wages in services increased only in the private sector and not at all in the public sector. In manufacturing, dominated by public enterprises, real wages rose at a pace well above that in services, but substantially below that in agriculture. While these trends generally confirm the deterioration of the Egyptian economy in the 1980s, their more interesting message is the difference found between real wages in the public and private sectors.

3.25   Government and by extension public enterprises faced a rising wage bill as the economy began to deteriorate in the early 1980s. The response was to slow down the growth of employment and nominal wage growth in the public sector. Government extended the waiting period for guaranteed jobs it offered graduates of secondary and post-secondary schools and released public enterprises from their commitment to this guarantee. As Government struggled to maintain a full employment economy, it did so by dividing the wage bill among an expanding workforce. Real wages plummeted as inflation surged. The real wages of workers in the public sector, seen in Graph 3.6, failed to keep pace with those in the private sector. Government workers suffered the largest reductions in real wages.

Graph 3.6 Real Wage Trends by Economic Sector

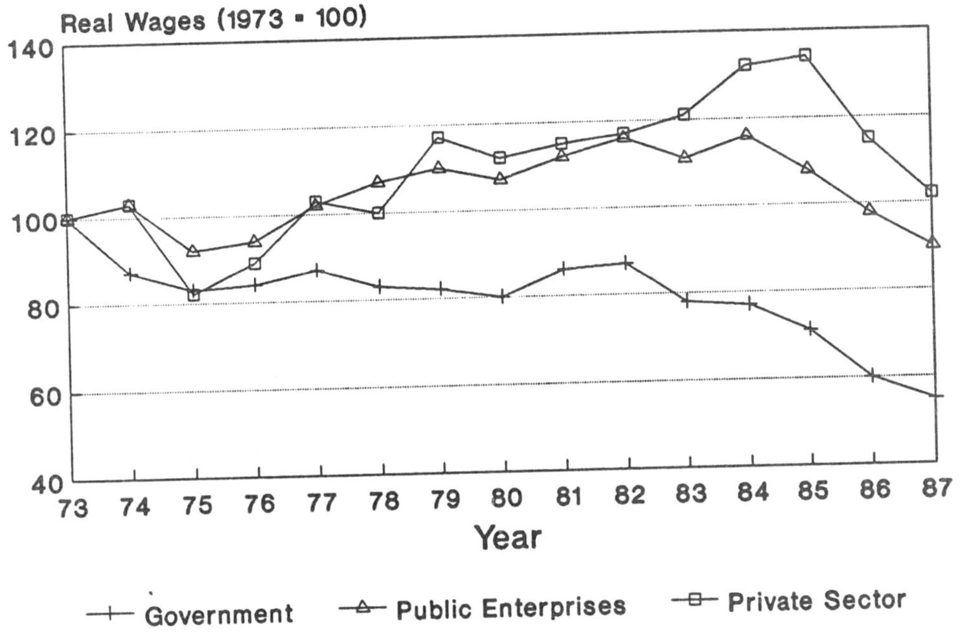

Source: Assad and Commander, 1989

3.26   With average wages exceeding those in other sectors of the economy, the decline of real wages in Government improved income equality, but it generally left workers in Government more vulnerable to economic hardship. This was reflected in the number of Government workers seeking second jobs in the 1980s. The same can be said for those in white collar occupations whose real wages declined in relation to wages in blue collar occupations. The compression of incomes at the upper end of the income distribution was matched at the lower end by the increase in real wages for agricultural workers relative to other sectors. Income from remittances, however, may have had an adverse impact on the equality of household incomes, at least in rural areas, as these incomes were earned mainly by upper income villagers (Adams, 1989).

3.27   These trends alter the picture of employment and poverty in Chapter 2 by suggesting the improvement of economic conditions in rural areas, particularly in agriculture. Household heads employed in agriculture represented 40% of poverty households in rural areas based on consumer expenditures in 1981-82. The improvement of real wages in agriculture as the decade continued plus the shift of farm workers out of agriculture were factors that would reduce the incidence of poverty in this sector. The pattern for workers in Government and public enterprises, however, confirms the picture provided in Chapter 2. Household heads employed in services and manufacturing, which are dominated by Government and public enterprises, accounted for slightly over 30% of urban poverty households based on the 1981-82 survey of consumer expenditures. The subsequent downturn of real wages in these sectors could only have made matters worse for these households.

3.28   As Egypt struggled to provide employment for a rapidly expanding population and labor force in the 1970's, it did so by using the public sector as an employer of last resort. As long as the economy remained strong, this worked. However, once the economy began to weaken, the solution started to unravel. The Government could no longer afford the cost of over-staffing employment in the public sector. Rather that displace workers, it chose to reduce real wages with Government workers bearing a major share of the cost. This increased the risk of labor market-related poverty for workers in Government and public enterprises. The problem Egypt faced in the creation of productive employment was deeply rooted in the pervasive role of Government in the economy as seen in distortionary labor market policies.

Government Labor Market Policies

3.29   Labor markets function in a macroeconomic framework that shapes incentives for competitive behavior in product and factor markets. This framework is closely linked with development strategies. For example, the adoption of an import-substitution strategy is sustained by macroeconomic policies that provide high levels of protection for domestic industries. These policies include the use of import quotas and tariffs, investment licensing, inflated exchange rates, price controls, and other measures that raise the cost of imports and provide domestic producers with shelter from foreign competition. By increasing the cost of imports, these policies make it more profitable to produce for domestic markets and discourage the growth of exports.

3.30   These policies characterize Egypt's economy in the 1970s and early 1980s (World Bank, 1989b). The failure to expand non-oil exports was linked to economic policies that distorted the incentive structure and encouraged production for domestic markets. The effects of this failure were twofold. First, with the decline of oil revenues in the early 1980s and the leveling off of foreign aid and worker remittances, Egypt experienced a shortage of foreign exchange that led to increased borrowing and external debt. The rising cost of debt made it difficult to sustain a full employment policy. Second, protectionist policies reduced incentives for competitive behavior in markets for goods and services and markets for capital and labor.

3.31   Capital markets were subject to controls and rationing. Interest rates were held below the inflation rate by controls that led to negative real interest rates. This, in turn, discouraged savings and capital formation while producing an excess demand for scarce capital. The excess demand led to the rationing of capital with a bias toward low-risk investments in public enterprises with protected markets (World Bank, 1989b). Access to low-cost financing was combined with an ambitious social insurance program funded with a tax on workers' wages that further increased the relative cost of labor. The combination produced capital-intensive development and low rates of employment growth in the modern sector represented by public enterprises. The distortion of capital markets in Egypt's labor surplus economy worked against the Government's goal of full employment.

3.32   This macroeconomic climate in the 1980s reduced incentives for maintaining competitive labor markets. Excess labor costs produced by market inefficiencies could be passed along to consumers in the form of higher prices for goods and services and lower levels of economic growth. With protectionist policies, there was little incentive for efficiency in production. In this climate, the Government adopted labor market policies and regulations that separated wages from productivity and created barriers to labor mobility. These policies and regulations produced labor market rigidities that impeded the economy's ability to respond quickly to new market incentives and external shocks and affected skills development and labor utilization (Fallon et al., 1989). These rigidities influenced employment and poverty in the Egyptian economy.

3.33   **Government as an Employer:** The public sector was Egypt's largest employer in the 1980s, accounting for nearly one-third of the nation's total employment. This employment included the administrative departments of national and local governmental units, 393 public enterprises, and 46 semi-autonomous economic authorities encompassing public utilities, the Suez Canal Authorities, and the General Petroleum Organization. Given its size and visibility, Government's employment policies played an important role in labor markets at all levels. These policies affected not only the public sector, but also the private sector through their impact on the labor supply. Government maintained an administered wage system and guaranteed employment to graduates of secondary and post-secondary schools. Both policies distorted employment incentives.

3.34   The labor policies applying to Government and public enterprises were unified in 1961. In 1962, the Government pay scale was adopted by public enterprises to maintain equality between employees in the two sectors (El-Salmi, 1983). In the years that followed, several laws were enacted to systematize and control employment and personnel affairs in Government and public enterprises. A unified structure of basic wages applies to both Government and public enterprises, although there is some flexibility in wages in the economic authorities. The most recent wage schedule was adopted in July 1984. The schedule covers 6 grades of labor, plus separate categories for Director Generals, Undersecretaries, and First Undersecretaries. This schedule replaced a 1978 wage schedule. The two are compared in Table 3.4.

Table 3.4
1984 Wage Schedule for Public Sector
Comparing Minimum Salaries with 1978

Salary in Egyptian Pounds (LE) per Year

Salary Grade	Salary Range	1978 Lower Limit (LE)
First Undersecretary	2,603	2,100
Undersecretary	1,680-2,493	1,500
Director General	1,500-2,364	1,320
Other Grades		
1	1,140,2,148	960
2	840-1,968	666
Grade 3	576-1,668	360
Grade 4	456-1,272	240
Grade 5	432-984	216
Grade 6	420-804	192

Source: Ministry of Labor

3.35 The schedules define basic wages for each grade of labor. Government workers may receive incentive payments of 15% to 25% on top of basic wages for improvements in productivity, cost-savings, and research, plus participation in extra activities such as committees. Beginning in 1987, a series of uniform adjustments were made, called social allowances, adjusting the 1984 schedule for inflation. By 1989, these allowances had increased basic wages by 50%, substantially below the rate of inflation. Workers paid 12% of their basic wages for workers compensation, pension, and health benefits. The Government and public enterprises in turn paid 20% of each worker's basic wages for these benefits. The 1984 wage schedule reflects the Government's social policy on wages.

3.36 When compared with the 1978 wage schedule, the 1984 schedule shows a social policy of wage compression and equalization. Comparisons in Graph 3.7 reveal that minimum salaries for Grade 6, the lowest skill level, increased by 119%, from 192 to 420 LE, while those for Grade 1, representing higher level skills, increased by a mere 19%, from 960 to 1,140 LE. This pattern of wage compression drastically reduced the real incomes of government officials in skilled positions compared with those in positions with lower skill levels. This compression occurred while Government wages in general were falling in real terms. Thus, faced with the need to control the size of the wage bill Government accomplished this by allowing real wages to fall with senior government officials bearing the major share of the burden. This pattern of compression was also evident in earlier wage schedules (Handoussa, 1988).

Graph 3.7 Rate of Growth of Public Sector Minimum Salaries: 1978-1984

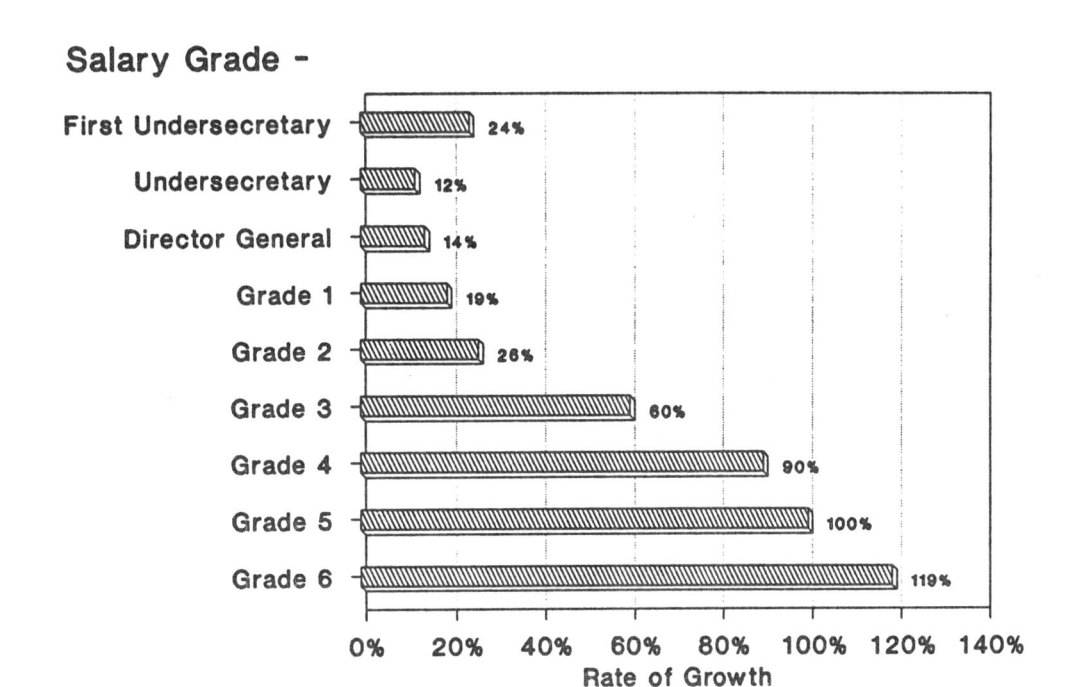

Salary Grade	Rate of Growth
First Undersecretary	24%
Undersecretary	12%
Director General	14%
Grade 1	19%
Grade 2	26%
Grade 3	60%
Grade 4	90%
Grade 5	100%
Grade 6	119%

Source: Ministry of Labor

3.37   Wages in Government and public enterprises, thus, had little connection with productivity, and instead, represented emerging budgetary pressures and a social policy favoring wage equalization. Descriptions of wage setting in Government agencies and public enterprises confirm this. Incentive payments, which are small to begin with, are spread uniformly among workers in most Government agencies and in many public enterprises. There is little differentiation in compensation by level of effort. When it occurs, it is frequently for activities that are only marginally related to productivity. For example, Government workers strive to participate on committees in their agencies for which they are paid extra. These committees have a very tenuous impact on productivity.

3.38   Some managers in public enterprises, however, attempt to use wage incentives. Thus, there is greater variation in wage setting in public enterprises than in Government agencies. The latitude for this, however, is limited within the administered wage schedule. The semi-autonomous economic authorities have more leeway in this regard as do public enterprises that are part of the Ministry of Defense production system. The latter represents a shadow economy within the public sector for which there is little or no public information available about its activities. The picture one draws from this brief look at wages in the public sector is that of a rigid system which has little connection with market conditions and productivity. It is basically driven by the Government's focus on education credentials as a condition for employment guarantees.

3.39   By comparison, wages in the private sector show more evidence of being set by market conditions. Comparisons are sketchy, however, because wages are reported only for private enterprises with 10 or more employees, which represent less than 10% of private nonagricultural employment. Wages in Government have exceeded those in the private sector, but the differential narrowed during the 1970s. The ratio of weekly wages in public and private sectors narrowed from 1.34 in 1970 to 1.07 in 1978. Recent trends in real wages in the two sectors, described earlier, suggest that this ratio may have even reversed. The narrowing, if not reversing of the relative wage in the two sectors reflects the growing scarcity of production labor in the free labor market and the wage flexibility of the private sector in relation to the public sector (Handoussa, 1988).

3.40   Government labor policies involving wages, covering administrative agencies and public enterprises, and to a lesser extent the economic authorities, have created a segmented labor market. The perceived security of Government employment has been a major factor in its attraction apart from its historical earnings advantage. The narrowing, if not elimination of this wage advantage, may dissolve this barrier and encourage a flow of redundant workers out of the public sector, but that remains to be seen. Meanwhile, in the 1980s, the attraction of government employment has driven up the wage costs of the private sector by restricting its labor supply and presumably reducing private employment creation potential. This may have been mitigated by Government allowing real wages to fall through the decade and its tacit acceptance of the practice of multiple job holding by civil servants.

3.41   Government employment guarantees for graduates of secondary and post-secondary institutions have added a second dimension of market segmentation. This guarantee in a labor surplus climate, reinforced by tuition-free education

Graph 3.8 Unemployment Share by Education (1986)

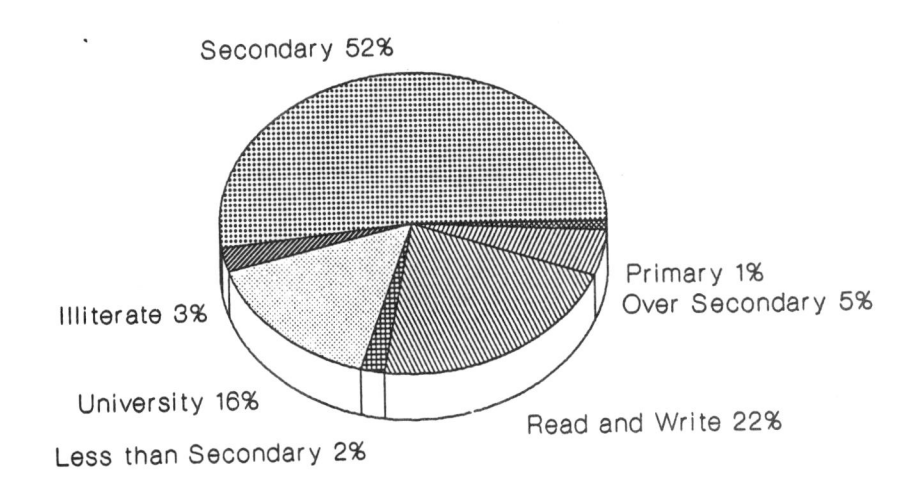

- Secondary 52%
- Primary 1%
- Over Secondary 5%
- Read and Write 22%
- Less than Secondary 2%
- University 16%
- Illiterate 3%

Source: CAPMAS

at all levels, has been a strong force behind the demand for education. Enrollment rates in post-secondary education in Egypt, for example, are 2 to 3 times those in neighboring Maghreb countries at similar stages of development. The effect of the incentive is revealed more directly by its impact on open unemployment. The guarantee creates an incentive to be registered as unemployed in order to claim the guarantee. This potentially biases upward unemployment statistics. In 1986, secondary and post-secondary graduates as shown in Graph 3.8 represented 84% of open unemployment, roughly 1 million out of 1.2 million unemployed.

3.42   <u>Government as a Regulator</u>: Government regulations directly affect employment in the private sector, although not necessarily in the smaller firms that may be hidden in the informal sector. Its regulation of layoffs and dismissals is a good example. The difficulty of dismissing workers under the cumbersome procedures of Public Law 137-1981 leads to labor being treated as a quasi-fixed factor of production. Two procedures exist to fire workers. The first, involving individual dismissals, requires the employer to submit the dismissal to a tri-partite committee encompassing a trade union representative, an official of the Ministry of Labor's employment service, and the employer. The decision of the committee is advisory. Should the employer ignore the advice, the dismissed worker can pursue the matter in a court of law. The second procedure, involving large scale layoffs, also involves a committee review of facts. The ruling of the committee is binding.

3.43   Private employers describe the individual procedure as a hassle. Some seek to avoid it by reaching a settlement with workers in which the worker is given a separation payment to leave quietly. Others seek to avoid the problem at the outset by hiring fewer workers than they need. They prefer instead to take on contract workers or even work 12 hour shifts with fewer people. This restriction has the perverse effect of encouraging capital intensive development in a labor surplus economy. Rather than create jobs, enterprises search for ways to mechanize and avoid taking on the obligation of more workers. Few employers seem to approach this in the fashion of the Japanese by offering retraining to keep the workforce flexible in adjusting to change.

3.44   The Ministry of Labor reports that the percentage of establishments allowed to restructure their employment between 1987 and 1989 ranged between 33% and 74%. For those who were not permitted to restructure and those who chose to delay presenting their case until forced by economic conditions to do so, this restriction acts as a barrier to mobility. It introduces a rigidity into the labor market affecting the movement of resources from less productive to more productive activities. It reduces the flexibility of enterprises to respond to a changing economic environment. Moreover, it reduces the incentive for employment creation in an economy that badly needs jobs. This and possibly other restrictions in a lengthy labor code work against the interest of employment creation and poverty alleviation.

3.45   One of the government's important functions is ensuring that the labor market functions smoothly as a clearing house for job seekers and employers. There appear to be problems in performing this function. Government through the Ministry of Labor maintains a monopoly on job placements in its employment offices. Workers have to be registered in one of these offices before they can be employed by an enterprise. Enterprises that hire an unregistered worker can be fined. The Ministry of Labor conducts inspections regularly for this purpose. If a private enterprise wants to recruit its own workforce, there are ways to work around this regulation by _ex post_ registration, but it nevertheless is an added burden to employment. The employment offices introduce their own labor market segmentation by retaining job vacancies only for their districts. They do not share information with other offices.

3.46   As a public good, government also has a role to play in producing labor market information for macroeconomic planning, planning for education and training, career counselling, and job placement. The principal sources of information are the annual labor force surveys and the census both produced by CAPMAS. Other information on migrants, training programs, registered unemployment and related statistics are produced by the Ministry of Labor. There is a severe shortage of timely and detailed labor market information available. The most recent data available from an annual labor force survey, for example, is from 1984. The detailed tabulations from the 1986 census were not released until late 1989. There are enormous problems in reconciling differences among the alternative sources (Assad, 1989). The activity-based labor force concepts employed, moreover, do not adequately reflect the role of women and children in the economy (ILO, 1988). Analysis of the data is limited in large part due to the lack of computers and access to the micro data. Publications are limited.

3.47   Taken one at a time, Government labor policies and regulations represent small impediments to the free operation of Egyptian labor markets. When combined, however, they create a massive burden affecting the efficient operation of labor markets and the economy. The pervasive role of Government in labor markets threatens the economy's ability to react quickly to new incentives and external shocks. The misallocation of labor inputs represents a significant waste of Egypt's most important economic resource, its labor force. The distortion of market signals increases the cost of production and of skills formation. Egypt's most serious problem has been employment creation for a rapidly expanding labor force. Government labor policies and regulations have discouraged this creation at every turn. Labor market rigidities arising from these policies and regulations in a framework of inward focused macroeconomic policies are a root cause of the country's poverty problem.

Income Transfers

Food Subsidies

3.48   The Egyptian Government operates an extensive food subsidy system which covers the vast majority of the population. As shown in table 3.5, approximately 93% of the population receives some form of ration card, with the major portion of the people receiving the full ration (green card).

Table 3.5
The Increase of Rationed Supply Cards during 1987-89

Description	1987 # of cards	1987 # of Indiv.	1988 # of cards	1988 # of indiv.	1989 # of cards	1989 # of indiv.
Full subsidy cards* (green)	9,662,842	45,741,255	9,874,730	46,766,062	10,395,114	47,085,001
Partial subsidy cards**(red)	281,592	1,354,870	288,999	1,379,721	300,404	1,416,013
TOTAL	9,944,434	47,096,125	10,163,729	48,145,783	10,439,154	48,501,014

Source: GASC, 1989

The detailed data relative to the types of foods, quantities and prices paid for the rationed commodities are presented in Annex A (Table A?). Each household is guaranteed a fixed monthly quota of rice, oil, sugar, tea and soap. If these items are not available in a given month, households can come back the following month to receive the prior month's commodities. The ration system is operated through government licensed supply shops called "Tamween" shops.

3.49   A second level of subsidy operates through state-owned cooperatives which distribute commodities at prices lower than the open market price. Items handled through the cooperatives include macaroni, eggs, oil, cheese, sugar, tea, and, on occasion, frozen chicken.

3.50   By far the biggest portion of the Egyptian subsidy budget goes for bread and wheat flour. There is no limit on the amount of bread that can be purchased and all consumers are subsidized regardless of income. The price of bread is heavily subsidized. For example, at the current exchange rate of 2.6 Egyptian pounds per U.S. dollar, a "balady" loaf of bread which is the least expensive available currently sells for five piasters per loaf; with no bread subsidy, the loaf would sell for 13 piasters.

3.51   To examine who are the real beneficiaries from this program, the International Food Policy Research Institute in conjunction with the Government of Egypt conducted an extensive analysis of the welfare effects of the ration/subsidy system (Alderman and von Braun, 1984). The results of this study are summarized in Table 3.6, which shows caloric intakes for urban and rural households broken down by quartiles of total expenditures and the share of food expenditures provided by different components of the ration/subsidy system.

Table 3.6 Calorie Consumption and Source of Calories for Urban and Rural Households

	Urban Expenditure Quartiles				All Urban Households	Rural Expenditure Quartiles				All Rural Households
	1	2	3	4		1	2	3	4	
Number of HH	245	245	245	245	980	347	348	347	347	1389
Total Monthly Expenditure (LE/capita)	14.48	25.35	38.11	82.52	36.33	9.37	15.08	22.09	43.62	20.92
% of Food Expenditure through Government channels	25.7	19.2	14.7	10.1	15.8	17.9	12.1	8.6	6.8	10.1
Caloric Intake	2343	2761	2915	3174	2798	2357	2574	2716	3149	2654
Source of Calories:					(Percent)					
Ration System	19	17	15	12	16	15	12	10	8	11
Cooperatives	5	6	6	7	6	1	1	1	2	1
Flour & Bread	49	45	42	35	42	34	25	19	19	23
Production by HH	--	--	--	--	--	8	13	13	14	12
Budget Share to Food	.63	.56	.51	.39	.48	.68	.65	.61	.48	.57

Source: Alderman and von Braun, 1984.
[a] Includes rations, purchases at cooperatives, government flour shops and licensed bakeries.

The following conclusions can be derived from these figures. First, the lowest income groups in both the urban and rural areas (expenditure quartile one) have a higher relative proportion of their food expenditures accounted for by government outlets. In particular, the ration system and bread/flour subsidy provides the biggest relative share of calories for the lowest income groups in the urban and rural areas. Second, it is clear that cooperatives benefit the upper income groups both relatively and absolutely more than the lower income groups. Third, caloric intake rises with income. Fourth, the lowest income quartile in the urban and rural areas are spending 63% and 68% of total expenditures on food.

3.52 In order to calculate the net impact of government policy on incomes- and ultimately on food consumption - it is necessary to examine not simply the ration/subsidy system on the consumer side, but the government policies on the production side. In order to avoid a decline in production as a result of the cheap food policy, the government has established a system of controlled area allotments for certain crops and enforced delivery quotas; rationed commodities such as rice, and sugar have controls on the production side (von Braun and de Haen, 1983). Many of the field crops have been implicitly taxed whereas farmers have benefitted from input subsidies including those on maize used for livestock feed and the production of meat and milk has historically been protected because of import restrictions.

3.53   As summarized in Table 3.7, the net impact of government food and agricultural policy varies by group.

Table 3.7 - Income transfers from food subsidies and distorted prices, by employment groups

(LE per year)

	Rural Households							Urban Households		
	Farm Households			Land-less Farm Labor	Non-farm Wage Labor	Non-farm Self-Employed	Others	Self-Employed	Wage Labor	Others
Sources of Transfer	Small Farms	Medium Size Farms	Large Farms							
Total transfer from production	6.13	-8.93	-80.65	2.38	1.37	3.08	-2.11	...	...	...
Total consumer	23.87	17.98	7.48	24.17	21.36	20.61	28.72	6.21	15.58	15.55
Total transfer	30.00	9.04	-73.16	26.56	22.74	23.69	26.61	6.21	15.58	15.55
Total annual expenditure	238.72	274.49	388.38	189.87	303.33	317.90	297.24	543.59	461.46	513.51

Sources: Data from the household survey made by the International Food Policy Research Institute and Institute of National Planning, Cairo, 1981/82.
Alderman and von Braun, 1984.

All groups have benefitted from the consumer transfer embedded in the ration/subsidy system. However the large farmers are net losers since the losses in production outweigh the gains from the food subsidy. A detailed breakdown of the production and consumption gains and losses from various types of households is provided in Annex D. The two lowest income groups - the landless and the small farmers (less than 1 feddan) benefit the most both relatively and absolutely from the total transfer. Thus the lowest income groups in the rural area are net gainers of the system.

3.54   The food subsidy system in Egypt is one of the most extensive in the world. One underlying assumption has been that since the ration system reaches approximately 93% of the population that the unserved 7% of the population are the non-nutritionally needy. This may not be the case. One recent survey with a small sample of 40 households found that it was the poorest of these households that typically did not have a ration card for various reasons (CRS, 1989). Many of the families without a ration card were illiterate and they indicated that they found the administrative steps in applying for the ration card an overwhelming obstacle. Another common reason given for not having the ration card was that the household did not have the necessary papers and did not know how to get them. This study cannot be extrapolated to the country as a whole but it does provide some information to suggest that not all food insecure households are benefitted by the current ration system.

3.55   Nevertheless, the very aggressive ration/subsidy policy pursued by the government has been effective in protecting the food security of the majority of the population. Food consumption levels, as described earlier, are significantly higher in Egypt than most developing countries and are higher than other countries in the region. In addition, the ration/subsidy system as it has operated favors the poor relatively more than the rich. In the urban areas, 12.7% of total expenditures of the lowest income households was contributed by the food subsidy system; in rural areas this income effect was even higher, reaching 18% of total expenditures (Alderman and von Braun, 1984).

Other Subsidies

3.56   Water. Household water consumption has traditionally been heavily subsidized with tariff revenues covering only a fraction of the operating costs of water supply companies. Up to 1985, a flat tariff of 1.2 piastres per cubic meter was charged to all consumers regardless of their actual consumption level. Recently, the Egyptian authorities have allowed steep increases in water tariffs, and more are planned in the near future, with the stated objective of covering the operation and maintenance costs of water utilities. Since 1985 prices have discriminated in favor of low users by charging a lower tariff for the first thirty cubic meters of consumption: 3 piastres per cubic meter for the 30 first cubic meters, and 5 piastres thereafter. Industrial and commercial users are subject to higher tariffs in principle. However, broad gauge meters are in short supply and many large users are still charged flat fees.

3.57   Because of low consumption levels, tariffs do not appear to have hurt low income households access to safe water. Where piped water is available, the main deterrent to water accessibility by low income household has been a hefty LE170 connection fee.

3.58   Electricity. Electricity consumption in Egypt is heavily subsidized. Both the household and industrial sectors pay tariffs that only permit partial recovery of the economic costs of production. The level of subsidies can be approximated by the difference between the long run marginal cost of production per KWH and the actual tariff per KWH. The estimates of the long run marginal cost of production in Egypt range from 13 to 17 piastras. The computations of subsidy levels for the household sector, as shown in Table 3.8, assume a long run marginal cost of 13.2 piastras per KWH.

Table 3.8
Electricity Subsidies to Households by Consumption Groups a/

Household Group by Monthly Consumption (1KWH/month)	Total Subsidy (LE 1,000)	Percent of Total Subsidy	Annual Subsidy per Household (LE)	Subsidy Rate (as percent of cost)
Up to 100	349,346.2	37.2	102.6	86.4
101 - 200	312,312.0	33.2	198.0	83.3
201 - 350	130,566.9	13.9	343.8	78.9
351 - 500	57,256.6	6.1	505.8	75.1
501 - 650	44,200.1	4.7	648.0	71.1
651 - 800	15,774.1	1.2	768.6	66.9
801 - 1,000	5,637.0	0.6	886.6	62.2
1,001 - 2,000	21,770.3	2.3	1,141.2	48.0
2,001 - 4,000	1,478.5	0.2	1,476.5	31.1
over - 4,000	900.4	0.1	1,523.9	19.2
TOTAL	939,511.9	100.0	168.0	80.2

Source: Adapted from "Residential Electricity: Consumption Rate Structure and subsidy "USAID/Egypt 1988.

a/ Subsidies are computed as the difference between a LRM cost of 13.2 piastras per KWH and the EEA's current electric tariffs.

In 1987-88, subsidized electricity consumption to households cost the government LE 939.5 million. On average, households paid one fifth of the economic cost of production for the electricity they consumed. But because of the progressive tariff structure and different consumption levels the distribution of benefits among households differs widely.

3.59   In absolute terms, 70.4% of the total subsidy went to households with monthly consumption of 200 KWH or less, of which 37.2% corresponds to households consuming 100 KWH or less per month. At the other extreme, because of much lower numbers, households consuming over 650 KWH per month received only 4.4% of the entire subsidy.

3.60   Given that the lower tariffs for lower levels of consumption apply to all small and large consumers, the annual subsidy per household increases sharply with consumption. The estimates in Table 3.8 show an annual subsidy of LE 102.6 for the average household consuming 100 or less KWH per month. This annual subsidy increases to LE 1,523.9 for the typical household consuming over 4,000 KWH per month.

3.61   _Oil Products_. Between 1982 and 1987, the regulated prices of most oil products, including gasoline and fuel oil, have increased somewhat faster than the consumer price index. But despite these price increases, oil products remain highly subsidized with prices just over one-third of world market prices.

3.62   Because of the lack of disaggregated information on consumption for oil products, it is not possible to establish precisely who are the main beneficiaries of oil subsidies. Nevertheless, based on the relative income level of oil product consumers in other countries, it is likely that the main beneficiaries are upper middle and high income households. Indirect subsidies to households through industrial and commercial users of oil products are much more difficult to establish.

3.63   The only two oil products which may be consumed more heavily by low income households in Egypt are fuel oil and kerosene. Fuel oil tends to be of importance in farming, fishing and small commercial and industrial businesses. Kerosene is an important consumption item for low income households. The 1986 Census reported that around 13 percent of all dwellings in Egypt used kerosene for lighting. While most of these dwellings were located in rural areas, some were also located in the urban slums. Kerosene also appears to be most frequently used by low income households for cooking purposes. Moreover, kerosene is the only fuel product that has experienced decreases in consumption in recent years. In 1987-88, kerosene represented a little less than 13 percent of the total consumption of fuel products. The negative income demand elasticity for kerosene is a sign of the higher relative share of this product in the budgets of low-income households.

3.64   _Transportation_. Passenger rail and public bus transportation are heavily subsidized in Egypt. Egyptian National Railways (ENR) data show that current revenues cover only a fraction of operation, maintenance and depreciation costs. The highest subsidy rates are for long-distance first class and second air-conditioned class passengers, 73 percent and 83 percent respectively. The lowest subsidy rate, 18 percent, is for long-distance third class passengers. Suburban commuting rail passengers have an average subsidy rate of 60 percent. There is less information on the level of subsidies in parastatal bus companies. However, the revenue from fares is less than operating costs for all parastatal bus companies.

3.65   No data are available on usage by income group of the different modes of public transportation. Therefore, it is not possible to establish directly the incidence of transportation subsidies. However, in the case of long-distance rail transportation, inferences can be made about benefit incidence because of the high level of product differentiation. Passengers using third class and many of those using non-air conditioned second class are likely to be low income households. Paradoxically, the richest passengers are those who benefit from the largest subsidy.

3.66   In the case of suburban commuting services, there is no such degree of service differentiation. Nevertheless, residential location patterns in urban areas show high and middle income groups residing in neighborhoods closer to the city center. Higher income households residing in the suburbs are also more likely to use their own automobile for commuting purposes. Thus, it seems likely that a significant share of suburban rail commuters are from lower income households.

3.67   The incidence of subsidies for public bus transportation in urban areas is probably mixed, but a significant share of the subsidy is likely received by low income households. The main reason is that lower income households are more likely to be users of public transportation. Higher income households have the ability to use more convenient modes of transportation including private automobiles, shared-taxis and minibus services.

Direct Transfers

3.68   Direct, non-contributory transfer payments are made both by the Government of Egypt, through the Ministry of Social Affairs, and by NGOs. In addition, the Ministry has another scheme for social assistance, called the Productive Families Programe, which is a training and employment/income rather than transfer payment program.

3.69   Government Social Assistance Schemes. The Ministry of Social Affairs handles transfer payments through the Department of Social Assistance. Payments of short term disaster relief and, more importantly, long term pension support are provided. A scheme known as the "Sadat Pension" was introduced in 1981 to reach a group not well covered by other schemes. Only persons over 65 years qualify; the great majority of recipients are women (widows).

3.70   Table 3.9 gives details of payments and the distribution of beneficiaries for 1984/85 and 1988/89. Comparable data on beneficiaries and types of payment are not available across the two years, but no significant changes have occurred in recent years in either respect.

Table 3.9

Social Assistance Schemes
Beneficiaries and Disbursements, 1984/85 and 1988/89

1. **1984/85: Payments by type of beneficiary**

	LEm	Number	Distribution (%)
Orphans	0.06	5,152	2.5
Widows	2.50	46,988	23
Divorced women	2.03	40,004	20
Children of divorced women	0.06	2,933	1.5
Disabled	1.82	58,988	29
Elderly	0.50	37,727	19
Miscellaneous	0.01	9,293	5
TOTAL	6.97*	201,085	100

Average payment per person: LE 35

2. **1988/89: Payments by type of payment**

	Disbursements LEm	No. of Beneficiaries
Pensions	7.38	129,833
Once-off relief payments	2.27	90,025
Assistance to Government employees & ex-employees	0.13	n.a.
TOTAL	9.78*	219,858

Average payment per person: LE 25
Average pension per person: LE 57

*Items do not add to total because of rounding errors.

Source: Ministry of Social Affairs

3.71   Women are the majority among the beneficiaries. Widows and divorced women together constitute the largest single group, and women are presumably included among the other main categories, the elderly and disabled. The number of persons receiving once-off relief support is only slightly less than the number of persons on indefinite pensions, but their pensions are much lower on average.

3.72   The Ministry has offices all over the country for delivery of assistance. Applications are reviewed by a committee of staff and social workers who make home visits if necessary. Both rural and urban project field workers report that the existence of support facilities is well known among the population and that contact with the local office is the main contact people have with government.

3.73   The Ministry has not made any assessment of the eligible population. It is possible to make a crude estimate of the coverage of the social transfer payment scheme, comparing the number of beneficiaries to the vulnerable groups identified above. In Cairo, approximately 120,000 elderly women live alone, constituting 7 percent of households. Another 15 percent of households are de facto female headed (i.e., either headed by a single parent or dependent on a women as main earner). Assuming half are poor, then in total about 190,000 women are Cairo are poor. If the situation in Cairo is typical, then three quarters of a million women in Egypt are in need of basic assistance. On the assumption that the 1984/85 composition of beneficiaries still holds, then approximately 100,000 women are currently given individual transfer payments. This is one out of 8 of the eligible female population. It seems reasonable to assume that coverage is better for the other two categories of the poor, elderly men and couples and the disabled; reaching 75 percent of these groups. On these assumptions, national coverage of the poorest groups through government payments assistance schemes is about 1 in 5 persons.

3.74   While a large number of persons throughout the country is certainly reached by social assistance schemes--whatever the shortfall on actual need - the total funds for assistance are small. The total budget for transfer payments was LE7m in 1984/85 and LE10m in 1988/89. Extremely low levels of individual benefits are provided. It is clear that the government is concerned about this situation, having increased the funds significantly since 1984/85. The average individual benefit has risen by almost a third and the number benefiting has increased by 10 percent. Still the situation is clearly unsatisfactory. The total average payment is a modest LE57 per annum in 1988/89, approximately half the statutory pension amount of about LE10 per month. This amount does not begin to approach an adequate subsistence payment. For the destitute, transfer payments from the state at this level can only be a supplement to other income. In that sense, and in view of the shortfall in coverage, **the government is clearly failing in its fundamental objective of providing a basic safety net for the poor.**

3.75   The incentive for individuals to apply for this level of support cannot be very great. This may partly explain the discrepancy in the numbers between those who apply for support and those who are in need. Many households nevertheless have transfer payments at this very low level as their main source of income (Hopkins, 1987). This testifies to the severity of poverty among many Egyptians, their vulnerability and their dependence on the government and other agencies for support.

3.76   **Non-Governmental Organizations (NGOs)**. The government program of social assistance is complemented by that of private non-governmental organizations (NGOs). NGOs are many in number and have a long history in Egypt. Their activities have three characteristics. These characteristics distinguish Egypt from other countries. The NGOs presence in the field of social assistance and social development is relatively less vigorous than in Asia and sub-Saharan Africa, in particular. Their orientation, in the main, is philanthropic rather than developmental; very few foreign based, international NGOs are active; and all NGOs' activities are closely regulated by the government under Law No. 32/1964.

3.77   All NGOs require official approval to operate from the Ministry of Social Affairs. They have to be registered either with the central Ministry, in cases where the operations are national in scope, or at the Governorate level. Only organizations dedicated to special groups, such as the handicapped, are centrally registered and given permission to operate nationally. They are in the minority: only about 150 out of a total of 14,000 registered. The rest are site-specific, registered with the governorate offices of the Ministry of Social Affairs and with their activities confined to particular urban neighborhoods or villages.

3.78   The financial affairs of NGOs are also subject to regulation, as regards both establishment and current fund raising. The number and financial strength of NGOs is limited by the restriction that endowment funds are not permissible. Informal representations have made the government aware that a potentially important source of finance is being missed here, and it is considering amending the legislation to permit the establishment of NGOs of this kind. All NGOs' fund-raising activities from the general public are subject to approval. Any specific fund raising project has to be approved by a high-level committee, and only a limited number are approved each year. There is a scheme of restricted sponsorship, whereby charities apply for the proceeds of sales through shops of stamps designated in their name. It seems clear that all these various rules seriously limit the fund raising capacity of NGOs.

3.79   Even so, the scale of operations of NGOs is impressively large. About two million people work for NGOs, most in a voluntary capacity. The government also gives financial support to all NGOs. On completion of an annual financial audit of operations and scrutiny of fund-raising and program plans, small operational grants are awarded from a special fund in the Ministry of Social Affairs. Currently, the government passes out approximately LE6m per annum on such grants. This compares favorably with the LE10m spent on direct transfer payments. But the government subvention accounts for only a small part of NGOs total disbursements. While information is not available for the country as a whole, in Cairo, NGOs' total expenditures were eight times the subvention from government. If this holds nationally, and all NGOs give direct income support to beneficiaries, it is clear that the quantum of income support to the poor in Egypt is much greater from the private sector than from the state.

3.80   Using earlier estimates of the vulnerable groups in the population, together with knowledge of the costs of subsistence/poverty line income, it is also possible to estimate the effectiveness of combined public and private social assistance schemes in alleviating poverty in Egypt. It was suggested that the state scheme covers about 1 in 4.5 of the eligible population, at a sub-subsistence level of about LE45 per year on average for once-off and pension relief combined. If the minimum income to provide basic needs for one adult is taken as five times that level (LE240m) (to equal the original value of the Sadat pension), then the total amount necessary to provide satisfactory coverage is more than twenty times greater than is currently provided by the Ministry (LE225 million per annum). For comparison, the government and NGOs may together provide about LE60m nationally. Their total disbursements need to be increased between three and four-fold to provide a complete safety net.

3.81   <u>Income Generating Schemes</u>. Moving beyond transfer payments, other activities of the Ministry of Social Affairs which provide support to household incomes should be mentioned. There are three main operations. The division of women's affairs is mostly concerned with education and income generating projects for rural women, mostly is collaboration with international aid agencies (UNFPA, UNICEF). Another division deals with children, and runs a nationwide system of daycare centers for pre-schoolers. In 1986, there were 2,969 nursery schools with a total registration of 145,050 (CAPMAS/UNICEF, 1988). Although this is a major effort, the quality of these institutions is variable. They lack a clear educational philosophy. Most are used by working women for their children and many provide no more than a custodial service.

3.82   Thirdly, there is the Productive Families Department, responsible for the Productive Families Programme (PFP). This is a major activity of government. It is a mixed training/loan/contract production and marketing system, currently benefiting about 200,000 people, or 1 million people, if the families of the beneficiaries are included. The activities supported cover sewing, crafts and livestock rearing, all of which show positive returns and which are estimated to increase beneficiaries' income significantly, typically by around 20 percent (Euroconsult, 1987). There is a waiting list on loans, which are given at rates below that of the commercial banks. The scheme is generally popular, and the government intends to expand it five-fold over the coming period.

3.83   The program has been the subject of several evaluations (LaTowsky, 1987, Euroconsult, 1987, Bol, 1986, Hailey, 1988). It is thought to be "reasonably effective in generating income at the level of relatively poor families in Egypt" (Bol, 1986). These improvements are significant in the context of the rapidly declining real value of wages and salaries in contemporary Egypt, especially for government employees (LaTowsky, 1987). In particular, the project is successful in reaching women who, for example, constituted 59 percent of the beneficiaries in Sohag Province (Euroconsult, 1987). Nevertheless, there are some reservations. The project does not operate on the smallest scale, and so does not reach the poorest. In Sohag Province, the poorest households accounted for only 19 percent of beneficiaries (Euroconsult, 1987). For the moderately poor who take most of the loans (66 percent in the same case), the PFP credit option was chosen because it gave cheaper credit than the commercial loans which were also available to them.

3.84   Moreover, the scheme may be over-ambitious in attempting to meet several objectives. As well as providing loans and training, it is developing into a direct employment service, providing equipment and materials to workers and organizing production and sale, mostly of crafts products, both in Egypt, and it is planned, abroad. As a production and marketing organization, however, it leaves a lot to be desired. The market research function is lacking and sales policy is ill-formulated. Quality control procedures are minimal. Sales are handled haphazardly, in many cases relying on casual drop-in visitors to the production centers. There is little attempt to match contracted quantities and product designs to consumer preferences; stocks accumulate as a result. In the circumstances, the launch into exports - which relies on contacts with Harrods, the London Department Stores owned by an Egyptian businessman -- is surely premature, except on the most limited basis and unless Harrods is prepared to give technical assistance and support for entering broader export markets.

Social Security

3.85   The Social Security System is comprised of a main scheme offering coverage to all government workers and most of the formal private sector employees, and three other schemes covering the self-employed, Egyptians working abroad, and domestic servants and temporary workers. The General System has a complete array of social welfare programs including old age, invalidity and death; sickness and maternity; work injury; and unemployment. The qualifying conditions, specific benefits, and other characteristics of the programs are summarized in Table 1 (Annex I).

3.86   The administration of social security services is fragmented. Although all programs are under the general supervision of the Ministry of Social Insurance, they are actually implemented by three semi-autonomous organizations. Old age and survivor programs and unemployment insurance for private sector workers are administered by the Social Insurance Organization. Old age and survivor programs for government workers are administered by a different institution, the Insurance and Pensions Organization. Government workers are not covered by unemployment insurance. Sickness, maternity and work injury benefits related to actual health care are administered by the Health Insurance Organization, which is under supervision of the Ministry of Health. Contributions and cash benefits for the health related programs are administered by the Social Insurance Organization and the Insurance Pensions Organizations.

3.87   Government contributions to the Social Security System amount to 1% of the payroll plus coverage of any deficit in the old age and survivor and the unemployment programs. The Government does not make contributions to either the sickness and maternity program or to the work injury program. Contributions to the General Scheme from the private sector amount to 40 percent of monthly salary up to LE 250, and to 35 percent of monthly salary from LE 250. The percentage of contributions earmarked for health insurance is very low.

3.88   Besides the General Scheme for government employees and formal private sector employees, the Egyptian social security system has three other minor schemes. The first, introduced by Law No. 108 in 1976, offers exclusively old age and survivor insurance to a broad spectrum of the self-employed, including professionals (doctors, lawyers, etc.), farmers owning 10 or more feddans of land, writers, artists, and members of the board of directors of private companies. The second subsidiary scheme was introduced by Law 112 in 1980 to extend also exclusively old age and survivor insurance to the working poor. Groups insured by this scheme include temporary workers, small farmers, fishermen and domestic servants. The individual's contribution to the scheme is very low, 30 piastres per month. The last subsidiary scheme also provides old age and survivor insurance to Egyptians working abroad. Enacted by Law 50 in 1978, this scheme is voluntary.

3.89   Benefits from old age and survivor insurance are quite similar among all schemes with pensions, amounting to about LE 30 for government employees at the bottom of the salary scale. Temporary workers/domestic servants scheme have a single pension benefit of LE 12 per month. Due to the lack of indexing, the effectiveness of social security pensions as part of the safety net for the elderly and dependent survivors has been eroded by inflation, especially in the last few years.

3.90   Unemployment benefits amount to 60 percent of the last month's wage and they are paid up to 16 or 28 weeks depending on the individual's contribution history. It appears that the unemployment insurance program does not play a major role in the system mostly because the vast majority of the unemployed are new entrants in the labor force who do not qualify for benefits.

3.91   The Health Insurance Organization provides curative care and treats work injuries for insured workers. Its coverage is limited to a small number of individuals within the general scheme of the Social Security System. In 1988, the Social Health Insurance covered 3.75 million individuals, of whom 11,000 were dependents and 113,000 pensioners and widows. While 85 percent of government employees are covered by health insurance, only about 30 percent of formal private sector workers are covered. The low coverage in the private sector is in part due to the existence of alternative plans fully paid by employers, and in part to the low quality of service provided by the Health Insurance Organization. Overall, the present insurance system covers only 8% of the population. Also, it is very difficult for workers to obtain coverage for their dependents. The evolution of the number of health insurance beneficiaries is shown in Graph 3.9.

**Graph 3.9 Number of Health Insurance Beneficiaries
(1977-1987)**

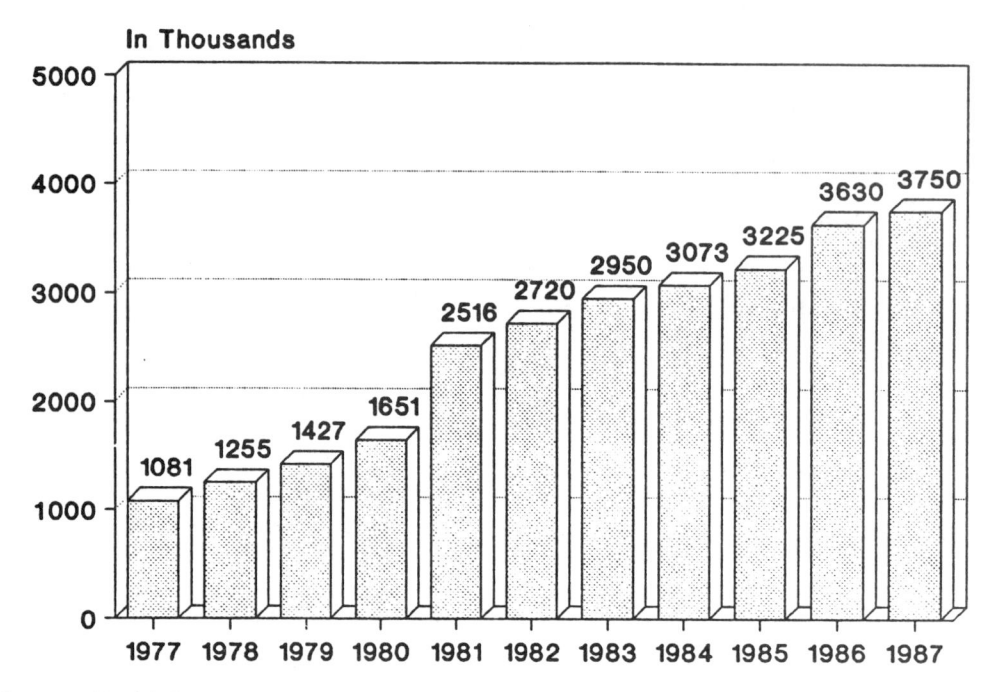

In Thousands

Year	Value
1977	1081
1978	1255
1979	1427
1980	1651
1981	2516
1982	2720
1983	2950
1984	3073
1985	3225
1986	3630
1987	3750

Source: Health Insurance Organ., 1987

3.92   The evolution of individual coverage for the four social insurance schemes over the 1980-89 period is presented in Graph 3.10. The general scheme covering government workers and formal private sector employees had 7.7 million insured individuals in 1988-89, representing 57 percent of total insured. At the other extreme, the migrant worker scheme had only 33,000 insured individuals, representing less than 0.3 percent of the total. The total number of insured in the four scheme grew at an average rate of 3.35 percent over the 1980-89 period. This is slightly higher than the rate of growth of the population of working age (15 to 65 year old); which was 2.75% over the same period. Some of the difference between the two rates may be explained by changes in female labor force participation, which increased from 6.6 to 8.2% from 1976 to 1986. The total number of insured individuals in 1988 was over 13 million. It appears therefore that almost all members of the Egyptian labor force are enrolled in one of the four social insurance schemes.

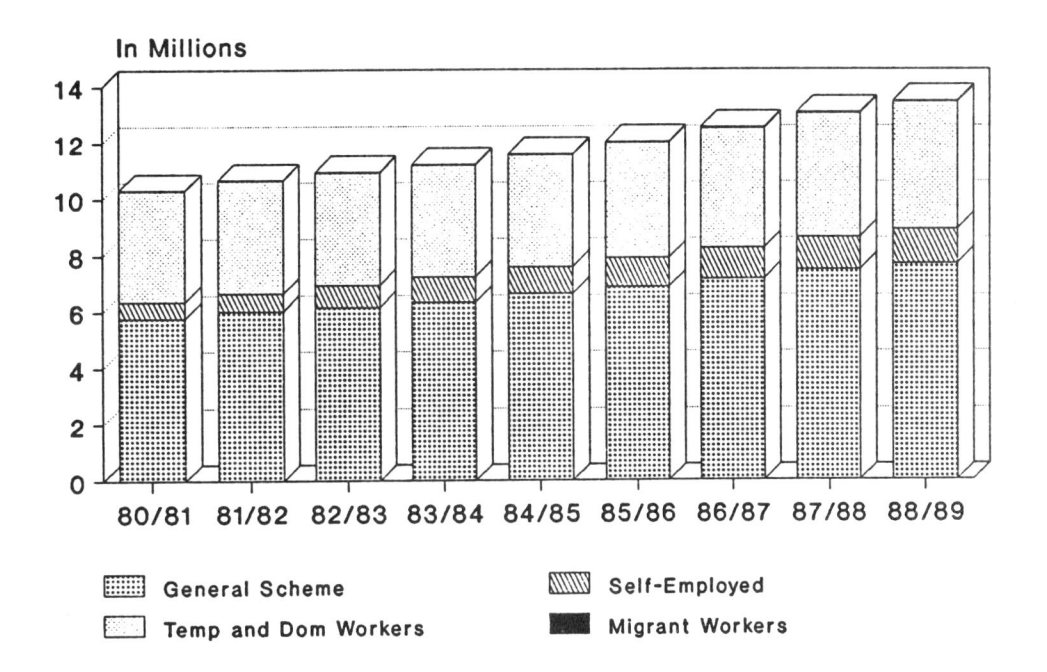

Graph 3.10 Number of Insured in Social Insurance Schemes

[Bar chart showing number of insured in millions from 80/81 to 88/89, with categories: General Scheme, Self-Employed, Temp and Dom Workers, Migrant Workers]

Source: Ministry of Social Insurance

3.93   The evolution of total earnings and expenditures for the entire system is presented in Graph 3.11 While for the 1980-89 period expenditures grew at an average rate of 15.7 percent, revenues grew at the higher rate of 17.8 percent. The system produced a current surplus in each year and the size of the surplus grew at an average rate of 23.1 percent over the decade. At the end of 1988-89, the accumulated surplus for the entire system amounted to LE 7,225 million, and 68.4 percent of it accrued over the 1980-89 period. It is quite clear from recent trends that without discretionary changes in benefits and contributions, the system will continue to accumulate surpluses well into the next decade.

Graph 3.11 Total Social Insurance Earnings and Expenditures 1980-1989

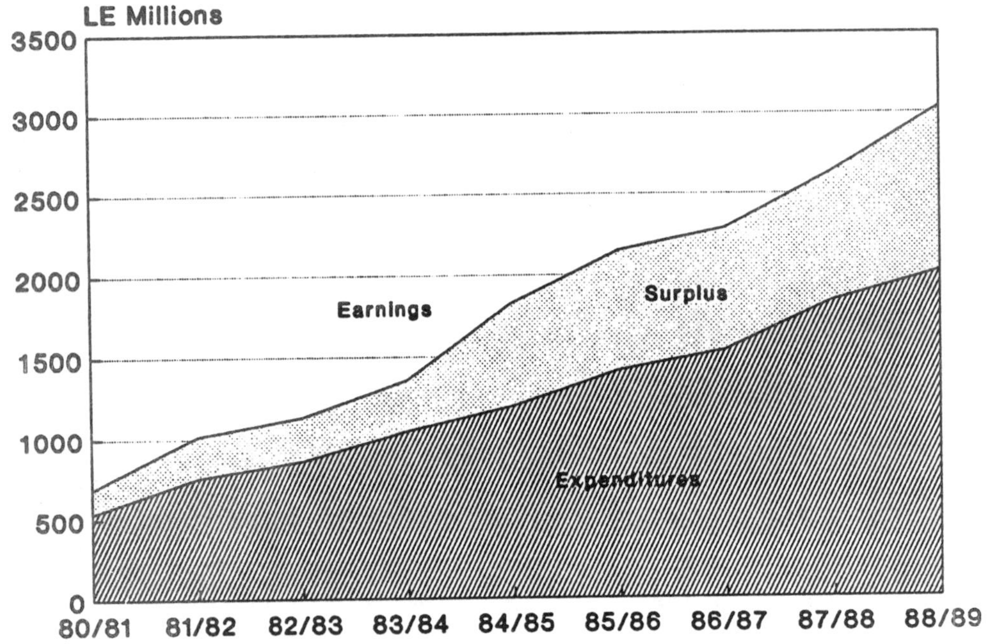

Source: Ministry of Social Insurance

3.94   This healthy picture of the system finances hides, however, several important caveats. The fact that the system has been able to generate current surpluses does not necessarily mean that the system is actuarially sound. As most other social security systems, the Egyptian system operates on a "pay-as-you-go" formula. Expenditures are paid out of current earnings and, it is expected that accumulated surpluses and earnings will in the future contribute to pay the retirement benefits of present contributors. The system is actuarially sound if for given (present) contribution rates, future revenues together with accumulated surpluses are large enough to finance (present) benefit levels of future beneficiaries. An audit conducted in 1982 found an actuarial deficit of LE 107.5 million despite accumulated operating surpluses by 1982 exceeding LE 2,500 million. A new audit of the system, being carried out at the present time, is also expected to yield a similar actuarial deficit.

3.95   A second caveat in the financial health of the system is that some schemes are not sufficiently funded on a current basis. Considerable cross-subsidization has gone on for years. Around 95 percent of all earnings in the past few years came from contributions to the general system, but only 90% of expenditures were made under the general system. In contrast, expenditures for the temporary workers scheme represented 10 percent of total social insurance expenditures. The temporary worker insurance scheme spent in 1988-89 over 11 times its earnings (Tables 5, Annex I).

3.96	In summary, the social security institutions appear, at least in principle, to offer some degree of broad and very shallow coverage to the bulk of the population. But the effective level of actual benefits and protection is low in many areas, notably pension benefits for widows and health insurance for dependents. Entire sectors of the population, specially those that are most vulnerable -- school age children, the elderly, widows -- have no health coverage. Moreover, even though legally both employers and employees make contributions to the social security system, the economic incidence or overall burden of both contributions is essentially borne by workers. The incidence of the payroll tax is therefore likely to be regressive because it falls only on labor income and because the highest salaries (above LE625 a month) are exempt.

Social Services for Human Capital Formation

Health

3.97	Egypt was one of the first countries of the region to start the development of rural health services throughout the country and this policy has been vigorously pursued over the last three decades. As a result, the Ministry of Health has been able to establish a network of facilities which provide adequate coverage and offer a balanced mix of preventive and curative health services.

3.98	As far as primary health care is concerned, the present network of 2,673 rural units is evenly distributed among the population, with a center for each 11,000 inhabitants (Table 5, Annex F). Ninety-nine percent of the population lives within a four kilometer radius of a health center. It can therefore be assumed that health services are accessible to almost everyone in the country, which is a very positive achievement.

3.99	The primary health care approach adopted in 1978 by the government places great emphasis on promotional and preventive activities while providing basic medical care and screening for patients needing a higher level of medical attention. For further expediency, a network of urban centers was developed to complement the rural units (Table 6, Annex F).

3.100	To address the important health problems identified in the previous chapter, the Ministry of Health has launched national disease control programs which retain a vertical management at the central and governorate levels and integrate their activities into the delivery of primary health care at the local level. Utilization of the primary health care units in the execution of disease control programs has proved to be quite effective. The extended program of immunization to protect children against tuberculosis, diphtheria, measles, pertussis, polio and tetanus has presently reached a satisfactory level of coverage (Table 7, Annex F). Reported cases of diphtheria, pertussis and polio are under decline and recent reports seem to indicate that, for the first time, the incidence of neonatal tetanus has decreased during the first six months of 1989. In diarrheal disease control, the early and proper management of acute cases by oral rehydration techniques has succeeded in reducing the number of deaths: since 1987, diarrhea has ceased to be the leading cause of early childhood mortality. The tuberculosis control through BAG vaccination, active case-finding and treatment of contagious cases has reduced the incidence of open pulmonary cases per 100,000 persons from 15.2 observed in 1984 to 11.3 in 1987. In bilharzia control, a new efficacious chemotherapy administered in a single oral dose has produced very encouraging results in control of S. Haematobia in Middle and Upper Egypt and is being applied presently to S. Haematobia and S. Mansoni in the Delta. Substantial progress in the reduction of prevalence rates has resulted in a shift in the control strategy of relying mostly on mass chemotherapy, while using mollusciciding intermittently and in selective areas, thereby greatly reducing the cost of control (Table 4, Annex F).

3.101 At the secondary level, government services are almost exclusively urban and curative. They are provided by 26 general hospitals, 165 central hospitals and 150 specialized hospitals (Table 8, Annex F). While the Ministry of Health is practically the sole provider of preventive services and primary health care, it shares the provision of secondary care with other ministries, the parastatal Curative Care Organizations in Cairo and Alexandria, the Social Security Health Insurance Organization and the private sector (Table 9, Annex F).

3.102 Government secondary level hospitals operate on a very tight budget. Most of them suffer from years of neglect in the repair and renovation of their physical facilities and upkeep of equipment. They generally experience a shortage of drugs and supplies which adversely affects the quality of care they can provide. However, they are fairly well utilized since they are the only solution for many poor persons. In 1986, there was an annual attendance at outpatient clinics of 1.9 per beneficiary (urban population only) and a bed occupancy rate of 58% (Table 10, Annex F).

3.103 At the tertiary level, services are provided by 25 university hospitals administered by the Ministry of Education (14,668 beds), 8 teaching hospitals (3358 beds) and 8 specialized institutes operated by the Ministry of Health (747 beds). A partial cost recovery system is applied as one-fourth of the beds are reserved for paying patients. All these establishments are largely subsidized by the government as they provide practical training to medical personnel. They are also involved in research. Establishments at this level are modernly equipped, properly maintained and receive adequate operational drugs and supplies. The professional standard of their medical and nursing personnel ensures the provision of a relatively satisfactory level of care. They have acquired the public's confidence and operate almost at full capacity (68% bed occupancy in Cairo University Hospital).

3.104 Admission process for inpatient care is quite selective. However, a small number of patients from low income groups are allowed to occupy free beds. They generally are urban or suburban poor living in the vicinity and admitted through the outpatient clinics.

3.105   Despite this overall positive picture of a health network with adequate coverage and access, the Egyptian public health system is plagued by two major shortcomings which have far-reaching implications from the viewpoint of the poorest groups in the population: (i) a poor performance of the primary health care services; and (ii) an inappropriate distribution of resources among the various types and levels of health care facilities.

3.106   In contrast to the results obtained in disease control, performance in the field of individual medical care is not impressive. Villagers complain of long waiting periods before being seen by doctors, of perfunctory examinations, and of shortage of drugs. In the rural areas, the provision of medical care takes place during hours which are not convenient for agricultural workers. Public dissatisfaction engenders low utilization of services. Rural beds are rarely used (2% of occupancy rate). The annual ratio of outpatient visits per beneficiary (1.6 annually) is one-third of the ratio registered among individuals covered by a health insurance schema. Whenever they can afford it, villagers go to a private practitioner or tend to ignore the rural and district units and pay their travel costs to go directly to a general hospital of the governorate, better equipped with diagnostic and treatment facilities, thus bypassing the normal referral system. But for the poorest among the rural population, there is no other option than to attend the government rural medical services. Those services should therefore be maintained at an acceptable standard. It has been established that the occurence of neonatal and infant mortality as well as of reproductive mortality among women could be reduced significantly if pregnant women were to receive antenatal care. Many studies have documented the overwhelming lack of medical care during pregnancy in both urban and rural areas, in spite of the widespread availability of such services (Capmas, 1988). It would be important for the Ministry of Health to be able to attract the non-user population in its primary health care centers.

3.107   In spite of its commitment to strengthen rural services and primary health care, the Ministry of Health is constrained by the extensive urban medical infrastructure inherited from the past. The financial consequences of this situation is that hospitals absorb a disproportionate share of the total health budget. Graph 3.12 indicates that hospitals account for 61% of the overall recurrent budget, primary health care for 22%, preventive services including the disease control programs for 15%, and the remaining 2% are for common administrative services. The present distribution of financial resources shows a heavy concentration of expenditures on curative services at the expense of preventive activities. Even within curative services, there is a strong urban bias as rural hospitals receive only 3% of the total budget versus 58% for urban hospitals.

Graph 3.12 Functional Distribution of MOH Recurrent Expenditures (1987)

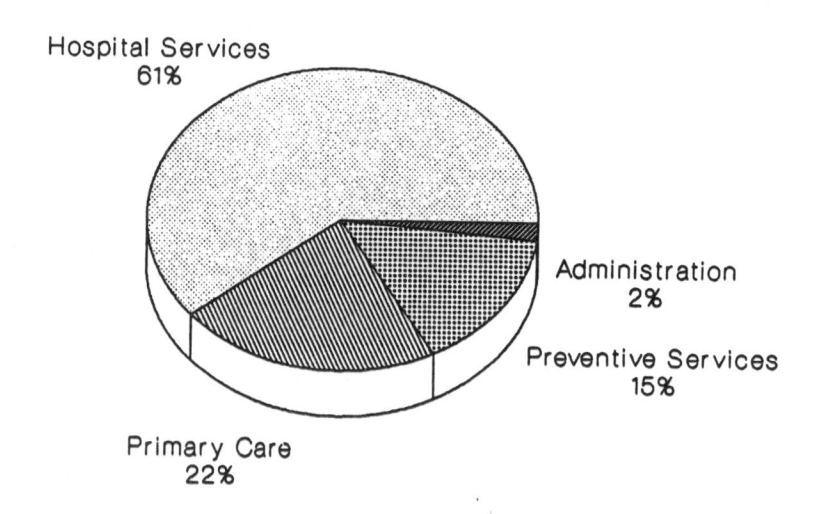

- Hospital Services 61%
- Administration 2%
- Preventive Services 15%
- Primary Care 22%

Source: Ministry of Health

3.108   The lesser proportion of resources allocated to the primary medical care level implies insufficient funding for the rural and urban health centers. The concrete implications are inadequate maintenance of buildings and sanitary facilities, insufficient provision of essential equipment and basic medical supplies and drugs, and limited transport means for the development of an effective outreach and referral system. In the rural areas, the difficult working and living conditions and the lack of opportunity for private practice to compensate for the low remuneration bring about low motivation and high turnover rates. This situation adversely affects the quality of care offered and creates public distrust, which in turn leads to underutilization of the facilities.

3.109   The distribution of health personnel follows the same pattern of imbalance as budgetary resources. The proportion of MOH doctors and nurses working in hospitals are 55% and 52% respectively, whereas only 24% and 30% are found in primary health care facilities.

Graph 3.13 Functional Distribution of MOH Personnel

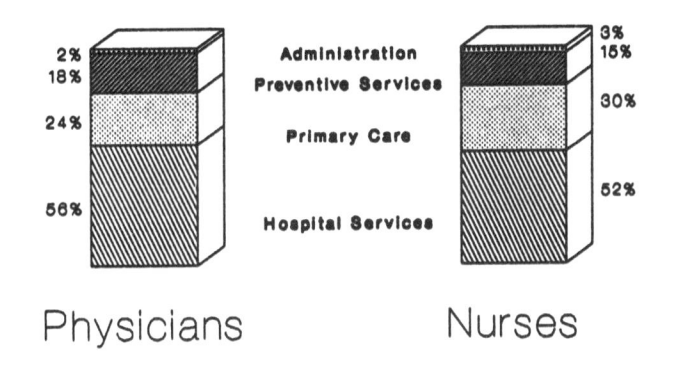

Physicians:
- Administration: 2%
- Preventive Services: 18%
- Primary Care: 24%
- Hospital Services: 56%

Nurses:
- Administration: 3%
- Preventive Services: 15%
- Primary Care: 30%
- Hospital Services: 52%

Source: Ministry of Health

In addition, there is a marked disproportion between the numbers of doctors and nurses. In 1988, the Ministry of Health employed 30,000 doctors and 27,000 nurses, equivalent to a ratio of 1.1 to 1. The accepted international norm for the physician/nurse ratio is in the order of 1 to 3. This top-heavy health manpower structure, which reflects the disproportionate share of curative facilities in the overall health network, is a source of increased costs because of the salary differentials between physicians and nurses.

Education

3.110   In an economy dominated by public sector employment where access to positions of status, wealth and power is determined primarily by educational attainment, it is important to analyze the distributional impact of government education policies to assess the link between poverty and the provision of education. The main indicators, for this purpose, are the degree of participation of various income groups and the pattern of allocation of education expenditures to these groups.

3.111   Education is one of the domains of public intervention in the social sectors where the most spectacular results have been achieved, as evidenced by the high rate of growth of enrollments at all levels (Table 1, Annex H). The considerable efforts put into the construction of primary schools throughout the country and the constitutional guarantee of free education at all levels have had a positive impact in terms of democratization of educational opportunities. It is clear that an increasing proportion of children from low-income class have been able to reach higher education and to gain access to well-remunerated positions in the modern sectors of the economy. A social mobility survey conducted in 1979 (Ibrahim, 1982) indicated that education has been a strong factor of upward social mobility during the Nasser era.

3.112   Nevertheless, the impressive expansion of the education system has still proved insufficient to reach universal primary education and suppress regional and gender inequalities of access. As indicated in the previous chapter, 10% of the primary school age population remained out of school in 1986 and half of the adult population is still illiterate. Even though a primary level enrollment ratio of 90% is a commendable achievement, there is cause for concern in as far as the remaining 10%, amounting to 160,000 children including a majority of girls, come undoubtedly from the poorest strata of society.

3.113   One of the characteristics of primary education in Egypt, until about five years ago when automatic promotion was introduced, was a relatively high repetition and dropout rate, in the 10 to 15% range. There are indications that dropouts between the fourth and sixth grade do not retain functional literacy and numeracy. This problem, which has affected mostly children from the poorest socioeconomic groups, was not caused only by learning difficulties. It reflected also the high opportunity cost of education for poor households in dire need of the additional income, small as it may be, that can be generated by working children. The importance of child labor in Egypt, which was documented in the previous chapter, bears witness to this phenomenon.

3.114   The widespread practice of private tutoring in secondary and higher education has reintroduced an element of social bias which partly defeats the democratic purpose embedded in the constitutional provision of free public education. As early as 1976, a survey had found that the proportion of students from low income families who could afford private lessons was much less than those from middle and upper income families (Ibrahim, 1982). Given the emphasis on rote learning, the ability to pay for private tutoring becomes a determinant of academic success. Researchers found that 80% of students of lower class origin got poor grades at the General Secondary Certificate Examination upon which access to higher education is based, versus 50% for students from upper class families (Ibrahim, 1982).

3.115   Looking at the pattern of allocation of educational expenditures, particularly in terms of subsidization of secondary and higher education, it would appear that middle and upper income groups benefit disproportionately from government spending on education. Research results (Abdel-Fadil, 1982) reveal that, from an equal opportunity perspective, i.e. focusing on inter-generational distribution effects, the proportional distribution of resources among students of various socioeconomic groups is skewed in favor of children of middle- and upper-income families. Similarly, in an attempt to measure the intragenerational distribution effects of education benefits by using estimates of the tax burden of various income groups, Abdel-Fadil (1982) came to the conclusion that middle-income families whose children attend higher education are subsidized by both low and high income groups.

3.116 To verify these trends, the differential pattern of allocation of educational expenditures can be observed by simulating the education journey of a theoretical cohort of students entering primary school in the beginning of the 1970s and going through the various steps of the educational ladder in the years after and working out the share of education expenditures received by various groups within that cohort. Based on data produced by Abdel-Fadil and official MOE statistics on promotion, failure and dropout rates, Graph 3.14 presents the outcome of this analysis which indicates clearly how those members of Egyptian society who obtain a university education are subsidized by the rest of the population. The implication of these data is that 70% of the population, representing people whose children were never schooled or did not go beyond primary education, receive only 20% of education expenditures. At the opposite

Graph 3.14 Distribution of Expenditures on Education by Level of Education

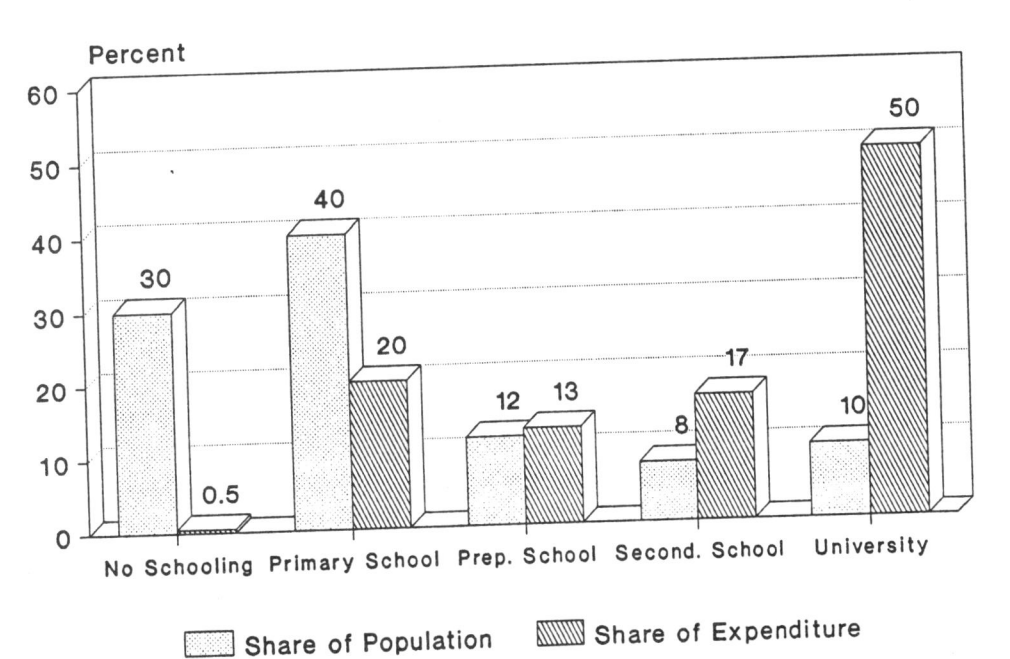

Level	Share of Population	Share of Expenditure
No Schooling	30	0.5
Primary School	40	20
Prep. School	12	13
Second. School	8	17
University	10	50

Source: Ministry of Education

end of the spectrum, university students who account for 10% of a given age-cohort benefit from 50% of total education expenditures. Budgetary data by category of expenditures reveal that non-wage expenditures per student are 50 times larger in higher education than in primary and secondary education (Table 4, Annex J).

3.117   The same methodology can be applied to introduce the socio-economic variable into the analysis (Annex L). Using the same 1970 cohort and data on the socioeconomic background of students presented in Abdel-Fadil's paper, Graph 3.15 confirms that the distribution of human capital investment in education among socioeconomic groups in Egyptian society is unequal.

Graph 3.15 Distribution of Education Expenditures by Socioeconomic Origin

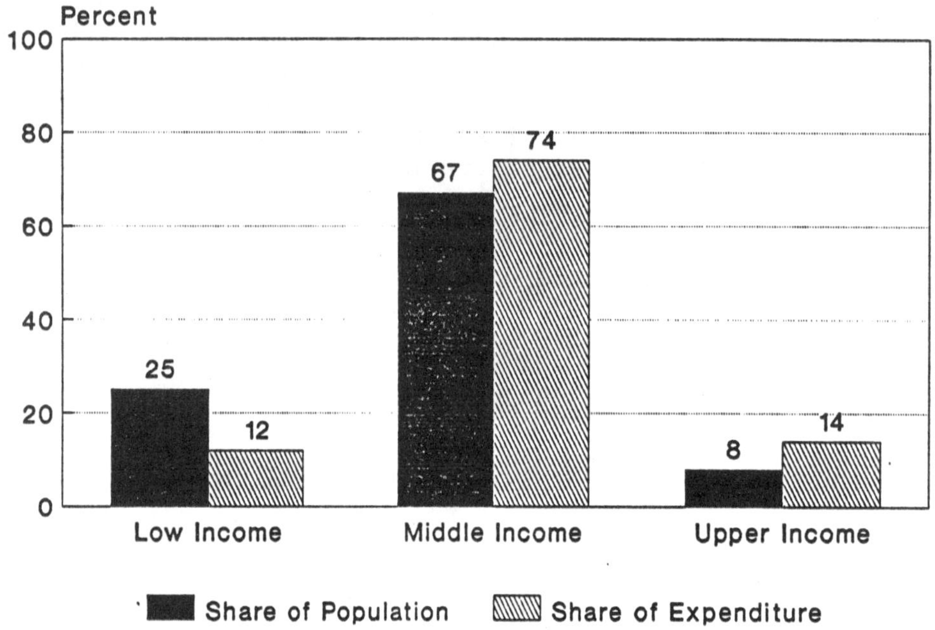

Socioeconomic Group	Share of Population	Share of Expenditure
Low Income	25	12
Middle Income	67	74
Upper Income	8	14

Source: Ministry of Education

While the share of education expenditures received by students from poor families represent only half their share in the population, students from rich households benefit from almost the double of their share in the population. This finding about the regressive nature of government spending in education is congruent with the results of an international study (Psacharopoulos, 1977) which had come to the conclusion that, in most countries, free higher education is a factor of aggravation rather than alleviation of social disparities.

3.118   The issue of gender disparities in education deserves special attention as another dimension of the distributional impact of government education policies and expenditures. It should be recognized that progress in this area has been very significant, especially in the last five years. During this period, without considering Cairo and Alexandria where the situation has always been better than the rest of the country, enrollments of girls in primary education have grown by 30% versus 20% for boys. Table 3.10 shows the long term trend of slow improvement in the proportion of girls at various levels of the education system.

Table 3.10. Proportion of Girls in Education

	1972/73	1981/82	1983/84	1985/86
Primary	38.0	40.9	42.2	44.1
Preparatory	33.4	38.5	39.4	40.3
General Secondary	32.1	36.7	37.0	37.6
University	29.9	32.0	34.6	35.0

Source: Ministry of Education

3.119 The budgetary implications of this situation of under-representation of girls can be assessed using the same methodology as for socioeconomic groups. The results of this analysis (Annex L) indicate that, in 1985/86, the female half of the Egyptian youth population received 39% of education expenditures versus 61% for the male half. These figures are a good measure of how gender imbalances in education access and participation are translated in inequalities in terms of financial benefits accruing to different population groups.

Population Pressure

3.120 The poverty problem faced by Egypt is compounded by rapid population growth. The continuous decrease in mortality (down to 8.6 per thousand in 1988) and the relative stability of the birth rate (still 37.5 per thousand in 1988) have led to an overall annual growth rate of 2.8%. The Egyptian population more than doubled between 1960 and 1989, from 26 to 55 million people. The population has also become increasingly young as a result of reduced infant mortality rates and emigration of adult workers to Arab countries. The preliminary results of the 1986 Census indicate that thirty-four percent of the population is under twelve.

3.121 The high rate of population growth translates into increased pressure on the economy: pressure for jobs, pressure for social services, and pressure for an increase in consumer subsidies. The labor force is growing at an even faster rate than the population. Its growth at an average rate of 5% per annum reflects the rising number of youths and women entering the labor force. The economy has not been able to keep up with the need for jobs. Nor has it been able to meet the demand for building additional schools and health facilities. The financial pressures created by this growth have prevented any significant improvement in the quality of social services. There is even concern that the continuation of these pressures will lead to further deterioration in the quality of education at all levels and in health services. At the same time, demographic pressures are making it increasingly difficult to sustain existing consumer subsidies, especially food subsidies.

3.122 After two decades of relative neglect of the population growth problem, the Government has been putting more emphasis on family planning activities. The rate of utilization of contraceptive methods grew from 34% in 1984 to almost 38% in 1988 according to the results of the latest Demographic and Health Survey. But the total fertility rate is still 4.5 and information and education programs on contraception issues remain insufficient. Much progress remains to be made to improve the availability of and access to contraceptives before the economic burden of rapid population growth can be seen to start decreasing.

Taxation

3.123 Establishing the overall distribution incidence of the tax system is a difficult task, especially in the case of Egypt, because of the complexity of its tax institutions and the degree of government intervention in the economy. This section presents some estimates of the tax burden distribution in Egypt for 1985-86, the last year for which actual tax data are available. The main tool of analysis is the "allocation method" which distributes the revenue collected from each tax among different income groups according to different assumptions about the incidence of the tax. For example, if a tax is assumed to be finally paid by consumers, consumer expenditure shares for the commodity are used to allocate tax collections among the different income groups. Although households differ in size both within the across income groups, data availability makes it necessary to take households as the unit of analysis and ignore differences in household composition.

3.124 Two past studies have made some attempts to establish the overall incidence of the Egyptian tax system. Using a Social Accounting Matrix, a team of researchers found in 1976 that taxes and transfers to government increased on a per capita basis with income across income classes, in a mildly progressive manner (Eckaus et al, 1976). This pattern was present in both urban and rural areas, but both burdens and the level of progressivity were lighter in rural areas. The second study was published in 1986 by the National Bank of Egypt. Based on general trends and shares of different taxes, it concluded that the Egyptian tax burden fell heavily on consumers with limited income because of its reliance on indirect taxation.

3.125   If direct taxes are more likely to be progressive and indirect taxes to be regressive, the Egyptian tax system should have become more regressive in the 1980s. Graph 3.16 which shows relative shares of direct and indirect taxes from 1980/81 to 1986/87, reveals that the relative importance of indirect taxes has been on the increase.

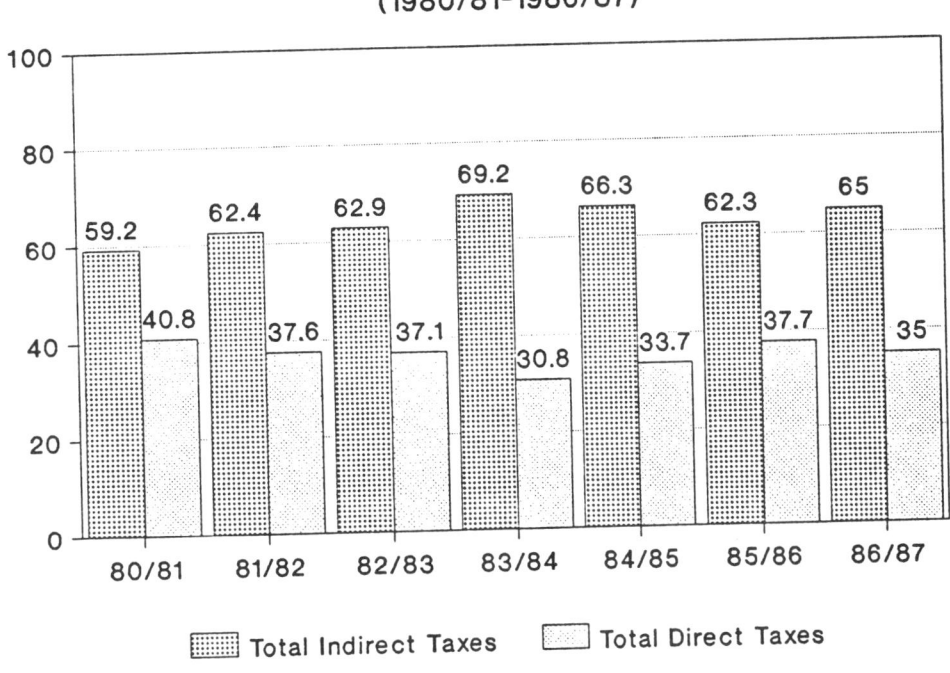

Graph 3.16 Composition of Egyptian Tax Revenue
(1980/81-1986/87)

Year	Total Indirect Taxes	Total Direct Taxes
80/81	59.2	40.8
81/82	62.4	37.6
82/83	62.9	37.1
83/84	69.2	30.8
84/85	66.3	33.7
85/86	62.3	37.7
86/87	65	35

Source: Ministry of Finance

In 1981/82 indirect taxes represented 59.2% of all tax revenues. In 1986/87, the figure was 65%. Preliminary data indicate that the relative importance of indirect taxes is unlikely to have decreased in 1988 and 1989. If the government goes ahead with its plan to introduce a broad based value-added tax, the relative share of indirect taxes in tax revenues should remain the same or augment.

3.126   *The Distribution of Income Before Taxes*. The analysis of tax burden distribution should be based on a comprehensive measure of individual income including, in an ideal world, gross income from wages and salaries, fringe benefits, transfer payments, income from capital including imputed income from owner-occupied housing, income-in-kind from government subsidies and in-farm consumption. Comprehensive income should also include estimates of the individual's share of corporate retained earnings and the part of the corporate income tax falling on owners of capital.

3.127   The task of allocating tax collection to households in different income groups is made difficult by data limitations. The lack of data on household income leaves no choice but to approximate income from the expenditure side, bearing in mind that total household expenditures as reported in the HBS are not a complete measure of disposable income (Box 2.1). All information available from the 1981/82 HBS distinguish always between rural and urban households. The two sectors are never aggregated. On the other hand, tax revenue data are only reported for the entire country, with no distinction between rural and urban sources. To compensate for the lack of an aggregate decile distribution for the entire country, the urban decile distribution is used here as a proxy for the entire country. The decile distribution of expenditures is a little less unequal among rural households than among urban households. Taking the urban distribution as representative of the entire country is not expected to introduce significant distortions.

3.128   Table 3.11 presents an approximate decile distribution of household expenditures for the urban sector computed from the original 1981/82 HBS published tables. These data are used to allocate taxes for 1985/86, the most recent year for which actual tax revenue data are available. The mismatch in years for the two data sets raises questions regarding the accuracy of the analysis, considering that changes in relative prices across commodity groups and increases in real income between 1981/82 and 1985/86 should have induced changes in household expenditure patterns. Commodities that experienced decreases in relative prices and/or those with larger than unitary income demand elasticities should have taken a more important role in households' budgets during the period. To adjust the 1981/82 HBS data for these changes is beyond the scope of this study. By not adjusting the data, the implicit assumption is made here that all income and price elasticities are unitary.

Table 3.11
(Approximate) Decile Distribution of Household
Expenditures in the Urban Sector in Egypt

Approximate Decile Expenditure Range (LE, 1981/82)	Share in Total Exp.	Exp. Share on Food & Beverage	Exp. Share on Tobacco	Exp. Share on Clothes & Footwear	Exp. Share on Housing	Exp. Share on Furniture Mat. & Serv.	Exp. Share on Health Services	Exp. Share on Transp. & Communic.	Exp. Share on Education	Exp. Share on Exports & Cult. Act.
I. Under - 600	2.91	3.46	1.90	1.97	4.21	1.41	2.59	0.78	0.64	0.20
II. 601- 800	5.19	6.00	4.88	4.37	6.19	2.66	3.78	2.34	2.32	1.27
III. 801-1,000	8.71	9.59	9.70	8.36	10.00	4.95	6.55	4.31	4.85	3.79
IV. 1,001-1,100	5.35	5.78	5.78	5.48	5.95	3.30	4.32	2.98	3.36	2.08
V. 1,101-1,300	11.37	12.07	12.56	12.00	12.19	7.68	9.41	6.92	8.55	5.90
VI. 1,301-1,400	5.79	6.13	6.02	6.17	5.97	3.92	5.06	3.89	5.29	3.47
VII. 1,401-1,600	10.99	11.40	11.93	12.00	10.85	9.43	10.26	7.35	9.79	6.85
VIII. 1,601-2,000	15.58	15.73	16.20	16.74	15.66	14.23	15.59	12.10	16.48	13.78
IX. 2,001-2,500	11.70	11.47	12.20	12.85	10.69	11.98	12.73	10.62	15.08	12.91
X. Over -2,500	22.40	18.35	18.83	20.06	18.29	40.43	29.71	48.71	33.64	49.75
TOTAL	100	100	100	100	100	100	100	100	100	100

a. This breakdown was necessary in order to use published tables from the HBS.
b. Columns may not add up due to rounding errors.

Source: Tabulations using data from the 1981/82 Household Budget Survey.

3.129   **Tax Sources in Egypt**. Fiscal revenues by type of tax and their relative importance in total collections in 1985/86 are listed in Table 3.12. Total tax revenues amounted to LE 6,518.8 million in 1985/86. Income taxes represented 37.3 % of total revenues. Within income taxes, the tax on corporate profits was relatively more important, representing 21.8% of total revenues. Personal income taxes accounted for 15.5% of total revenues, schedular taxes (income taxes by source of income) alone representing 13.4% of total tax revenues. Egypt does not have a payroll tax. Fees (or taxes) for social security are administered outside the Ministry of Finance and are not considered part of the government tax revenues.

Table 3.12
Current Revenues 1985/86
(In millions of Egyptian pounds)

	Tax Source	Amount	% of Total Revenue
I.	**Income Taxes**	2,433.2	37.3
	1. _Individual_	1,012.9	15.5
	a. Schedular Taxes	874.9	13.4
	(Salaries)	(144.5)	2.2
	(Professionals)	(20.0)	0.3
	(Commercials & Industrial)	(531.1)	8.1
	(Capital Income)	(179.3)	2.8
	b. General Tax	57.0	0.9
	c. Others (including some Social Security Charges)	81.0	1.2
	2. _Corporation_	1,420.3	21.8
	(Oil Sector)	(411.5)	6.3
	(Suez Canal)	(184.1)	2.8
	(Others)	(824.7)	12.6
II.	**Property Taxes**	43.3	0.6
	(Agricultural land)	(34.5)	0.5
	(Buildings)	(5.3)	0.0
	(Unused Land)	(3.5)	0.0
III.	**Estate and Inheritance Taxes**	18.8	0.2
	(Estate Duty)	(12.0)	0.1
	(Inheritance Tax)	(6.8)	0.0
IV.	**Stamp Duties** 1/	383.0	5.9
V.	**Consumption Tax**	1,489.0	22.8
	(Taxes on Food & Beverage)	(347.6)	5.3
	(Taxes on Tobacco)	(387.4)	5.9
	(Taxes on Cloth & Footwear)	(52.9)	0.8
	(Taxes on Furniture & Household goods)	(142.1)	2.2

1/   Includes revenue from net wealth tax, property transfers tax, and a few indirect taxes

Table 3.12 (cont'd)

	Tax Source	Amount	% of Total Revenue
	(Taxes on Medicaments & Health products)	(30.3)	0.4
	(Taxes on Oil, Transp. & Communication)	(318.7)	4.9
	(Other)	(210)	3.2
VI.	Import Duties	1,807.8	27.7
	(Tobacco and Cigarettes)	(277.9)	4.3
	(Motor Vehicles)	(133.8)	2.1
	(Other)	(1,396.1)	21.4
VII.	Other Taxes	343.7	5.3
	TOTAL	6,518.8	100

Source: IMF: "Egypt: Possibilities for mobilizing Tax Revenue and improving the Elasticity of the Tax System" 1988, and computations.

3.130   Property taxes and estate and inheritance taxes, also considered direct taxes, are a minor part of government tax revenues, 0.6% and 0.2% of total revenues respectively. There is also a stamp duty which is considered part of direct taxes. This tax is levied on contracts and transfers of assets in a variety of ways, and represents 5.9% of total tax revenues.

3.131   Indirect taxes which include the consumption tax, (22.8% of total tax revenues) and custom duties (27.7% of total revenues) represent the bulk of Egyptian tax revenues. The consumption tax is levied in a variety of forms and rates on both domestically manufactured goods and imported goods.

3.132   *The Incidence of Indirect Taxes*. It is generally assumed that indirect taxes are shifted forward to consumers. Under this assumption, household expenditure patterns can be used to allocate tax burdens among taxpayers. To find the tax paid by households in a particular decile (say, on food), total tax revenues from that tax source are multiplied by the households' expenditure share on the particular commodity as listed in Table 3.11. The computed tax paid by households in the decile is then divided by the share of GDP assigned to these households. The latter is the proxy for the total income of the households in the decile. For lack of better data, the decile shares in total expenditure in Table 3.11 are used to allocate the 1985/89 nominal GDP of LE 36,039 million. Allocating income (GDP) by total expenditure shares is likely to overstate incomes at the lower range of the income distribution and understate then, at the higher range of the income distribution. The ratio of taxes paid to estimated income are listed in Table 3.13 for all indirect taxes.

Table 3.13
1985/86 Indirect Tax Burden by (Approximate) Expenditure Decile
(as percent of estimated income)

Approximate Decile Expenditure Range (LE, 1981/82)	CONSUMPTION TAX							IMPORT DUTIES		TOTAL
	Exp. Share on Food & Beverage	Exp. Share on Tobacco	Exp. Share Clothing & Health	Exp. Share on Furniture & Household goods	Exp. Share on Medicam. & Health	Exp. Share on Oil Prod. & Transport	Total Consump. Tax	Exp. Share on Tobacco	Exp. Share on Motor Vehic.	Total Import Duties	Total Indirect Taxes
I. Under - 600	0.64	0.70	0.10	0.19	0.07	0.23	2.51	0.50	0.09	4.46	6.97
II. 601- 800	1.12	1.01	0.12	0.20	0.06	0.40	3.49	0.72	0.17	4.76	9.20
III. 801-1,000	1.06	1.20	0.14	0.22	0.06	0.44	3.70	0.85	0.18	4.90	9.55
IV. 1,001-1,100	1.04	1.16	0.15	0.24	0.07	0.49	3.73	0.83	0.21	4.91	9.59
V. 1,101-1,300	1.02	1.19	0.15	0.26	0.07	0.54	3.81	0.85	0.23	4.95	9.71
VI. 1,301-1,400	1.02	1.12	0.16	0.27	0.07	0.59	3.81	0.80	0.25	4.92	9.68
VII. 1,401-1,600	1.00	1.16	0.16	0.34	0.08	0.59	3.91	0.84	0.25	4.96	9.82
VIII. 1,601-2,000	0.97	1.12	0.16	0.36	0.08	0.69	3.96	0.80	0.28	4.95	9.86
IX. 2,001-2,500	0.94	1.12	0.16	0.40	0.09	0.80	4.09	0.80	0.34	5.01	10.05
X. Over -2,500	0.79	0.90	0.13	0.71	0.11	1.92	5.14	0.65	0.81	5.33	11.42
All Households	0.96	1.07	0.15	0.39	0.08	0.88	4.11	0.77	0.37	5.01	10.07

Source: Bank's mission based on 1981/82 HBS data, IMF, and data provided by the Egyptian authorities.

3.133   As far as the consumption tax is concerned, two important groups of commodities in the budgets of low income households, food and beverage and tobacco products, exhibit a regressive tax burden distribution as shown in the first two columns of Table 3.13. The regressivity appears to be more pronounced in the case of food and beverages. For the other groups of commodities for which desegregated household survey data were available, clothing and footwear, furniture and household goods, medicaments, and oil products and transportation, the tax burden impact is proportional or progressive. Similarly, the overall distribution of consumption tax burdens is mildly progressive.

3.134   For import duties, desegregated information is available only for two groups of commodities. Customs duties on tobacco products were allocated according to household expenditure shares on tobacco and cigarettes. As in the case of the consumption tax, the distribution of burdens for custom duties on cigarettes is mildly regressive. The second group of desegregate revenues, custom duties on motor vehicles, were allocated according to household expenditure shares on transport and communication. The distribution of tax burden is in this case progressive. The balance of import duty revenues were allocated according to households' shares in total expenditures. Overall, the distribution of tax burdens from import duties appear to be slightly progressive.

3.135   The last column of Table 3.13 reports the overall tax burden distribution for indirect taxes. This column which is obtained by adding across consumption taxes and custom duties, indicates that the burden distribution of indirect taxes in Egypt appears to be mildly progressive.

3.136   *The Incidence of Direct Taxes*. To analyze the incidence of most direct taxes, it is necessary to have representative samples of tax returns for the year under study. Because of the lack of data, the following paragraphs comment only on the likely incidence of each of the Egyptian direct taxes based on the structure of the taxes and on conventional assumptions about the final shifting of these taxes.

3.137   The conventional assumption for individual income taxes is that they are not shifted but are borne by households. Egypt has four scheduled individual income taxes, falling respectively on wages and salaries, professional income, income from individual commercial and industrial activities, and capital income. There is also a general individual income tax falling on global income. The global income tax represents less than 6% of all revenues from individual income taxes. Because of the relatively high exemption level, the nature of the deductions and the highly progressive tax rate schedule, the final incidence of the global income tax is expected to be progressive. Among the schedular taxes, the most important source of revenue is the tax on income from individual commercial and industrial activities. This tax represents over 60% of all schedular tax revenues. Because the source of revenue for this tax requires at least some asset holdings, and because its structure has some built-in progressivity, it can be expected that the tax on industrial and commercial income to have a moderately progressive impact on income distribution. The same arguments can be used and the same conclusions reached for the schedular tax on capital income, although this tax represents a more modest source of revenue. The schedular tax on wage and salary income is also a relatively modest source of revenue. About 14% of all individual income tax revenues come from the tax on wage and salary income. This is the income tax with the highest potential for having a proportional or even regressive impact on income distribution. But given the relatively high exemption levels in Egypt, the impact of the schedular tax on wage and salary income is also likely to be moderately progressive.

3.138   The equity issue with all individual income taxes and in particular with the schedular tax on wage and salary income is not expected to be vertical equity but instead horizontal equity. In part because of tax design (different deductions and rates), and more importantly, because of very different degrees of tax compliance, households with equal incomes are expected to pay quite different individual income taxes. While wage income of government employees and others is subject to withholding, professionals have a much easier time evading taxes. These different levels of evasion are probably reflected in the fact that taxes on professionals' income represent less than 2% of all individual income tax revenues.

3.139   The corporate income tax is a more important source of tax revenue in Egypt than individual taxes (21.8% of tax revenues versus 15.5%). Establishing the incidence of the corporate income tax is also more complex. To start with, an important source of corporate income tax revenues is the public sector itself, where price and other controls constrain public enterprises behavior. Close to 42% of corporate tax collections come from the oil sector and the Suez Canal. Depending on a number of economic conditions including the mobility of capital and the existence of pure economic rents in the corporate sector, the corporate income tax may be paid by owners of capital in the corporate sector, all owners of capital in Egypt, or the tax may be partially or fully shifted to consumers of the commodities produced in the corporate sector. If it were the case that capital owners pay all or part of the corporate tax, this burden would be allocated among households in the highest decile of the income distribution, and the corporate income tax would be a contributor to the overall progressivity of the Egyptian tax system. The portion of the corporate income tax that is shifted to consumers generally is allocated according to households' share in total expenditure. Because higher income households spend a smaller share of their incomes than lower income households, the part of the corporate income tax shifted to consumers may have a regressive element in it. It should be noted that part of the corporate tax burden may be exported to foreign consumers and/or capital owners. In the present analysis, the impact of the tax shifted to consumers would be proportional because income has been approximated by households' shares in total expenditures.

3.140   Egypt's property tax is levied on the annual assessed rental value of agricultural land, the annual (assessed) rental value of buildings in major urban districts, and the estimated capital value of unimproved land in urban areas. All property tax revenues are earmarked to local governments. Assessments lag behind many years, rates are low, and enforcement is lacking. Overall tax revenues from property taxes are extremely modest; they represent only 0.6% of all tax revenues. Over four fifths of these revenues came from the agricultural land tax. Since properties of less than 3 feddans are exempt and around 80% of rural households own a land area of less than 3 feddans, the property tax is not expected to affect the income of poor households adversely.

In addition, property taxes may get capitalized into property values, and thus the modest property taxes may have been paid by the original owners of land when the tax was first introduced.

3.141   Egypt also has an estate tax, levied on the total value of the estate of deceased persons, and a succession or inheritance duty payable by persons to whom a succession accrues. Annual tax revenues represented only 0.2% of all tax revenues. The first LE 5,000 of the estate are exempt and the first LE 500 of the inheritance are also exempt. These two taxes are likely to be progressive, although they play a very minor role in making the distribution of income less unequal.

3.142   The final two direct taxes in Egypt's tax structure are a stamp tax on transfers of stocks, bonds, and company shares both domestic and foreign, and a net wealth tax. Together these two taxes represent close to 6% of all tax revenues. The incidence of these two taxes should be progressive.

3.143   **Summary of Findings**. This analysis of the overall incidence of the Egyptian tax system has to be considered preliminary because of the significant data problems encountered. Nevertheless, most of the conclusions reached are expected to stand after a more exhaustive study of tax burden distribution for Egypt. Although several indirect taxes, namely consumption taxes falling on food and cigarettes, were found to be regressive, overall the burden distribution of indirect taxes appears to be mildly progressive. The lack of data makes it impossible to quantify the burden distribution of direct taxes. But the review of tax bases, tax structures, and the likely incidence of these taxes indicate that Egyptian direct taxes should be progressive. Therefore, it is expected that the Egyptian tax system has, overall, a moderately progressive to progressive impact on income distribution.

Conclusion: The Limits of the Egyptian Welfare State

3.144   Since the 1952 revolution, the Egyptian leadership has placed much emphasis on social development to foster greater equality and increased wealth. The implementation of successive land reforms and business nationalization measures, the establishment of an egalitarian wage structure and the pursuit of generous employment policies in the public sector which dominates the economy, the operation of a moderately progressive taxation system, the construction of a national public health network and a comprehensive education and training system, and the introduction of direct and implicit subsidies in a wide range of economic and social sectors have all contributed to improvements in standards of living of the bulk of the population.

3.145   These well-intentioned policies from a distributional viewpoint have probably slowed down economic growth in Egypt and may have actually decreased overall welfare. The multiplication of unproductive government jobs and the proliferation of subsidies throughout the economy has been costly and the burden on the budget has been very heavy. This strategy has resulted in the diversion of large amounts of resources away from productive purposes and has created important distortions in the economy. The ensuring pattern of resource misallocation has had adverse social effects, in particular in terms of obstacles to employment creation in the productive sectors.

3.146   Furthermore, the coverage of the various social programs and transfer mechanisms has not been universal as they have failed to protect the poorest members of Egyptian society. Some of the poorest households are not among the beneficiaries of the food ration program. Opportunities to gain access to self-sustaining income-earning opportunities and to raise individual productivity through human capital formation have not been available for the most needy. The lack of access to productive assets, notably land in rural areas, and the unavailability of alternative sources of steady income through regular wage employment explains the persistence of chronic poverty among potentially productive groups. Even most of the direct welfare programs administered by the Ministry of Social Affairs have not effectively reached the ultrapoor in terms of coverage of the target population and adequacy of the level of financial assistance offered. In the light of the failure of the welfare system built over the last decades to serve as an adequate safety net to protect the most vulnerable groups in the population, there is concern that the present economic crisis could bring about increased hardship for many households.

IV. From Economic Crisis to Reform: Assessing the Social Costs of Adjustment

Introduction: From Recession To Adjustment

4.01   Following the launching of the Open Door policy in late 1973, Egypt was able to achieve rapid economic growth until the early 1980s. Average real GDP growth between 1974 and 1981 was 9% per annum. But the prosperity of the economy was based on excessive reliance on oil revenues while the production of tradeable goods outside the petroleum sector failed to expand. Furthermore, the combination of rigid price controls, low energy prices, strict import restrictions, and an over-valued exchange rate created distortions resulting in growing inefficiencies in resource allocation and utilization. These structural imbalances were however hidden by large inflows of foreign exchange generated by oil revenues, income from shipping traffic in the reopened Suez Canal, increased remittances from workers aborad, and expanding foreign aid.

4.02   The decline of oil-related sources of foreign exchange after 1982 led to a slowdown of the economy, despite the government's attempts to maintain an expansionary fiscal policy. The reluctance of government to reduce its expenditures and the failure of non-oil exports to replace stagnating growth in foreign exchange led to a rising budget deficit and an increase in external debt. The situation deteriorated further with the decline of worker remittances and the leveling off of foreign aid. The current account deficit grew to a peak of $5.3 billion in 1986, about 15% of GDP. External debt increased rapidly, reaching $47 billion by end 1989. The budget deficit has remained at about 15% of GDP and inflation is estimated at 20% a year.

4.03   In 1987, the government responded to the deteriorating situation with a series of economic reforms to reduce the budget and external account deficit. The reforms included steps to reduce barriers to trade and price distortions in the economy. By increasing exports, the Government hoped to increase access to foreign exchange and reduce external debt. At the same time, reducing price subsidies was expected to encourage the efficient use of resources and consumption of goods and services. The reduction of subsidies would further improve the budget deficit.

4.04   The continued decline of the economy, however, with growth rates well below 3%, has placed new pressures on Egypt. In discussions with the World Bank, in 1989, the Government agreed in principle to broaden and accelerate economic reforms to restore conditions favorable to economic growth. The package of reforms, as proposed, will include increased autonomy for public enterprises with the closing of some that are unprofitable and the privatizing of others. It will remove investment licensing controls as a barrier to entry in the private sector and it will reform financial markets to improve access to capital. Resource and producer prices will be adjusted toward world price levels. Prices for agriculture export crops will be increased and delivery quotas eliminated.

Graph 4.1 The Need for Adjustment in Egypt

GDP Growth vs. Budget Deficit

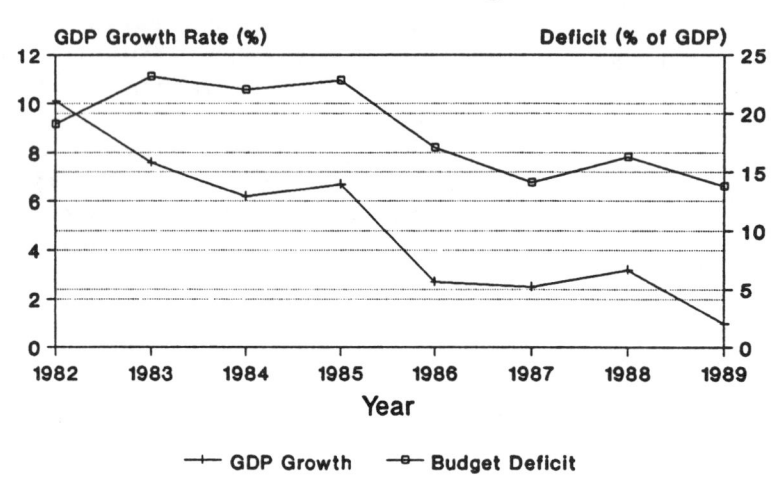

GDP Growth vs. Current Acct Deficit

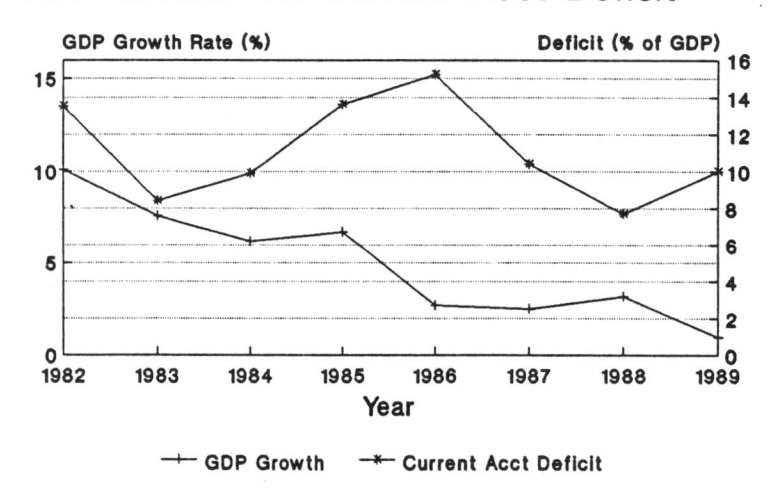

Source: Assad and Commander, 1989
Mission Estimates

Measures to liberalize foreign trade will be taken with an emphasis on the lifting of quantitative import restrictions, the rationalization of tariff protection, and the removal of biases against exports. The expansionary effect of government spending will be lessened by limiting the budget deficit to less than 10% of GDP. Government subsidies to the transport sector will be reduced. Public investment will be held to 11% of GDP and targeted to core governmental responsibilities of maintenance, renovation, and rehabilitation.

4.05   The principal effects of these reforms, if successfully implemented, will be the creation of a leveling playing field for public and private enterprises, improvements in production and consumption efficiency through an increased reliance on markets, an expansion of import capacity through increased exports, and a reduction of government's visibility in the economy and improvements in its fiscal condition. The combination of reforms is expected to create conditions favorable to economic growth for Egypt.

4.06   However, the implementation of the envisaged economic reform program would bring not only benefits to members of Egyptian society, but also some substantial costs. Moreover, the hardship associated with the costs of adjustment is likely to be felt before the intended beneficial effects. It is therefore important, in order to determine the degree of social equity and political sustainability of the reforms under consideration, to make an overall assessment of how various population groups are likely to fare during the adjustment period.

4.07   There are two main groups of potential losers as a result of the proposed macroeconomic adjustment measures. The first comprises all those who have been benefiting from existing distortions in the economy such as import licenses, protectionism, price controls or non-productive activities. The second category includes, on the one hand, people who are already poor and are at risk of becoming poorer and, on the other hand, persons in a vulnerable position who might become poor as a result of the crisis and the structural adjustment measures. This chapter concentrates essentially on the costs borne by groups in the second category, i.e. the poorest and most vulnerable segments in the Egyptian population.

4.08   Adjustment measures can hurt population groups from three angles. First, as earners of income through the productive activities they are engaged in, people can lose their employment or see their remuneration fall when they are wage-earners, or their income can be adversely affected through changing output level and prices when they are self-employed. Second, as consumers, their standard of living can suffer from changes in the price of goods and services, for example through price increases brought about by price liberalization measures or through the removal of subsidies. Third, as beneficiaries of government social services, the level and type of benefits available to them may change for the worse as a direct consequence of budget cuts affecting the provision of public services.

Impacts on Producers

Employment Effects

4.09   In the midst of a favorable economic climate in the late 1970s, large numbers of jobs were created in Government and public enterprises in an effort to maintain full employment. This led to distortions in the allocation of labor and the over-staffing of Government and public enterprises. The deterioration of the economy in the early 1980's made it increasingly difficult to sustain a full employment policy. The failure of the economy to stimulate private investment and employment outside the informal sector compounded the problem. Events in the Gulf also weakened the safety valve of external migration. Thus, as the 1980's progressed, labor force growth out-paced the creation of employment opportunities.

4.10   **Employment in Crisis**. By 1986, open unemployment had risen and real wages were falling with the sharpest declines for government employees. Government restrictions on layoffs and dismissals shaped the employment response to economic events. These restrictions made it difficult to displace workers. Enterprises were left with wages as the only adjustment mechanism available. The sharp decline of real wages throughout the economy in mid-decade, seen in Annex A, was intensified by the inability of enterprises to reduce costs through adjustments in employment. The Ministry of Social Insurance, for example, reported no significant increase in unemployment benefits for displaced workers in the mid-1980's. Instead, the increase in open unemployment was concentrated among new labor force entrants whose wait for guaranteed jobs was extended.

4.11   Open unemployment climbed to 9.2% in 1986, an increase from 7.4% in 1976 as seen in Table 8 (Annex D). Three-quarters of the 1.2 million labor force participants looking for work in 1986 were 16 to 25 years of age and slightly over 84% were graduates of secondary and post-secondary schools. In addition to being young and relatively well educated, the incidence of unemployment in 1986 was higher among women than men. This incidence, however, varied for urban and rural areas. For women, the open unemployment rate in rural areas exceeded that in urban areas, while for men the opposite was true. Trends in open unemployment seen in Graph 4.2 show that the gap in open unemployment rates for men and women in urban and rural areas narrowed between 1976 and 1986. The full impact of the economic downturn appeared to fall entirely on men. Open unemployment rates for men rose over the period, while those for women actually fell in both urban and rural areas.

Graph 4.2 Open Unemployment Rates for Men and Women in Urban and Rural Areas (1976-1986)

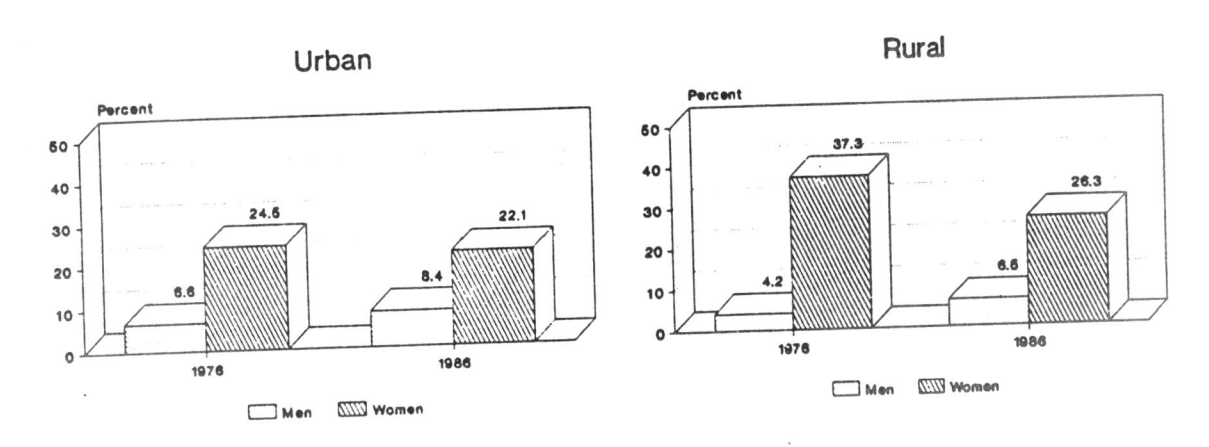

Urban

Year	Men	Women
1976	6.6	24.5
1986	8.4	22.1

Rural

Year	Men	Women
1976	4.2	37.3
1986	6.5	26.3

Source: Census, 1976 and 1986

4.12   In many industrialized countries, adjustments to external shocks are divided between reductions in real wages and layoffs. Egypt, however, chose a different path. Its restrictions on layoffs forced the full impact of the recession on real wages and new entrants to the labor force. The cost of the economic downturn was distributed through the economy in the form of reduced real incomes for those who were employed. Labor was treated as a fixed input in production. Its cost could only be adjusted by allowing nominal wages to fall behind inflation. Government workers incurred a disproportionate share of this cost. Rather than laying off Government workers, real wages in 1987 were permitted to fall to nearly half their 1973 level. Managers and senior level civil servants sustained the largest share of the decline.

4.13   Workers in public enterprises did not share equally in the decline of real wages. The real wages of those employed in public enterprises in 1987 fell to 90% of their 1973 level. Without public accounting for profits and losses in these enterprises, it is difficult to know how many were incurring losses as the recession deepened. Anecdotal evidence indicates that a large number were experiencing losses. Some of these losses were shifted to workers in the form of lower real wages, but a larger share was transferred to the Government, further enlarging the budget deficit. Depending on the scope of these losses, this placed additional pressure on the Government's wage bill. Although not confirmed, the case can be argued that the wages of Government workers were used as the principal adjustment mechanism for the public sector and its response to the growing economic crisis.

4.14   As the economy continued to deteriorate, the rising number of new entrants waiting for jobs created a problem for employment offices of the Ministry of Labor. The severity of the problem is seen in the number of registrants relative to the number of placements. Numbers were collected for a 3-month period in 1989 in a typical employment office in the suburbs of Cairo. Registrants were recorded as skilled and nonskilled with graduates listed separately. The ratio of registrants to placements in each of these categories was 10 to 1 during this period. As an example, 1,294 graduates were registered as unemployed in the 3-month period. During the same period the employment office placed 129 graduates in jobs. A similar shortage of jobs was observed in other employment offices.

4.15   These offices faced the task of rationing a scarce number of jobs among a growing body of job seekers. In this difficult situation, the emphasis was on ensuring all persons waiting in the queue equal access to the limited number of jobs available. Job seekers were referred to announced vacancies in the order they registered as unemployed. The emphasis was on equity rather than efficiency in this environment. Enterprises that hired an unregistered worker were subject to a fine. Job seekers who were not placed within 12 months were required to re-register or they were dropped from the queue. Rising open unemployment among youths as the economy slowed was joined by anecdotal evidence of increasing child labor. School officials reported a rising dropout rate among young boys whose families needed their labor incomes.

4.16   <u>Adjusting to the Crisis</u>. GDP growth slowed to 2.6% per annum from 1986 to 1988. Faced with a deteriorating economy, Egypt's population and labor force developed strategies for adjusting to the crisis. The sharp decline in real wages for Government workers made multiple job holding a necessity for financial survival as the economic crisis developed. This was reflected regularly in conversations with Government workers and supervisors. By law, it is illegal to hold a second job, but in practice it appears to be widespread among Government workers. Estimates are that 1 out of 5 Government workers hold a second job. Although no firm statistics are available, observers indicate that the number grew as the real wages of Government workers fell. In many second jobs, Government workers were able to earn several times their Government wages.

4.17   The Government tacitly accepted multiple job holding. The workday ends at 2:00 p.m. leaving 6 to 7 hours for work on a second job. Supervisors who approve the practice argue that it improves the worker's performance on the Government job. In other cases, it recognizes that the failure to approve a second job could mean the loss of a key employee. And in some cases, it is accepted by supervisors who themselves are engaged in a second job. With less flexible schedules, however, workers in public enterprises are generally not engaged in multiple job holding. Multiple job holding is especially prevalent among teachers. Government has virtually institutionalized the second job for teachers. The teacher will merely move to another Government school or accept employment in the afternoon session of the same school having worked in the morning session.

4.18   New labor force entrants also developed survival techniques as the economy deteriorated and the queue for guaranteed jobs grew longer. Most of the new entrants were graduates of secondary and post-secondary schools who were

BOX 4.1

The Story of a Government Worker and Multiple Job-Holding

The young woman, a civil servant in her mid-20's, looked about nervously when asked if she held a second job. For workers in other countries, holding a second job is an accepted practice, but not for Government workers in Egypt. Moonlighting for civil servants is unlawful, except when approved by a supervisor. With Government wages falling sharply in real terms, more and more Government workers have turned to second jobs to make ends meet, with or without a supervisor's approval. The young woman was among those whose supervisor had approved her second job.

A talented computer systems expert as described by her co-workers, the young woman responded, "yes," she held another job in the private sector. Like other civil servants, she finished her work at 2:00 p.m. each day, which left her ample time for moonlighting. The second job, she said, involved 6 to 7 hours each day and paid her 3 times her Government salary. Did other colleagues holding outside employment do as well? "No, probably not," she smiled. Her skills in designing computer systems for offices were in high demand.

With this kind of opportunity, she was asked, why do you keep your Government job? She laughed and turned uneasily to her supervisor who sat nearby. "She keeps the job because the business climate is uncertain," he said. "We do not know if employment in private companies will continue. Her job offers security." She nodded her agreement.

Why did you agree to her holding a second job, the supervisor was asked? "Two reasons," he replied. "Her Government salary is not enough to live on and like our other employees, she needs the income. Also, the experience she gains in her outside work makes her more valuable to our office." Moving to a more delicate question, the young woman responded, "no," when asked if her private employer paid her social insurance. She worked like many others, she said, "off the books".

waiting for a guaranteed job. Government faced with a mounting wage bill extended the wait up to 5 years. This, however, did not immediately translate into economic hardship for those forced to wait for jobs. In discussions with graduates and officials in CAPMAS responsible for the measurement of unemployment, many youths chose to register as unemployed, but worked in the informal sector while waiting for a Government job.

4.19   In the early 1980's, migration to the Gulf provided a safety valve for Egypt's labor surplus economy. As the economy deteriorated, however, workers were less frequently able to employ this strategy as a solution to rising open unemployment. Opportunities for external migration declined as oil incomes in the Gulf States fell in the mid-1980's and war disrupted Iraq's economy. These events did not immediately lead to large numbers of return migrants, but they removed the safety valve of expanding external migration just as Egypt's economy slowed. For the families of workers who remained in the Gulf, remittances became an important element in the strategy for survival. For workers who had returned from the Gulf, the savings from remittances provided a cushion against economic hardship.

4.20   **Anticipating the Impact of Reforms**. In 1986, the Government began to introduce a series of economic reforms to reduce the budget deficit. The reforms included steps to reduce barriers to trade and price distortions in the economy. By increasing exports, the Government hoped to increase access to foreign exchange and reduce external debt. At the same time, reducing price subsidies was expected to encourage the efficient use of resources and consumption of goods and services. The reduction of subsidies would further improve the budget deficit. These reforms were accompanied by labor market reforms further extending the wait for guaranteed Government employment by graduates of secondary and post-secondary schools. These reforms, however, did not remove barriers to labor mobility.

4.21   Restrictions on layoffs and dismissals remained in place as did the system of administered relative wages in public enterprises. These reforms were implemented gradually to spread their cost over time. The goal was to restructure the public sector through attrition rather than mass layoffs. This assumed, of course, that the Government budget could afford to wait for this transition to occur. It also assumed that labor force growth would not overwhelm the economy during the interim and that existing wages would efficiently allocate labor. The continuing decline of the economy led Egypt in 1989 to enter discussions with the World Bank. The Government agreed in principle to broaden and accelerate economic reforms in order to restore conditions favorable to economic growth. The impact of these reforms on employment is difficult to project.

4.22   The impact will depend in part on the pace of reforms. One of the important consequences is expected to be the reduction of the economy's capital bias. The capital bias of its ecoomic policies has contributed to the slowing of employment growth in the modern sector. The failure of the economy to create productive jobs has prompted Government and public enterprises to act as an employer of last resort. The over-staffing of public enterprises in the 1970's resulted in the perverse situation of enterprises being both capital and labor intensive. Capital market reforms and increased autonomy for public enterprises will shift the modern economy toward more labor intensive development with an expansion of productive employment in public enterprises. This will offset in part the likely displacement of surplus labor in these enterprises.

4.23   The over-staffing of public enterprises is significant. In steel and cement, for example, estimates of over-staffing based on international standards, imply displacement rates varying from 20% to 80% of the workforce. The likelihood of this depends again on the pace of reforms and the degree of liberalization of labor markets including restrictions on layoffs and dismissals. As part of public enterprise reforms, it is anticipated that wage and employment policies will be uncoupled from those of the Government, giving management more autonomy in hiring and firing. If restrictions on layoffs are not removed, it is likely that management will continue to use wages as the adjustment mechanism for labor costs. Real wages will fall further in public enterprises. Management's ability to displace labor could mitigate this decline.

4.24   While it is likely that public enterprises will become less capital intensive as a consequence of economic reforms, it is also possible that private enterprises, 90% of which are in the informal sector, will become less labor intensive. The strong record of employment growth in private enterprises has been encouraged by the capital constraints facing this sector. Studies of the informal sector have shown its capital cost to be higher than those of favored public enterprises with differences exceeding expected risk premiums. Access to capital is often through personal resources and informal capital markets. This has encouraged labor intensive development in private enterprises. Capital market reforms are expected to reverse this and possibly slow the rate of private sector employment creation. The displacement of labor from public enterprises, however, could reduce the labor cost of private enterprises and offset the bias toward capital.

4.25   Economic development on balance is likely to become more labor intensive. Employment will shift from public to private sectors. There will be pressures for workers to move from less productive to more productive activities. In the public sector, there will be incentives to reduce the over-staffing that exists as a consequence of full employment policies in the 1970's. Continued restrictions on this displacement will increase the pressure on wages in this sector as an adjustment mechanism. If restrictions on labor displacement are removed, then the pace of the reforms will determine the rate of labor displacement. Accelerated reforms will lead to significant labor displacement from over-staffed public enterprises in the short run. This would increase the importance of having economic safety nets in place to protect the incomes of those displaced and to facilitate their movement to new employment.

4.26   There are also potential employment effects in Government and agriculture. Reforms to reduce the budget deficit will continue to constrain Government's ability to guarantee full employment. This will affect open unemployment among new labor force entrants. The current slowdown of Government employment creation has lengthened the queue of new entrants, the majority of whom are graduates of secondary and post-secondary schools waiting to take a guaranteed Government job. If Government acknowledges its inability to sustain this policy and announces a continued phasing out of the guarantee, its effect on open unemployment will be uncertain. There is strong reason to believe that current statistics are biased upward by the incentive to be registered as unemployed. Anecdotal evidence points to the economic activity in the informal sector of many of those registered as unemployed.

4.27   Phasing out the Government employment guarantee for graduates could have the effect of actually reducing registered open unemployment and accelerating the entry of youths into productive activities. Budget pressures will also force government to reexamine its wage and employment policies. Current policies have placed government in an untenable position. Its effort to serve as an employer of last resort for graduates remains in open conflict with pressures to reduce the budget deficit. These pressures have forced it to use wages as an adjustment mechanism leading to sharp declines in the real wages of government workers. The shifting of these reductions to senior officials has grossly distorted their employment incentives resulting in increased multiple job holding. This policy is distracting to the core of talent that Government needs to manage its affairs effectively.

4.28   With continuing pressure to reduce the budget deficit, government will be faced with the need to rationalize its wage and employment policies. It cannot continue to allow real wages of Government workers to fall with the burden placed disproportionately on senior officials without risking the demise of effective Government. With economic reforms shifting more responsibility to markets for managing the economy, this implies a smaller government. Egypt will therefore confront the need to downsize its employment and reduce its overstaffing, while raising salaries in order to retain the most skilled professionals. There is no good measure of the scope of downsizing needed until government's roles in the economy are fully rationalized.

4.29   Agriculture through the 1980's has declined in importance as a source of employment. Commodity pricing policies have shifted incentives away from the production of tradeable goods. Economic reforms would restructure these incentives and encourage once more the production of commodities for export. It is doubtful, however, that this will reverse employment trends in agriculture making it a source of employment creation. A recent study shows that allowing agricultural commodities to be priced at international prices would lead to a reallocation of crops and a dramatic positive change in the agricultural balance of trade (Richards, 1989b). A very simple calculation assuming fixed labor coefficients suggests this would have relatively little impact on the demand for labor. Continuing mechanization of harvest and control-intensive operations will further reduce the demand for labor.

4.30   The complete picture for employment, then, is that the proposed economic reforms will in the long run lead to a more labor intensive economy with new jobs created in the private sector and autonomous public enterprises. Government employment will decrease as will employment in agriculture. However, in reaching this state there will be short run transitional costs in the form of labor displacement as the economy is restructured. Given past employment policies, this displacement will be heavily concentrated in public enterprises and Government which together represent one-third of the economy's total employment, approximately 3.8 million workers.

4.31   The level of transitional costs associated with structural adjustment will be determined by the pace of the reforms and the degree of liberalization of the labor market removing barriers to labor mobility. The persistence of these barriers will slow the adjustment process and likely increase its total cost. The impact of these costs, given the location of Government and public enterprises, will affect urban areas disproportionately. Approximately 30% of the urban poor are employed in social services and manufacturing making them vulnerable to the restructuring of employment in Government and public enterprises. An economic safety net targeted to these sectors would protect these workers and reduce resistance to beneficial reforms.

BOX 4.2
Labor Market Analysis in Egypt is Difficult

The analysis of trends in labor force activity and earnings in Egypt is made difficult by the absence of timely, comparable, detailed information. In 1989, for example, labor market analysts were using data from 3 sources: the 1986 population census (PC), the 1984 labor force sample survey (LFSS), and the 1982 employment, wages, and hours worked (EWHW) survey. The final report of the 1986 population census was not actually released until late 1989. More recent labor force sample surveys taken in 1987 and 1988 were not yet available. Similarly, more recent surveys of employment, wages and hours through 1988 had not yet been released. This delay in access to timely information impedes the use of labor force data in macroeconomic policy development and manpower planning.

The coverage and timing of the PC and LFSS differ which affects the comparison of their statistics. The PC defines the labor force as those 6 years of age and older, while the LFSS uses the definition of 12 to 64 years of age. Comparison of the two requires adjusting the PC to fit the LFSS age definition. Within the PC, the reporting of key labor force characteristics uses different age cohorts. For example, the education of the labor force is reported for those 10 years and older. The occupational distribution of the labor force is reported only for those 15 years and older. The absence of a uniform age definition for the labor force complicates labor market analysis. The different treatment of in-school youths further affects this analysis. The PC excludes from the labor force youths under 15 who work and attend school. The LFSS, however, retains these youths in the labor force.

The measurement of labor force activity is affected in the PC and the LFSS by seasonality. The PC is conducted in November when employment in agriculture is low. Until 1985, the LFSS was conducted in May when agricultural employment is high. This seasonality is reflected in the measurement of labor force participation and unemployment in the two surveys, particularly of women and children in agriculture. The LFSS is not conducted in census years. In 1987, the LFSS was converted to a quarterly survey and its content expanded. When it becomes available, this will provide information on employment seasonality. The EWHW suffers a different kind of problem. There are gaps in the annual series. The Central Agency for Public Mobilization and Statistics (CAPMAS) which produces all 3 series will simply skip survey years for the EWHW when it falls behind. This has happened in 1980, 1981, 1983, and 1986. The analyst is forced to interpolate for missing years.

The most serious constraint to labor market analysis is the absence of appropriate concepts of labor utilization. The labor force is based on the conventional definition of those who are working or actively searching for employment. Those actively searching for employment are identified as the open unemployed. As a measure of labor utilization, open unemployment fails to capture the scope of Egypt's employment problem. It overlooks the problem of those engaged in marginal employment activities in agriculture and the informal sector who are working fewer hours than desired. It excludes those whose skills are not being fully utilized in over-staffed government and public enterprises. It ignores those who want a job, but who have given up looking for one in Egypt's labor surplus economy.

The absence of information related to these problems leads to an understatement of Egypt's employment problem. The failure to collect individual information on hours of work and reasons for part-time employment, earnings and characteristics of employment, and desire for work among those classified out of the labor force, as provided in other countries, precludes an understanding of the real dimensions of Egypt's employment problem. Even for information collected on open unemployment there are deficiencies in detail. There is no information, for example, on the duration of unemployment as a guide to macroeconomic policies. These deficiencies greatly limit the scope and content of labor market analysis in Egypt.

Agricultural Prices and Farmers

4.32   In mid-1986, the government started implementing a reform program in the agricultural sector. A number of measures were taken to increase production and efficiency in the sector: (i) removal of delivery quotas at fixed procurement prices; (ii) substitution of floor prices for the prices of formerly controlled crops such as wheat and lentils for example; (iii) suppression of the public sector monopoly on import of animal feed grains and agricultural inputs; (iv) removal of restrictions on private sector exports of agricultural commodities; (v) increase in prices of inputs and stabilization of nominal value of input subsidies; and (vi) transfer of the responsibility for land reclamation development to the private sector. These measures apply to all crops except cotton, rice and sugar cane. It is expected that the government will expand these policies over the next few years to include cotton and rice and completely eliminate input subsidies so that international prices and market forces would guide farmers' decisions on investment, production and prices.

4.33   It is too early to observe the distributional impact of the recent reforms and to assess the likely effects of the planned changes for cotton, rice and sugarcane. Obviously, the outcome for different categories of farmers will vary depending on the evolution of the balance between input and output prices in each specific case. As long as the reduction in input subsidies and the increase in output prices go in parallel, the income effect should be neutral. Moreover, on the input side, farmers will have the possibility to cut down on the utilization of fertilizers and pesticides which had been boosted by the high level of subsidies, maybe beyond real needs as will be revealed under real market prices. An important risk factor for the poorest farmers is that the lack of access to cheap credit and marketing assistance would prevent them from shifting to more profitable crops and benefiting from technological change. What will happen to the livestock market is also important. This market has been protected up to now and the smaller farmers have benefited most from this protection.

Impacts on Consumers

Food Products

4.34   From 1970 until recently, the cost of the ration/subsidy program grew dramatically, to the point where in the mid-1980's the cost was almost 20% of the total government budget. As its cost was becoming prohibitive, the Egyptian government began to make changes in the program, examining ways to reduce coverage and even dismantle the system while at the same time ensuring the food security of the most vulnerable segments of the population.

4.35   Some changes in the ration/subsidy system have already been made as a way to reduce the budget deficit. The projected cost of the 1989/1990 program is approximately 1/2 that of the 1984/1985 program in nominal terms. The cost containment measures have involved three components: raising ration/subsidy prices, reducing the number of items included, and reducing the quantities subsidized. Table 4.1 presents recent data on the prices of rationed, subsidized and open market commodities. Clearly prices for many ration and coop foods have increased substantially. In addition, the Balady bread price increased by 150% between January and June, 1989.

Table 4.1. Prices of Selected Basic Consumer Products (Prices in Pt/Kg except as noted)

Item	Jan. 1989	July 1989	Percent Change July 88/89	Percent Change January/ July 89
Bread (Pt/Loaf)	2.0	5.0	N/A	150.0
Rice				
- Green Card Ration	37.0	37.0	146.7	0.0
- Coops	40.0	80.0	66.7	100.0
Macaroni				
- Coops	50.0	60.0	20.0	20.0
- Free Market	150.0	180.0	N/A	13.3
Fava Beans	80.0	120.00	20.0	50.0
Lentils	125.0	150.0	0.0	20.0
Chicken (Frozen)				
- Coops	320.0	360.0	N/A	12.5
- Free Market	430.0	430.0	N/A	0.0
Eggs (Ft/Egg)				
- Free Market	14.0	15.0	131.5	7.1
- Coops	9.0	9.0	N/A	0.0
Vegetable Oil				
- Green Ration	24.7	31.3	26.7	26.7
- Coops	80.0	235.0	193.8	193.8
White Cheese				
- Coops	250.0	250.0	N/A	0.0
- Free Market	350.0	420.0	N/A	20.0

Source: GASC (1989), Field visits, 1989.

4.36   The mix of subsidized foods has also changed. Table 4.2 contrasts the range of ration/subsidized foods available in 1980/1981 and those available in 1989. For example, maize, beans and lentils are no longer provided at subsidized prices and the amount of government budget allocated to other food items has decreased.

Table 4.2 Allotment for Subsidized Commodities in the 1980/81 and 1989/90 Budgets[1]

Description	1980/81	Subsidies in Millions/E 1989/1990
Wheat and Flour	511.0	258,674
Sugar	97.8	244,077
Maize	63.7	--
Tea	742.0	3,645
Frozen meat [1]	--	17,115
Frozen fish [2]	--	15,726
Cooking oil) Palm oil) Coconut Oil) Shortenings (animal fat))	125.4	245,100
Others) Butter) Poultry) Powdered Milk) Sheep) Tomato sauce)	254.4	188,447
Total	1,794.3	972,784

[1] Source: 1980/1981 data from Alderman and von Braun, 1984.
    1989/1990 data provided by GASC, 1989.

[2] Frozen meat and fish included under other.

4.37   Finally as an additional cost containment measure, the government has reduced the size of the Balady loaf from 160 grams to 130 grams. This has increased the effective price per calorie purchased by the household from .003 piasters to .0096 piasters per calorie. The cost has more than tripled. These food price increases have had a marked effect on the food expenditures of the poor, as shown in Graph 4.3.

Graph 4.3 Consumer Price Index in Cairo (1989)

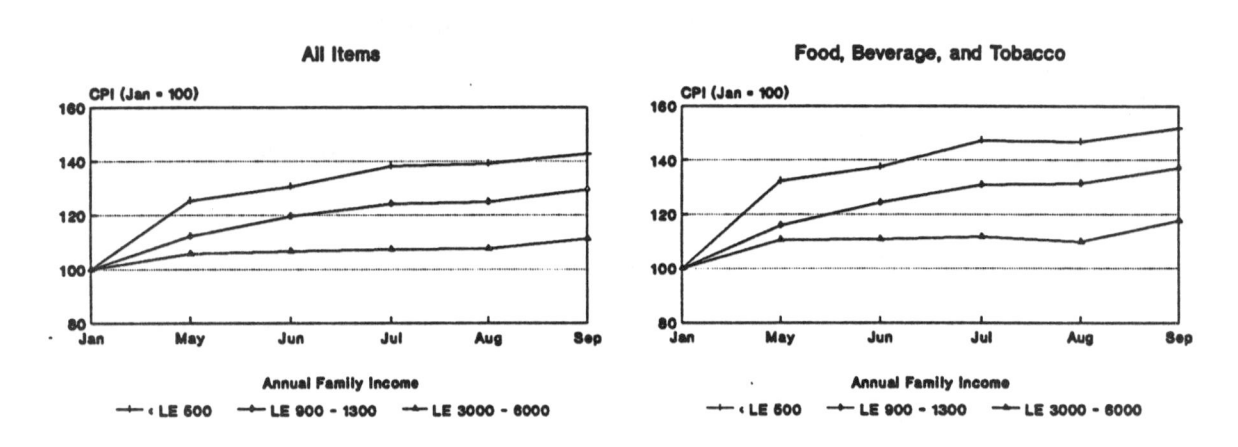

Source: GASC, 1989, Field Visits, 1989

Between January and September 1989, the average increase in the all Egypt Consumer Price Index has been 20%. However, the increase in the food and beverage consumer price index in Cairo for the lowest income category of household has been 51.7%. About 80% of this increase is due to the increased price of Balady bread which accounts for approximately 50 to 60% of the calories in the lowest income households (Alderman et al., 1984, Galal et al., 1984). Clearly the increase in food prices has affected the purchasing power of the lowest income group more than Egyptian households as a whole. Some recent evidence (CRS, 1989) suggests that the majority of households have been decreasing their food consumption in response to these food price increases.

4.38   It is likely that further increases in the price of bread and other basic commodities will hurt the low income groups more than other income groups since food occupies a larger share of total expenditures for the poor. Large farmers should not be hurt as some of the proposed changes in agricultural pricing policies will benefit them. Over the next three to five years prices paid to producers for cotton, rice, sugarcane will be increased substantially. These changes will occur concurrently with the removal of farm input subsidies. Large farmers have been relatively more taxed by the area allotments and enforced quotas for certain crops since these crops occupy a larger share of their farmland (Table 6, Annex E).

4.39   The small and medium sized farmers and the landless farmers are however net purchasers of food. Table 7 (Annex E) shows source of major staples (own production versus purchase) in the diet. Any gains in income for small farmers from the proposed producer pricing changes are likely to be more than offset by the lowering or in some cases elimination of food subsidy.

4.40   The matrix presented below attempts to summarize the potential food security effects of the changes that have been made and are being proposed in the consumer ration/subsidy system and the government's agricultural policy. Clearly all consumers - both rural and urban - will be negatively affected by the elimination or reduction of subsidies. However, some groups can adapt more easily by switching to a cheaper source of calories and/or increasing household expenditure on food. This adaptation is not possible for the lowest income urban household (approximately the bottom quartile) since they are already spending 75 to 80% of their income on food. In the rural areas, the small farmers (less than 1 feddan) and landless will be negatively affected. Since they are net purchasers of food, any increases in income due to the new agricultural policy could be outweighed by food price increases.

Matrix of Food Security Winners and Losers from Changes in Consumer and Agricultural Producer Policies

	Rural Areas	Urban Areas
Small farmer (< 1 feddan)	-	
Modern farmer 1/ (1-5 feddan)	0 or weakly -	
Large farmer (> 5 feddans)	+	
Landless Laborer	-	
Lowest Quartile		-
Second Quartile		Weakly -
Third Quartile		0
Fourth Quartile		0

1/ Effect will vary depending on farm size holding.

4.41   In conclusion, it is important to emphasize again that malnutrition and hunger are different. It is clear that the ration/subsidy system has been a major contributor to the food intake of the population. The raising food prices and cutbacks in the subsidized quantities will hurt the lowest income households. However it is less clear what the implications of these policies changes are for the vulnerable household members - children and women. Historically most of the malnutrition in children has not been related to inadequate foods supplies but rather to the maldistribution of food within the family. However, if household food intake has fallen in response to the higher food prices, it is plausible to assume that the food consumption of children and women might also decrease. The impact of government policies on women and children will therefore need to be carefully monitored.

Other Goods and Services

4.42   To reduce the budget deficit, the government is committed to continue its policy of fiscal adjustment which involves further reductions in subsidies and increases in revenues. As a result, substantial price increases are likely to take place, notably on water and electricity tariffs, fuel products, and transportation. Water tariffs have already doubled for the first tranche of consumption, from 3 to 6 Piastres a cubic meter, and have gone from 5 to 7 piastres for consumption above 30 cubic meters. The Electricity Authority plans to raise tariffs so as to be able to recover the long run marginal cost of production by 1995. A 30% increase is envisaged in 1990, with regular adjustments in the following years. Similarly, the government intends to raise the domestic price of oil products so as to reach the international price level by 1995. Transport tariffs will be adjusted over the next five years with the objective to cover eventually all operating costs.

4.43   While all these increases will undoubtedly be felt by the bulk of the population, the effects on the poorest segments are likely to vary depending on the goods and services concerned. As most of the poor in rural areas have no access to publicly distributed potable water and are not connected to the electricity network, utility tariff increases are not likely to have a detrimental impact. For the urban poor, however, tariff increases will necessarily erode their income further. Higher fuel prices would not affect the poor directly, except in the case of kerosene which is used a lot for cooking purposes. In terms of transportation costs, low income households will be particularly hurt by increases in suburban train and intracity bus tariffs. But raising the price of first and second class trains and luxury buses would not affect them.

Incidence of New Tax Measures

4.44   Since 1986, the Egyptian government has introduced a number of tax changes which are summarized in Box 4.3. The tax on cigarettes has been increased every year between 1986 and 1989, generating additional revenues of LE 1,370 million to be compared with LE 387.4 million in 1986 for cigarette tax and LE 1,489 for all revenues from consumption taxes. An important distributional consequence of the increasing reliance on the tax on cigarettes as a source of tax revenue is the relative regressivity of this tax.

Box 4.3

Tax Measures Introduced Since 1986

Consumption Tax on Cigarettes

July 1986   - tax increase of LE 0.1 per pack of 20.

May 1987   - tax increase of LE 0.1 per pack of 20.

August 1988 - tax increase of LE 0.15 per pack of 20.

June 1989   - tax increase of LE 0.2 average per pack of 20.

Consumption Tax in General

July 1989, increases in the number of goods subject to the tax and increases in some rates.

Stamp Taxes

December 1986 - stamp tax rates were increased by some 50-100 percent.

July 1989   - all specific and ad-valorem stamp duty rates were doubled.

Other Direct Taxes

July 1989, imposition of a development surcharge on corporate profits, and imposition of a new tax on immigrant workers incomes.

Source: Ministry of Finance

4.45   There is little information available about the July 1989 changes in the consumption tax. The number of commodities covered by the tax was increased and some tax rates were also increased; but more information will be needed to conjecture about the impact of these changes on the distribution of tax burdens. The changes in stamp duty rates in December 1986 and July 1989 are not expected to affect the progressivity of the tax structure because they fall mostly on holdings or transactions of financial assets. Again little information is available on the new tax on immigrant worker incomes to make any judgement about its ditributional impact.

4.46   The Egyptian authorities appear to be considering a major overhaul of the tax system. One change that has been frequently mentioned is the substitution of a value-added tax for the present collection of consumption and sales taxes. Experience from other countries where a similar policy change has taken place shows that the impact of such a change on income distribution can go either way. In the case of Egypt, the substitution could potentially increase the overall progressivity of the tax system if a number of basic commodities which play a significant role in the budgets of low income households, especially basic food items, are exempt from the new value-added tax. Careful simulations should be undertaken to assess the incidence of the proposed tax on different products and different income groups.

Social Security Benefits

4.47   The real value of benefits received by retirees and other insured through the general social security system is increasingly threatened by inflation in the absence of mechanisms to adjust benefits. The sharp decrease in real wages in recent years is an indication of probably worse declines in the real purchasing power of pensions and other social security benefits. The fact that employer and employee contributions are already relatively high at the present time as a proportion of wages would make it difficult to offset increased system expenditures with discretionary increased earnings.

4.48   In addition, the social security system's financial health is faced, in the long term, with the risk of future non-availability of accumulated funds, given the trend toward increasing borrowing by the central government, the low nominal rates of return earned by the system's trust funds, and increasing inflation rates. Thirty percent of total borrowing by the central government in 1987 was from the social security system. Investment of the trust funds in government securities earned for many years a 6% interest rate; this rate has now been increased to 8%. But with inflation rates well into the double digits, the future real purchasing power of the system's accumulated surpluses has continued to erode. Central government inflationary financing coupled with limited investment alternatives, threatens to wipe out the system's reserves in real terms and its ability to comply with its statutory future obligations when increased pressures on the system's finances are likely to come from improvements in the life expectancy of beneficiaries and more modern and costlier health care standards.

4.49   Finally, if measures are taken to liberalize the labor market by removing restrictions on dismissals, and if more workers become unemployed as a result of public sector restructuring, compensation under unemployment insurance could become a major drain on the resources of the social security system in the absence of offsetting measures.

Provision of Social Services

4.50   The fall in oil receipts and other government revenues after 1982, combined with expansionary expenditure policies, led to a large fiscal deficit (23% in 1986). The reform program adopted in 1987 by the government included as one of its key elements the objective of reducing this fiscal deficit. Despite substantial cuts in the last four years, the deficit has remained high and the government has undertaken, as part of the adjustment program under negotiation with the Fund and the Bank, to further reduce it. Against this background of tight resources, the government is confronted with the challenge of having to make additional cuts in public spending while maintaining human capital formation through expenditures in health and education and protecting the poorest through its social welfare programs.

4.51   The share of public expenditures for the social sectors as a proportion of GDP and of the budget constitutes a first indicator to assess how government activities in these sectors have been affected by the economic crisis and by budget cuts. Graph 4.4 presents the evolution of these shares, based on budgetary data concerning the Ministries of Education, Higher Education, Health and Social Affairs throughout the 1980s.

Graph 4.4 Evolution of Social Sectors Budget (1980-1989)

Share of GDP

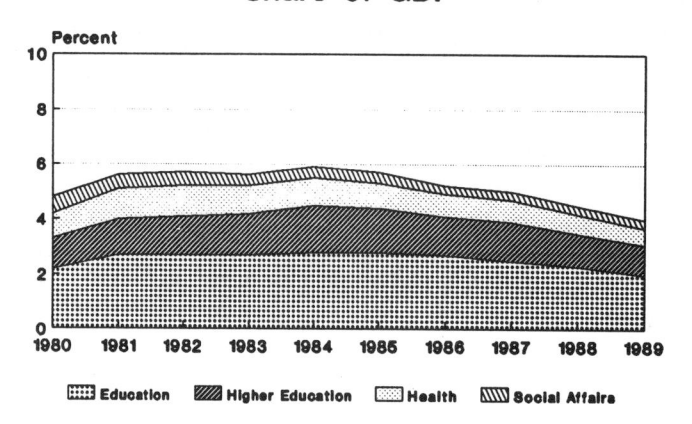

Share of Government Budget

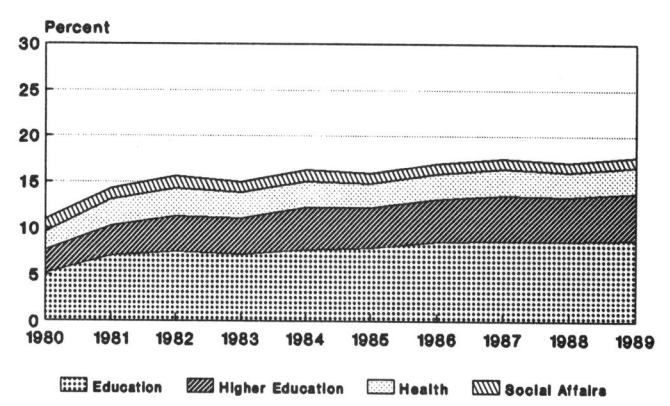

Source: Ministry of Finance

Two important observations are suggested by these figures. First, as could be expected, the share of social expenditures in GDP has decreased over the years, although there are sectoral variations. Total social expenditures have come down from a peak of 5.9% of GDP in 1984/85 to 4% in fiscal year 1990, reflecting the overall reduction in government expenditures. The most significant drops have affected the Ministries of Social Affairs and Health. The trend has been less drastic for both Ministries of Education.

4.52   Second, it comes as a positive surprise that the government has succeeded in actually increasing the share of the social sectors in the overall budget despite the economic difficulties and the necessity to decrease the fiscal deficit through reduced expenditures. The data indicate a steady increase since the beginning of the 1980s, from 11% to almost 18%. On a sectoral basis, however, this is not true of the budget of the Ministry of Social Affairs whose share has slightly fallen (from 1.4% to 1.1%). But the other three ministries, especially the education ones, have been able to attract a growing proportion of government resources. Higher education, for instance, has doubled from 2.5% in 1980 to 5.1% in 1989.

4.53   While the fact that the social ministries's share in the overall budget has been preserved is a positive result in itself, it is necessary to examine what happened to each ministry's budget in real terms, given the high rate of inflation in the last few years. Graph 4.5 presents the evolution, in real terms, of per capita budgets for the Ministries of Social Affairs and Health, and of expenditures per student enrolled for the Ministries of Education and Higher Education. The deflator used is a compound index based on the evolution of real wages for the salary part of the budget and the CPI for supplies and other expenditures (Table 8-11, Annex J). At first glance, the evolution looks very satisfactory as in all four ministries expenditures have substantially increased in real terms. But these figures are misleading due to the strong bias which the importance of salaries in total expenditures and the considerable fall in real wages (down 44% in relation to their 1980 level) introduces in the results. It is necessary to analyze the budgetary situation by category of expenditures to obtain an objective picture of the real evolution.

Graph 4.5 Social Sector Expenditures Per Capita/Per Student
(in 1980 Egyptian Pounds)

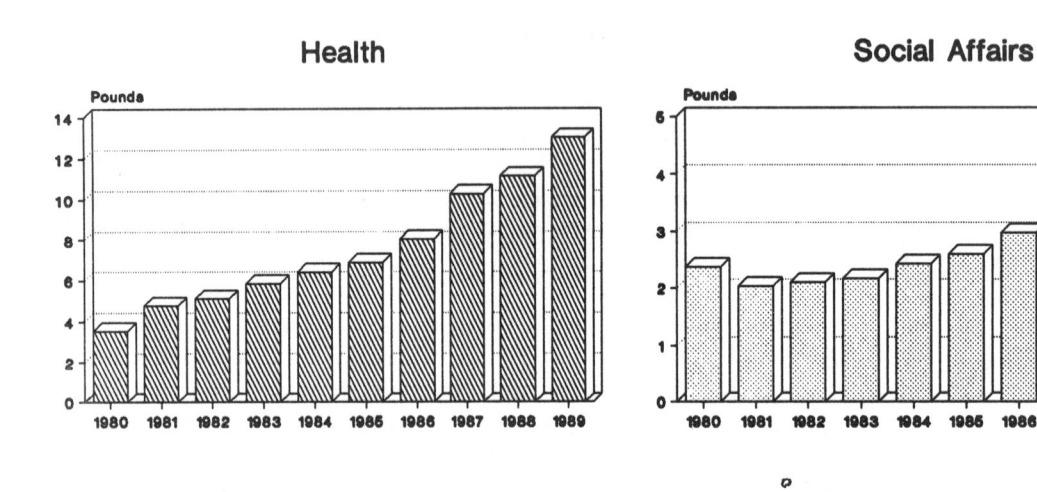

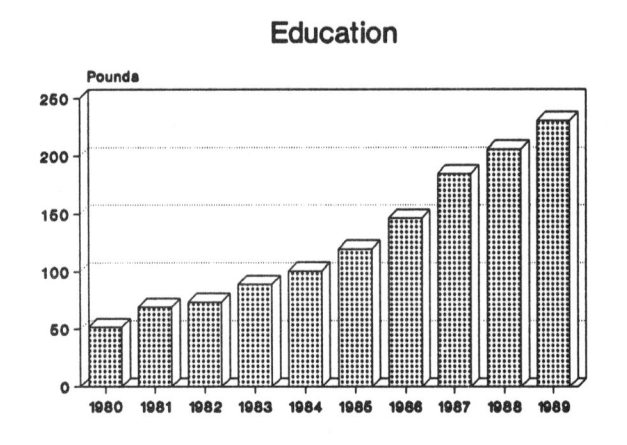

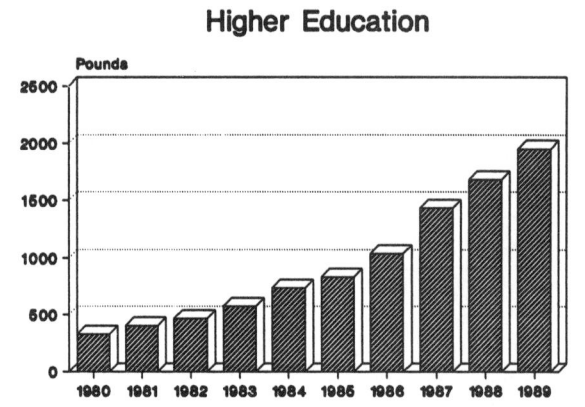

Health

Social Affairs

Education

Higher Education

Source: Ministry of Finance

4.54   Indeed, the most striking feature linked to the impact of the budgetary crisis on the social sectors is the growing share of salaries in total spending to the detriment of other categories of expenditures. Graph 4.6, which represents the evolution of the distribution of expenditures by category for the four social ministries, illustrates this trend quite clearly. The proportion of salaries in 1989/90 is particularly high for both ministries of education: 94% for education and 70% for higher education. The situation of the Ministry of Health is no less worrisome, with the wage bill amounting to 78% of the budget. The international standard is approximately 65% in the health sector.

Graph 4.6   Social Sectors Budget by Expenditure Category

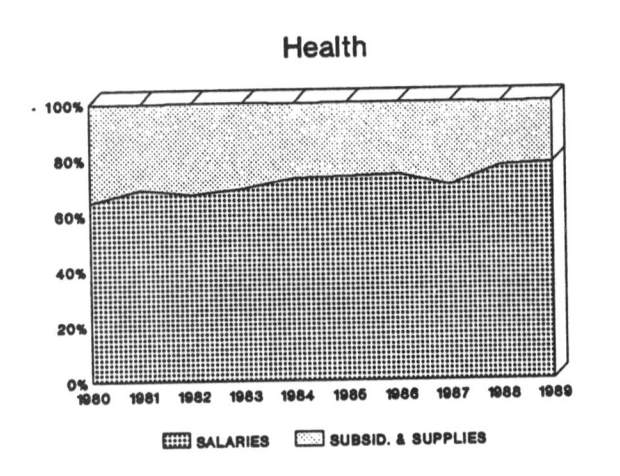

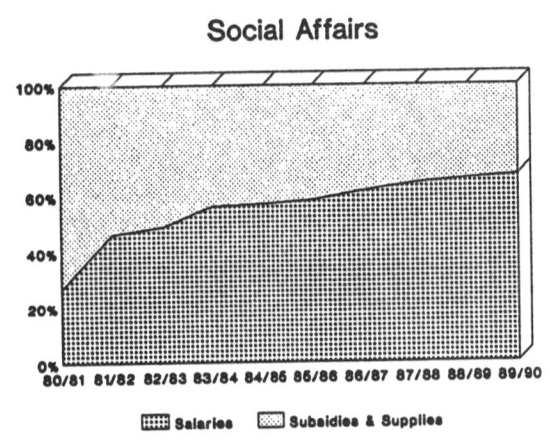

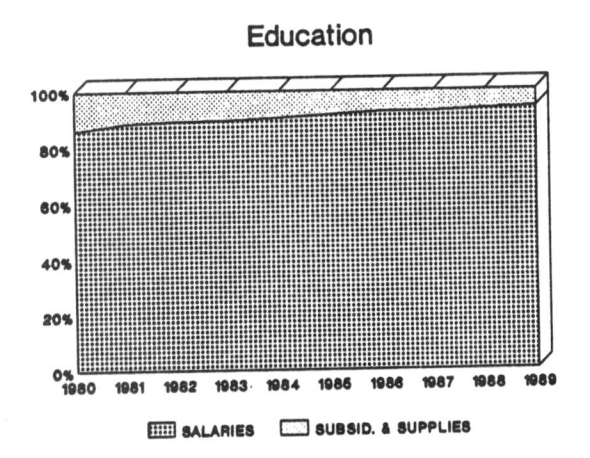

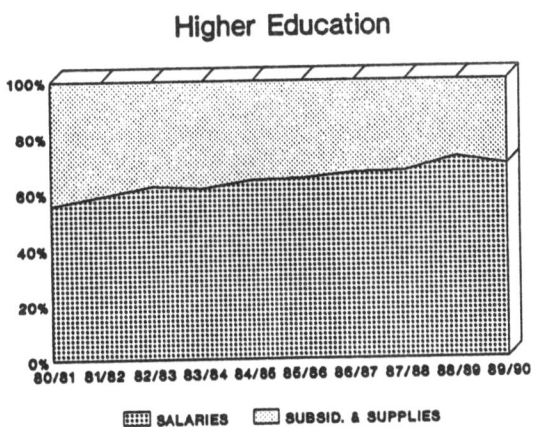

Source: Ministry of Finance

4.55   The direct implication of this imbalance is that all these ministries are under-funded to purchase the supplies needed for normal operation and conduct the maintenance and repair activities necessary to prevent further deterioration of the physical infrastructure (hospitals, health centers, schools and universities). The evolution of per capita real expenditures on non-wage items in the Ministries of Health and Social Affairs and of per student expenditures in the Ministries of Education and Higher Education, which is depicted in Graph 4.7, reflects indeed a very disturbing trend.

Graph 4.7   Non-Wage Real Expenditures Per Capita/Per Student
(In 1980 Egyptian Pounds)

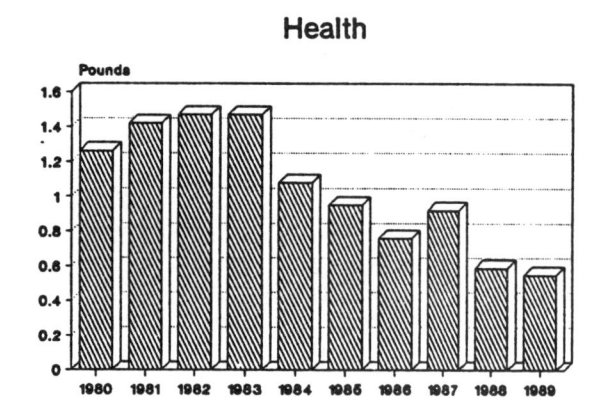

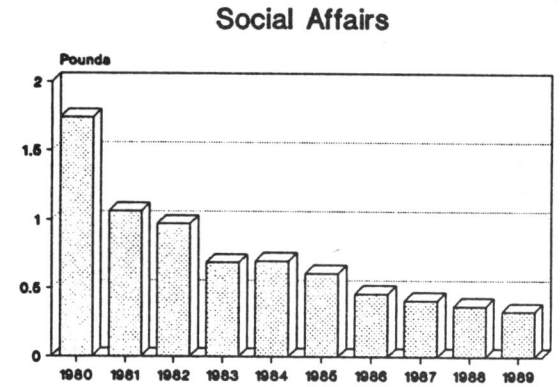

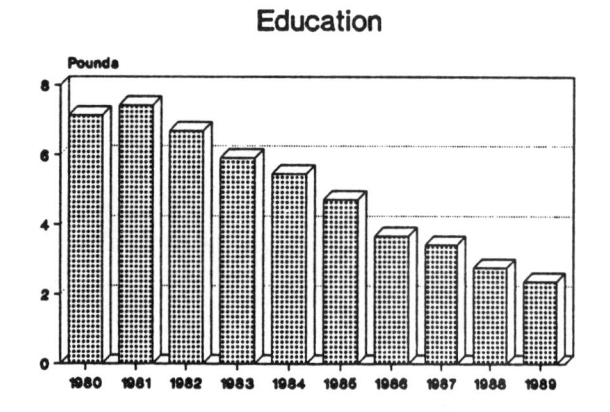

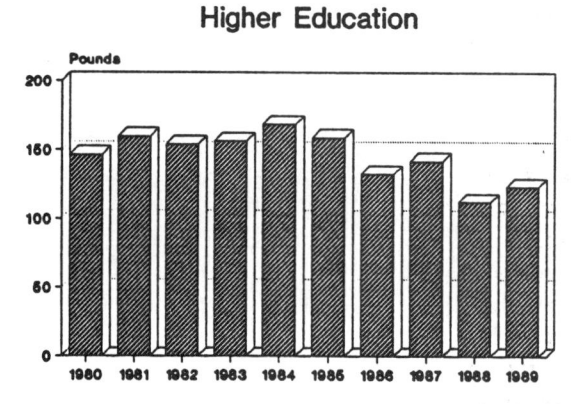

Source: Ministry of Finance

For the Ministries of Social Affairs and Education, per capita or per student expenditures are now five times smaller than at the beginning of the decade; for the Ministry of Health, they are three times lower. The Ministry of Higher Education is the only one where the decline has been relatively minimal, which can be attributed to a deliberate policy of slow reduction in enrollments implemented for the last four years.

4.56   The social ministries are faced with the paradox of spending most of their budget on salaries at the expense of indispensable supplies and other non-wage expenditures while, at the same time, being unable to offer a level of remuneration sufficient to motivate their teaching force and health personnel. The magnitude of the moonlighting phenomenon discussed at the beginning of this chapter is a direct result of this problem. This situation also reflects the fact that these ministries have been considered as employers of last resort by a government committed to guaranteed employment for all graduates.

4.57   The general trend described in the preceding paragraphs has different implications for each sector. In health, the shortage of supplies has become so acute at general and central hospitals that it is not uncommon for patients admitted to surgery to be asked to furnish bandages, syringes, or even small surgical equipment. In some instances, those who can afford to bring these items may have priority over those who cannot. The unavailability of drugs and operational supplies are a cause of public dissatisfaction and under-utilization of health services. A good indicator of the difficulties faced by the Ministry of Health in the administration of its establishments is the fact that the annual running costs of a bed in a general hospital are estimated at LE 700 compared to LE 2,200 for a bed at Cairo University Hospital, and more than LE 15,000 at the Cairo Curative Organization. The lack of transport facilities at the district level also appears to prevent the operation of an effective referral system.

4.58   To offset these budgetary problems and improve hospital management, the Ministry of Health is progressively introducing cost-recovery schemes in a number of secondary and tertiary level curative care facilities. Although provision has been made for reserving a certain proportion of beds to non-paying patients, there is concern that a two-class system could result from these schemes, with significant differences in terms of availability and quality of care.

4.59   In education, the authorities have instituted modest fees at all levels to compensate for the decline in budgetary allocations for supplies and other non-wage expenditures. But this decision can be potentially harmful when applied across the board. While the introduction of cost-recovery measures in higher education is justifiable from an equity standpoint and should be further strengthened, the opposite is true of fees in basic education. There is increasing evidence that the cost of education is becoming prohibitive for parents in the poorest population groups and that dropout rates in low income areas are on the rise as a direct consequence. In addition to the compulsory fee which ranges from 20 to 30 Egyptian Pounds per child in primary education, representing 5 to 7.5% of the yearly income of a government employee, the

Ministry of Education has recently institutionalized the practice of private tutoring within public schools to compete with private lessons organized outside on an informal basis. Under the new system, the school management organizes and monitors private lessons given by the students' teachers on school premises at a fixed rate. It is estimated that half of the students are enrolled in these institutionalized "private" lessons, at a cost of 3 to 5 Egyptian Pounds per subject per month.

4.60   Another equity issue that has been exacerbated by the economic crisis is the problem of overcrowding in primary and preparatory education. The high cost of urban land and the lack of recurrent funds to rent additional facilities are reflected in the increasing degree of overcrowding in urban schools. At the primary level, the national average is 45 per classroom. In some cases, a primary school teacher must take care of up to 60 students at the same time, which makes for less than ideal learning conditions and makes private tutoring all the more decisive in terms of educational achievement.

4.61   As far as the Ministry of Social Affairs is concerned, one of the main sources of worry is the dramatic fall in the real value of the direct transfers given to indigent people. For example, the nominal amount of the Sadat pension, currently 8 Egyptian Pounds a month, has not been changed since the introduction of the scheme in 1981, when its purchasing power was approximately four times the current level.

4.62   To conclude, there is concern that additional reductions in real salaries and non-wage expenditures might compromise further the coverage and quality of programs in health, education and social affairs.

Conclusion: Adequacy of the Existing Safety Net?

4.63   The results of the analysis conducted in this chapter are summarized in the following matrix which identifies the social impacts, on the most vulnerable groups in Egyptian society, of the economic changes likely to take place as a result of the macroeconomic adjustment program envisaged. The matrix focuses on three specific groups: (i) the ultrapoor who are entirely economically dependent on transfer income; (ii) the chronic poor who are engaged in economic activities but whose earnings are insufficient; and (iii) the new poor, i.e. those households who are likely to suffer most from the economic restructuring and who are at risk of falling in poverty during the transition phase.

SOCIAL IMPACTS OF ADJUSTMENT MATRIX
(WINNERS AND LOSERS AMONG VULNERABLE GROUPS)

	ULTRAPOOR Rural Households	ULTRAPOOR Urban Households	CHRONIC POOR Landless Farmers	CHRONIC POOR Agricultural Laborers	CHRONIC POOR Low level Government Employees	CHRONIC POOR Urban Unemployed or Marginally Employed	CHRONIC POOR Other Urban Wage Workers	NEW POOR Small Farmers	NEW POOR Laid-off Workers	NEW POOR Unemployed Graduates
I. IMPACT ON PRODUCTIVE ACTIVITIES										
- Dismissals in public sector					-				--	
- Decline in real wages in public sector					--		-			
- Increased waiting period for graduates										-
- Employment growth in private modern sector					+	+	+		++	++
- Slower employment growth in informal sector						-	-		-	-
- Change in prices of agricultural inputs			--	-				-		
- Removal of crop control mechanisms and increase of agricultural outputs in price of agricultural outputs			++	+				+		
II. IMPACT ON DELIVERY OF SOCIAL SERVICES										
Health										
- Inappropriate Funding	-	-	-	-	-	-	-	-	-	-
- Increased Cost Recovery	--	--	-	-	-	-	-	-	-	-
Education										
- Increased Cost Recovery	--	--	--	--	-	--	-		-	
- Deterioration of Quality	-	-	-	-	-	-	-		-	
Social Affairs										
- Fall in real value of Sadat Pension		--								
- Inappropriate Funding for Other Social programs	--	--				--				
III. IMPACT ON CONSUMERS										
- Reduction in Food Subsidies	--	--	-	-	-	-	-	-	-	
- Increase in price of kerosene	--	--	-	-						
- Increase in intracity bus and suburban railways tariffs		-			--	--	--		-	
- Increase in electricity and water tariffs		-			--	--	--	-	-	
- Increase in price of other goods and services	-	--	-	--	--	--	--	-	-	
- Exemption of basic goods from value-added tax		+			+	+	+		+	+

Note: — Deterioration
       + Improvement

4.64   As emphasized by this matrix of losers and winners, the economic crisis and the adjustment reforms under consideration have wide-ranging social implications, both positive and negative. Even though the reform program, if successfully implemented, should restore growth and bring about economy-wide benefits in the long term, the transition period is likely to produce considerable social costs. Most population groups are likely to suffer from price increases and from reductions in the coverage and quality of social services. For the poorest of the poor, the decline in the real value of their social benefits, for those who get financial assistance from the State, will represent an additional burden. Tensions on the employment side and falling wages will affect the chronic poor. Furthermore, restructuring measures that would cause loss of employment could create poverty for the households of those concerned.

4.65   In conformity with its long-standing commitment on behalf of social justice and development, the Egyptian government has responded so far to the adverse social effects of the economic crisis by spreading hardship rather than penalizing certain groups more than others. This is reflected in the emphasis on real wage compression instead of staff reductions and in the efforts to use subsidies, especially food subsidies, to protect the purchasing power of consumers threatened by falling real wages. Thus, the degree of hardship likely to befall various groups in the Egyptian population during the transitory adjustment period will depend to a great extent upon the evolution of this fragile balance among salaries, employment and subsidies.

4.66   So far as can be determined on the basis of all macroeconomic indicators, it is unlikely that this strategy aimed at protecting the whole population can be sustained much longer. The prospect of rupture of the prevailing social equilibrium raises concern about the adequacy of the existing safety net. The lack of information and monitoring systems to get rapid feedback on the social implications of economic trends (income, employment, etc), the absence of well-functioning employment services to assist displaced workers with retraining and job search programs, and the inexistence of targeting mechanisms to ensure that budgetary reductions in subsidies and social expenditures do not affect the poorest point to the need to put in place efficient social protection mechanisms to cushion the most needy and vulnerable groups.

4.67   At the same time, it is crucial to stress tht the social situation is unlikely to improve should the reform program not be implemented. On the contrary, the negative social consequences of the economic crisis are expected to be even stronger in the absence of any significant structural change. In the event of a slow down in the implementation of the Government's reform program, the economy would slide further into a recession, with little chance for a renewal of growth in the medium term. GDP growth would become nil or even negative and per capita income and consumption would further decline in real terms. Thus the costs of non adjustment, in terms of increased unemployment and falling income, could have severe social consequences.

SOCIAL IMPACTS OF ADJUSTMENT MATRIX
(WINNERS AND LOSERS AMONG VULNERABLE GROUPS)

	ULTRAPOOR		CHRONIC POOR					NEW POOR		
	Rural Households	Urban Households	Landless Farmers	Agricultural Laborers	Low level Government Employees	Urban Unemployed or Marginally Employed	Other Urban Wage Workers	Small Farmers	Laid-off Workers	Unemployed Graduates
I. IMPACT ON PRODUCTIVE ACTIVITIES										
- Dismissals in public sector					−				−−	
- Decline in real wages in public sector					−−		−			
- Increased waiting period for graduates										−
- Employment growth in private modern sector					+	+	+		++	++
- Slower employment growth in informal sector						−	−		−	−
- Change in prices of agricultural inputs			−−	−				−		
- Removal of crop control mechanisms and increase of agricultural outputs in price of agricultural outputs			++	+				+		
II. IMPACT ON DELIVERY OF SOCIAL SERVICES										
Health										
- Inappropriate Funding	−	−	−	−	−	−	−	−	−	−
- Increased Cost Recovery	−−	−−	−	−	−	−	−	−	−	−
Education										
- Increased Cost Recovery	−−	−−	−−	−−	−	−−	−	−		
- Deterioration of Quality	−	−	−	−	−	−	−	−		
Social Affairs										
- Fall in real value of Sadat Pension		−−								
- Inappropriate Funding for Other Social programs	−−	−−				−−				
III. IMPACT ON CONSUMERS										
- Reduction in Food Subsidies	−−	−−	−	−	−	−	−	−	−	
- Increase in price of kerosene	−−	−−	−	−						
- Increase in intracity bus and suburban railways tariffs		−			−−	−−	−−	−		
- Increase in electricity and water tariffs		−			−−	−−	−−	−	−	
- Increase in price of other goods and services	−	−−	−	−−	−−	−−	−−	−	−	
- Exemption of basic goods from value-added tax		+			+	+	+		+	+

Note: − Deterioration
+ Improvement

4.64   As emphasized by this matrix of losers and winners, the economic crisis and the adjustment reforms under consideration have wide-ranging social implications, both positive and negative. Even though the reform program, if successfully implemented, should restore growth and bring about economy-wide benefits in the long term, the transition period is likely to produce considerable social costs. Most population groups are likely to suffer from price increases and from reductions in the coverage and quality of social services. For the poorest of the poor, the decline in the real value of their social benefits, for those who get financial assistance from the State, will represent an additional burden. Tensions on the employment side and falling wages will affect the chronic poor. Furthermore, restructuring measures that would cause loss of employment could create poverty for the households of those concerned.

4.65   In conformity with its long-standing commitment on behalf of social justice and development, the Egyptian government has responded so far to the adverse social effects of the economic crisis by spreading hardship rather than penalizing certain groups more than others. This is reflected in the emphasis on real wage compression instead of staff reductions and in the efforts to use subsidies, especially food subsidies, to protect the purchasing power of consumers threatened by falling real wages. Thus, the degree of hardship likely to befall various groups in the Egyptian population during the transitory adjustment period will depend to a great extent upon the evolution of this fragile balance among salaries, employment and subsidies.

4.66   So far as can be determined on the basis of all macroeconomic indicators, it is unlikely that this strategy aimed at protecting the whole population can be sustained much longer. The prospect of rupture of the prevailing social equilibrium raises concern about the adequacy of the existing safety net. The lack of information and monitoring systems to get rapid feedback on the social implications of economic trends (income, employment, etc), the absence of well-functioning employment services to assist displaced workers with retraining and job search programs, and the inexistence of targeting mechanisms to ensure that budgetary reductions in subsidies and social expenditures do not affect the poorest point to the need to put in place efficient social protection mechanisms to cushion the most needy and vulnerable groups.

4.67   At the same time, it is crucial to stress tht the social situation is unlikely to improve should the reform program not be implemented. On the contrary, the negative social consequences of the economic crisis are expected to be even stronger in the absence of any significant structural change. In the event of a slow down in the implementation of the Government's reform program, the economy would slide further into a recession, with little chance for a renewal of growth in the medium term. GDP growth would become nil or even negative and per capita income and consumption would further decline in real terms. Thus the costs of non adjustment, in terms of increased unemployment and falling income, could have severe social consequences.

V. Toward a Poverty Alleviation Strategy

> "...adjustment does not have to lower basic human standards ... the more adjustment efforts give proper weight to social realities --especially the implications for the poorest -- the more successful they are likely to be."
>
> Michel Camdessus, IMF Managing Director

> "An important general priority is the design of programs to address long-term poverty issues..., programs which expand the opportunities for employment and the availability of services for the poor. Our approach to poverty alleviation has three main elements: first, to restore growth which is essential to raising incomes of the poor; second, to design our sector interventions in education, health and other human resource development in ways which benefit the poor; third, where appropriate, to design specifically-targeted programs to address the needs of the poor."
>
> W. Thalwitz, Senior Vice-President, The World Bank, Presentation to the Executive Directors, January 11, 1989.

Introduction: Presentation of the Overall Strategy

5.01   Despite commendable improvements in the standards of living and well-being of the majority of the Egyptian people as a result of thirty years of efforts to promote economic and social development, poverty remains a significant problem. Even under the most conservative standard poverty affects between one fifth and one fourth of the population. The present economic crisis and the macroeconomic reforms needed to restructure the Egyptian economy threaten, in the short term, to aggravate the plight of the existing poor and, possibly, to create new poor. Paradoxically, the need to protect the poor is becoming more pressing at a time when the economic recession and budgetary constraints make it more difficult to set aside resources for distributive purposes.

5.02   The 1990 World Development Report on poverty emphasizes the fact that, historically, social progress has been achieved only when there is a satisfactory combination of substantial economic growth and an appropriate pattern of growth. Economic recovery is therefore the first condition of success for any poverty alleviation strategy in Egypt. Without restoration of economic growth, there is no basis for improving income-earning opportunities for the poor and mobilizing resources for income redistribution. The second important condition is an adequate pattern of growth from the viewpoint of the distribution of the benefits of economic growth. The history of the last two decades in Egypt shows that economic growth alone is not sufficient to eradicate poverty, even when the State is as committed to the promotion of social justice and welfare as the Egyptian government has been. As R. McNamara remarked in an address to the World Bank's Board of Directors in 1977, "economic growth cannot assist the poor if it does not reach the poor." The design of a poverty alleviation strategy for Egypt needs therefore to reflect this dual preoccupation of increased economic growth and appropriate pattern of growth.

5.03   In terms of configuration of the proposed poverty alleviation strategy itself, the following three dimensions are important in the present Egyptian context: (i) the range of possible policy measures; (ii) the diversity of groups at risk; and (iii) the time horizon.

5.04   Poverty alleviation could be approached in three ways: from a welfare, human capital, or economic viewpoint. A welfare approach would consist of making direct income transfers to the most needy, either through cash payments or through subsidized goods and services. A human capital approach would aim at increasing the poor's potential earnings by raising their productivity through nutrition, health, education and training programs. Finally, an economic approach would focus on interventions designed to improve income-earning for the poor, for example by providing easier access to productive employment or assets and by promoting a better remuneration of their productive activities.

5.05   These three types of partially overlapping interventions are not equally desirable. Establishing an order of priority among them is important for operational purposes. Although the welfare approach has traditionally been the preferred option in many countries including Egypt, the economic approach appears to be the most appropriate. It confronts directly the roots of poverty which are linked to the lack of sufficiently remunerating primary income. Only measures to improve access to sustainable income can make people move from poverty to economic self-sufficiency. Moreover, these types of interventions can be limited in time as, once the conditions for improved participation of the poor in economic life are set right, government assistance can be phased out gradually. Although the human capital approach does not improve directly the income of the poor, it is complementary to the economic approach in so far as it helps the poor increase their potential for a better productive life.

5.06   The welfare approach is the most costly and least effective method of poverty alleviation. While providing for protection of the poorest against the lack of regular income, it does not reduce their level of economic dependency. In Egypt, the welfare approach has had many shortcomings. The most needy have been ignored in the absence of targeting mechanisms and a real safety net. Furthermore, this strategy has resulted in the diversion of large amounts of resources away from productive purposes. The multiplication of unproductive government jobs and the proliferation of subsidies throughout the economy have had a high budgetary cost and created serious distortions.

5.07   However, the introduction of a hierarchical order among these approaches does not imply that they are entirely mutually exclusive and that the welfare approach should be rejected altogether. Given the heterogeneity of the groups in poverty in Egypt, it is necessary to adopt a diversified approach to poverty eradication. It is important to recognize that, before the poor can respond to policy incentives provided by the macroeconomic reform program, they may require initial help for the satisfaction of their basic needs, notably in terms of food, health, and access to productive employment. Similarly, in the case of the ultrapoor, the welfare approach is likely to remain predominant considering the difficulties involved in attempting to integrate older people, widows with young children, and handicapped or sick people in mainstream economic activities. For the chronic poor, on the other hand, the economic approach should prevail as this group is made up of people who are already engaged in economic activities but whose incomes are too low. Human capital formation is crucial for all vulnerable members of society, but its impact is dependent on the success of reforms on the economic side as improvements in the human capital of the poor can be translated into productivity gains only if there is an economic demand to use the labor force effectively. **Ideally, the strategy adopted should combine all three forms of intervention with a different emphasis depending on the degree and type of poverty of each target group.**

5.08   Both the short term and the long term requirements of a poverty alleviation strategy must be considered. Short of rapid and massive income transfers which would not be desirable per se and would be impossible to consider under the prevailing economic conditions, there is no short term answer to the kind of chronic poverty which has persisted in Egypt for at least three decades. Effective as they may be, measures to provide better income-earning opportunities for the poor have a long maturation span. Similarly, interventions to improve access of the poor to public services in health or education take a long time to bear their fruits. By definition, the very structure of the delivery systems and the patterns of resource allocation need to be reformed and the reorientation of investment in hospitals or universities for example is a long term process. At the same time, however, it is impossible to ignore the immediate adverse effects of the economic crisis, notably the growing unemployment, falling wages, and higher prices, and the need to protect the human resources of the poor as early as possible. Therefore, the goals of the poverty alleviation strategy should be not only to suppress chronic poverty in the long run, but also to ease the burden of the economic crisis and reduce the social costs of structural adjustment on the economically vulnerable members of the population.

5.09   Taking these dimensions into consideration, the poor should be seen not as a burden, but as a potential resource. A comprehensive Poverty Alleviation Strategy should include the following elements:

- structural measures to increase income-earning opportunities for the poor through improved access to productive employment and assets;

- structural measures to improve the equity and cost-effectiveness of public expenditures in health and education to increase opportunities for human capital formation for the poor;

- structural measures to achieve a more equitable and efficient targeting of all secondary income transfers, including consumer subsidies, producer subsidies and direct welfare transfers; and

- an Emergency Social Fund to enhance the above efforts and to protect the low-income population groups directly affected during implementation of macroeconomic reforms.

5.10   While all these measures are equally important to achieve the overall goal of poverty alleviation, their implementation schedules would vary significantly. In the short term, the government's priority is obviously to set up the Social Fund and to initiate emergency measures to protect the poor during the adjustment period. The next priority would be to work on the targeting aspects in order to establish mechanisms which are both more efficient and more equitable. Introducing reforms in public expenditures allocation and utilization in the social sectors and improving access of the poor to productive employment and assets are measures with a longer term horizon.

5.11   Effective targeting is a fundamental determinant of success and cost-effectiveness of government intervention under each of the four components. Moving toward selective targeting would represent a significant departure from past practices based on the belief that generous equal opportunity policies would automatically benefit the whole population. Both the persistence of poverty and the financial unsustainability of present social policies of generalized subsidies, access to free health and education, government employment guarantee and egalitarian salary scales regardless of actual need, ability, performance or merit underline the urgency of designing appropriate targeting mechanisms. This would make it possible to ensure that resources reach the most needy groups, increase the benefits to the targeted population and, at the same time, lower the cost of the programs to the government.

5.12   The availability of timely and accurate information is a sine qua non condition for any attempt to improve targeting. At the present time, the possibility to reach the poor is constrained by the ability to identify them and to monitor the evolution of their living conditions. Among other agencies, the Ministries of Social Affairs (Sadat pension), Education (scholarships and fees), Health (cost-recovery), Supply (food subsidies), Energy (electricity and fuel subsidies), Housing (water tariffs) and Labor (employment and retraining) would benefit from the capacity to target their programs to protect the most vulnerable groups. As illustrated by the matrix of winners and losers at the end of chapter 4, the effects of the planned reforms are likely to differ widely among various categories of poor households. This should be reflected in the focus of the specific interventions for each of these groups. The establishment of monitoring mechanisms will therefore be an integral part of the poverty alleviation strategy.

5.13   In deciding which targeting mechanisms would be appropriate, the Egyptian authorities will face the challenge of finding the right balance between the administrative cost of targeting and the degree of acceptable leakage. All the cost of targeting will be determined by the size of the program envisaged, the number of beneficiaries in the target groups and the level of precision expected in the identification of these beneficiaries. The amount of leakage is linked to the degree of "undercoverage" or "overcoverage" of the program. This implies looking at alternatives based either on direct targeting mechanisms or on indirect targeting using characteristics of the poor as proxies, depending on data availability and the cost of information collection in each specific case. Flexibility should also be a feature of the targeting system to provide the capacity to admit new households or remove old households as their income situations change over time.

Income Generation Policies

5.14   Strategies for income generation will focus on employment promotion and measures to improve access of the poor to productive assets.

Employment Promotion Policies

5.15   Egypt's economy has struggled to provide productive employment for its rapidly expanding population and labor force. In an effort to maintain full employment, it has overstaffed government and public enterprises. With the downturn of the economy in the 1980's, this policy is no longer sustainable. The economic reforms planned with the support of the World Bank will create incentives for the restructuring of employment and the movement of workers from less productive to more productive jobs. This will include a restructuring of employment in government and public enterprises. Both are expected to experience a downsizing of employment. The speed with which the economy responds to new production incentives and creates alternative employment opportunities for displaced workers will affect the social costs of the economic reforms and their impact on the poor.

5.16   The social costs of economic reforms and the distribution of these costs will shape government's response to structural adjustment. Employment promotion is a key element in any strategy to reduce the social costs of economic reforms and their impacts on the poor. The availability of productive jobs for displaced workers will reduce their loss of income and resistance to structural adjustment. Without this, displaced workers will need protection from economic hardship. If this protection is not offered, worker resistance to adjustment can be expected. This protection is justified on equity grounds. It represents society's transfer of a share of the benefits of adjustment to those who bear its cost. These benefits come to consumers in the form of lower prices for goods and services and in expanding employment, although not necessarily in the same communities where workers are displaced.

5.17	Employment promotion can reduce the social cost of adjustment. This promotion is encouraged by (i) financial market reforms, (ii) labor market reforms, (iii) emphasis on technology and productivity in the enterprise, (iv) support for small and medium-sized enterprises, and (v) direct expenditures on transitional employment. Financial market reforms are essential to reducing the capital bias of the modern sector. Improving the efficiency of labor markets will facilitate the economy's response to new production incentives and employment creation. Management's choice of appropriate production technologies and organization of the work process will increase labor productivity and incentives for employment creation. Support for small and medium-sized enterprises can be an important means for employment creation. While the economy is adjusting, the government can use public works to create transitional employment for displaced workers.

5.18	**Financial Market Reforms.** The World Bank's proposed program of financial market reforms will address laws, policies and practices which have stifled capital market activity and distorted the allocation of scarce capital resources in favor of large public enterprises. The reforms are expected to improve the mobilization of capital resources and increase the level of private investment. As part of broader economic reforms, financial market reforms will help restore a level playing field for the public and private sectors. This will have an important impact on incentives for employment creation in both sectors. In the current economic climate, large public enterprises receive favored treatment in their access to scarce capital resources. Egypt's experience in this case is similar to that of other developing countries. Capital tends to flow to "low risk" investments in public enterprises whose markets are protected from trade competition and whose deficits are covered by the state budget.

5.19	The description of capital flows in Chapter 3 confirm this pattern. Small private enterprises experience higher capital costs than larger public enterprises, costs that exceed expected risk premiums. The cost of borrowing for public enterprises has been kept below the rate of inflation, resulting in negative real interest rates. This has, on the one hand, discouraged private savings, and on the other hand, encouraged investments with rates of return well below the social opportunity cost of capital. By increasing the demand for capital and by discouraging savings, this has created an excess demand for capital which has produced a need for capital rationing. Capital rationing is carried out through mechanisms such as letters of credit for foreign exchange and the licensing and restriction of investment.

5.20	The access of public enterprises to low cost capital has increased incentives for capital intensive investments. The leveling of the playing field for public and private sectors in their access to capital will increase the incentive for labor intensive production and employment creation in restructured public enterprises. In the private sector, financial market reforms, by improving access to capital, are expected to increase the capital intensity of production in this sector. This will lower the employment elasticity of private sector growth, but sharply increase the level of private investment and employment overall. Financial market reforms will therefore play a critical role in balancing the use of capital and labor in the economy and encouraging employment promotion for displaced workers.

5.21 **Labor Market Reforms.** An efficient labor market will facilitate change in the economy and reduce the social cost of adjustment. It will permit faster rates of economic growth and employment creation without accelerating inflationary pressures. An efficient labor market requires flexible wages linked to productivity and low barriers to labor mobility. The analysis of Chapter 3 identifies 6 types of labor reforms to improve the efficiency of Egyptian labor markets. These reforms are listed in Box 5.1 along with a tentative schedule for implementation. The reforms address government's role as an employer and as a regulator of labor market activity. As an employer, government will need to restrict the growth of its wage bill as part of economic reforms to reduce the budget deficit. This will force a restructuring of government wage and employment policies.

BOX 5.1
Labor Market Reforms

Reforms	FY90	FY91	FY92	FY93
1. Phase out government employment guarantees	X			
2. Introduce civil service reform				X
3. Uncouple wage and employment policies in public enterprises	X			
4. Repeal restrictions on worker hiring and dismissals			X	
5. Remove government monopoly on labor exchange			X	
6. Improve labor market information			X	

5.22   The government continues to grow through its guarantee of employment to graduates of secondary and post-secondary schools. Given restrictions on the wage bill, this growth cannot be sustained without further reductions in real wages for government workers. However, the real wages of government workers have already experienced substantial cuts in an effort to reduce the deficit with the wages of managers and skilled workers bearing a disproportionate share of this reduction. It is doubtful that government can further reduce real wages in this manner without damaging the efficacy of government itself. The restriction of the wage bill will therefore encourage the government to consider a downsizing of its workforce and a restructuring of wages once alternative private employment opportunities are created. This will require civil service reform.

5.23   Government can reduce pressure on the wage bill by announcing that it is phasing out the guarantee of employment for graduates of secondary schools nd universities. The current waiting period of 5 years could be increased one year for each year to graduation. The guarantee would be dropped altogether for those who had not entered a secondary school or university at the time of the announcement. This would allow those who are approaching the schooling decision to adjust their expectations, while protecting the interests of those now pursuing one of these degrees. It could improve the effectiveness of this reform by coupling it with additional cost recovery in post-secondary education and a general hiring freeze. The delay, moreover, would allow time for the economy to adjust to new production incentives and expand private sector employment creation. The proposed expansion of the private sector implies a smaller government in the future. Phasing out the employment guarantee and freezing new hires would be consistent with this goal.

5.24   Government is overstaffed as a consequence of past employment policies. Pressures on the wage bill can be further eased by rationalizing this employment. This requires a plan for the organizational and personnel structure of government, policies for merit selection and determination of the redundant workforce, programs for the integration of redundant workers into the private sector, and procedures for implementation of the reform. This reform should include a restructuring of the wage system whereby savings from displacement can be shifted into improved salaries for those who remain with increased incentives for management and skilled workers.

5.25   These reforms have been implemented successfully in other countries as part of structural adjustment without mass displacement of workers. In most cases, it has been possible to provide incentives that have encouraged voluntary separations along with natural attrition. Civil service reform has been a prominent feature of structural adjustment in countries like Bangladesh, Cameroon, Central African Republic, Costa Rica, Cote d'Ivoire, Ghana, Guinea, and Senegal. The result of civil service reform is a reduction in barriers to labor mobility created by government employment policies, an increase in market efficiency through the linking of wages and productivity, and an improvement in government's fiscal condition. Merit selection and the linking of wages with productivity increase government efficacy.

5.26   One of the goals of civil service reform is to improve the link between wages and productivity. Public enterprise reform should also have this as a goal. Public enterprises should be free to set wage and employment policies consistent with market conditions. The increased autonomy of public enterprises should include the uncoupling of wage and employment policies in these enterprises from those of government under Public Law 48. This uncoupling will increase wage flexibility and encourage the closer connection of wages and productivity. The decentralization of wage determination will represent an important shift in wage policy as wages are now set nationally by law. Under Public Law 137-1981, the Egyptian Trade Union Federation plays an advisory role in wage setting at the national level. There would be no basis for this under a decentralized, market-based system of wage determination. After further review of the market power of large public enterprises, Egypt may wish to revise its law on collective bargaining to balance this power from the supply side of the market.

5.27   As a regulator of labor market activity, government interventions should be limited to cases where there is a legitimate public interest to protect, e.g. worker safety and health, child labor. In other cases labor markets should be deregulated. Government should focus on improving the functioning of labor markets and avoid interventions that distort the operation and efficiency of these markets. In this context, the government monopoly on job placements through the Ministry of Labor and its employment service should be eliminated. Enterprises are already using other means of recruitment for their workforce. Their willingness to pay fines to do this is a measure of the relative efficiency of these means. Government should remove its restraint on this activity and even encourage the operation of private employment services. The experience of other countries shows that government employment services at their best will account for only 30% of job placements.

5.28   Government can improve the efficiency of labor markets by improving access to labor market information. The weakness of the information now available is in its timeliness and detail. This information is important to macroeconomic planning, planning for education and training, career counselling, and job placement. It will also be important to monitoring the consequences of structural adjustment. A special government task force should be created to make recommendations for improving the labor market information provided by CAPMAS and the Ministry of Labor. The task force should focus on identification of appropriate concepts and data needs, technical issues in the collection and processing of data, and strategies for administration of the system and the presentation and dissemination of its information on employment and incomes.

5.29   The Government's regulation of dismissals in Public Law 137-1981 is a barrier to labor mobility and should be repealed. By making it difficult to displace redundant labor, enterprises are forced to treat labor as a fixed resource. In an economic environment of uncertainty, this discourages employment creation. In the case of large scale layoffs, however, a case can be made to require prior notice giving public officials adequate time to organize services to meet the needs of displaced workers. This has been used in countries like Canada to provide time for mobilizing a special task force to deliver employment services to redundant workers. The services include job search assistance, career counselling, training grants, and assistance with unemployment and early retirement benefits. A general review of the labor code should be conducted to identify other laws for amendment or repeal that fail the test of protecting legitimate public interests.

5.30   **Technology and Productivity in the Enterprise.** Against the background of changing relative factor prices that will favor labor intensive development, managers must choose appropriate production technologies and methods of organizing the work environment. On the supply side of the labor market, investments in skills development to improve worker productivity assume that the appropriate complementary resources will be introduced by enterprise managers. However, managers that lack skills to select appropriate technologies or to organize the workplace to use workers efficiently will reduce the economy's potential rate of growth and employment creation. Thus, an employment promotion strategy should include assistance for managers in choosing appropriate production technologies and forms of work organization.

5.31   This element of the employment promotion strategy will be particularly important during the transition phase of structural adjustment as enterprises respond to new market signals. Emphasis on technology and productivity in the enterprise has been a feature in other middle-income countries with national training agencies, particularly among the newly industrialized countries in Asia. Examples are also found in Latin America. Technology choices and training needs are related concerns. National training agencies separate government responsibility for skills training from that for education. They typically are managed by tri-partite committees involving representatives of government, management, and labor. The establishment of a national training agency in Egypt would provide an effective institutional setting for technical assistance to public and private enterprises in technology choices and work organization.

5.32   An alternative for Egypt would be to establish productivity centers within the Ministry of Industry and its Productivity and Vocational Training Department that would be linked to specific sectors of economic activity, e.g. construction, industry, and services. These centers would provide technical assistance to enterprises engaged in restructuring with advice on appropriate production technologies and work organization. This in turn would be tied to assistance with training. The centers would maintain a core staff for administrative operations, but rely on international specialists to provide enterprises with technical assistance. These specialists would be engaged on short-term contracts for specific tasks to ensure flexibility. Because this may create inter-ministerial conflicts, an alternative arrangement would have these centers established as a public enterprise outside government administration. This would enhance their operational flexibility.

5.33   This technical assistance might be funded initially under the Emergency Social Fund established with the support of the Bank with a sliding scale of cost-sharing favoring small and medium-sized enterprises. The purpose of these centers would be to facilitate structural adjustment. Given the social benefits of this adjustment, government might expect to heavily subsidize this activity during the initial phase of structural adjustment. This would reduce the private cost of adjustment to enterprises and facilitate change. After an initial adjustment phase of 4 to 5 years, these centers should become primarily self-supporting. Models for these centers are found in the national training agencies for Brazil, Peru, and Argentina. Brazil now has 10 such centers for its manufacturing sector. [1]

5.34   **Support for Small and Medium-Sized Enterprises.** SME's have been an important source of employment creation in Egypt during the 1970's and early 1980's. Small enterprises, defined as those with less than 10 workers, tend to be clustered in the informal sector, while medium-sized enterprises, representing those with 10 to 50 workers, are more likely to be in the modern sector. Approximately 97% of private sector establishments fall into the small enterprise category which grew rapidly through 1986. SME's have characteristics that make them attractive for economic development and employment promotion (Handoussa, 1989). SME's tend to be more labor intensive than larger enterprises. Thus, they offer considerable employment potential. They also draw heavily on self-financing for capital and are an important stimulus for savings and capital accumulation.

5.35   SME's develop skills through apprenticeship and do not place heavy demands on pre-employment training. Their production is based largely on domestic resources, reducing the demand for scarce foreign exchange. Likewise, their demands for infrastructure related to roads, schools, telecommunications are limited and less costly from the government's perspective. Their products are frequently sold to low income consumers meeting an important market segment of needs. The average employment in small enterprises is under 2 persons per establishment and in medium enterprises it is 18 persons. Preliminary estimates from the 1986 establishment survey indicate that the number of small and medium-sized establishments has increased since 1976 by 50% which is consistent with the observed growth of private employment in the 1986 census.

5.36   The support of SME's offers considerable potential for employment promotion. Issues affecting the growth of these enterprises in Egypt include credit access, labor constraints, technical knowledge, and marketing skills (Jones, 1988). The general economic reforms removing government's pervasive hand from the economy will encourage the growth of SME's and employment creation. In particular, financial market reforms will improve access to capital. Labor market liberalization will reduce the fixed cost nature of labor and improve its mobility. Other reforms will reduce government interventions in price setting, licensing of investment, allocation of raw materials and foreign exchange. The general liberalization of the economic climate will remove many of the incentives for SME's to remain small, hidden from government's regulation. These general reforms will encourage the movement of some SME's into the modern sector.

---

[1]   CINTERFOR, 1989. <u>Regional Review of Vocational Training in Latin America.</u> a report prepared for the World Bank, Washington, D.C. (mimeo).

5.37   Government can also take specific steps to support SME's and open the path to new employment for displaced workers. It can do the following: (i) allow the capitalization of job separation benefits giving displaced workers a source of capital for private investment; (ii) assist the banking system in establishing credit mechanisms for small enterprises; (iii) create an SME division within the productivity centers above offering entrepreneurs technical assistance involving technology choices, productivity, and marketing, plus access to management training; and (iv) provide an infrastructure of services and facilities to launch new SME's. The latter is referred to as an incubator system and has been employed successfully in the United States and other industrialized countries to encourage the growth of SME's (Temali et al., 1984).

5.38   **Transitional Employment.** The government will naturally want to avoid sharp increases in open unemployment during structural adjustment. This will occur where new jobs are not created in the same sequence as workers are displaced. Some industrialized countries have used public works to create transitional employment to avoid this outcome. A displaced worker is expected to find employment in the private sector after a fixed period of time in a transitional job. The worker may receive training in the transitional job along with other employment counselling and job search assistance. The key word in this case is "transitional." The jobs are not intended to be permanent and are typically up to 6 months or a year in duration.

5.39   These jobs will delay reductions in the government's wage bill, but they provide an important means to reduce the worker's loss of income and resistance to structural adjustment. The use of redundant labor in public works actually increases the output of government. By labeling these jobs as transitional, this changes worker expectations and encourages their transition into the private sector. Some industrialized countries have allowed displaced workers to capitalize the benefits of these jobs as a means to encourage their entry into private employment. The capitalized sum becomes a basis for private investment. The risk of these jobs is that governments will not treat them as transitional thereby producing a new class of government employment.

5.40   Temporary employment in public works programs can also be used to provide income for the unemployed in poverty households. Targeting these jobs on the economically vulnerable members of the population can be facilitated by selecting projects in low income communities and keeping wages low. Workers who have better employment options will exercise these options, while others will use these jobs as the employment of last resort. Apart from the danger of treating these jobs as a new class of government employment, there is also the danger of exceeding the capacity of local governmental units to implement effective public works projects. These projects require considerable advance planning and supervision. Care should be taken to avoid exceeding this capacity.

Access to Productive Assets

5.41   Provision of small scale credit technical assistance and training, especially to women, has a great potential for income generation. In other adjustment compensation programs, credit schemes play a prominent role. Plenty of examples of successful pilot project schemes exist in Egypt, in both urban and rural settings, some in the public sector, others administered by NGOs (El Kholy, 1987, EQI, 1988, UNICEF internal documents, Oldham, 1988). The objective should be to ensure that every person in the country has access to credit on reasonable terms even for the smallest undertaking. The smaller the loan, the proportionately larger the potential gain to the borrower; it is the poorest groups who use the smallest loans, and thus the higher the welfare impact of a given increment in income; and the poorest, especially women, are the group which has had least access to credit up to now.

5.42   The government should commission the preparation of a review of such schemes with a view to understanding best practice methods and deciding on the appropriate implementing agency in different cases.

5.43   Some likely conditions for success can be suggested. First, small loans for women can best be established and administered if a group lending mechanism is used. Several of the existing schemes in Egypt are of this kind; repayment rates are much higher than on commercial loans. Among other virtues, this mechanism avoids the need for collateral, which is a major obstacle in women's access to credit through formal financial institutions. Second, for women, loans need to be combined with technical assistance, in literacy, numeracy, bookkeeping and management skills as well as in the production process itself (see Oldham, 1988). Third, for any project involving livestock, which seems presently to be the majority of projects for women in both urban and rural areas, an insurance element is essential to cover losses from disease.

5.44   The development of credit institutions should be combined with the deposit-taking function. Collier (1988) notes that in countries where women's rights to property are limited, as in Egypt, it is only through building up a record (and accumulating funds) as a depositor that women can establish a credit rating. The prevalence of small savings circles ("jamiyat") among women in Egypt, indicates that this objective is feasible (see for example Ibrahim in Zurayk and Shorter, 1987).

5.45   Furthermore, the existence of savings circles demonstrates the widespread capacity for savings mobilization in Egypt, and suggests that the credit operations can set fees at a cost-recovering level. Whatever the nominal rate of interest charged, which may have to be tied to subsidized formal market rates, experience shows that borrowers are willing and able to pay realistic fees for specific credit related services.

5.46   The government can increase its involvement and effectiveness in the field of small scale credit in any of three ways:

- first, consideration should be given to extending the scope of existing financial institutions, eg., the Village Banks. This might be done, not directly with beneficiaries, which would involve excessive administrative costs and radical changes in procedures, but indirectly, through village and neighborhood Community Development Associations.

- second, the Productive Families Program might be modified so as better to serve the poorest groups, not by reducing the cost of credit to borrowers -- studies show that borrowers see a good return on their activities and in NGO projects accept higher charges without difficulty -- but by lowering the size of loans.

- third, consideration should be given to concentrating the activities of the Productive Families Program entirely on the training and loans side, and either delegating the direct employment and production aspect to the private sector entirely, or dropping it altogether. It is far less risky and costly for the state to disburse a given fund in credit than in direct production: credit schemes can benefit from the diversity of activities among borrowers and from coopting the interests of borrowers in achieving high returns.

5.47   NGOs have an important place to play in small scale credit, as the success of innovative projects has proved. However, NGOs' success rests ultimately on intimate familiarity with particular communities, which is expensive to attain. There is in this way a considerable subsidy element in many projects. One way to spread these costs is for the government to ensure that knowledge of the methods of successful projects is well disseminated, and that good procedural manuals and training materials for staff and beneficiaries alike are made available to all credit projects.

5.48   It has been shown that Community Development Associations (CDAs) can take over successful projects and operate them on their own behalf (EQI, 1988). This practice should be encouraged. The legislation governing CDAs (and other NGOs) should be amended to allow them to carry out income generating projects of their own to finance the operating costs of loans schemes. As suggested above, the Village Banks could be the channel for receipt of government start-up funding, and could also provide financial technical assistance to CDA officers.

5.49   To ensure that CDAs perform well in reaching women borrowers, it is recommended that local targets be set for the proportion of females to be reached, and regular monitoring of performance be instituted. One means of improving performance in this respect might be to have a women's officer on the CDA board. It is recommended that an experiment be set up, comparing the effectiveness in reaching women of matched sets of CDAs with and without women's officers. If the women's officers prove instrumental in ensuring good performance, then there should be a standing requirement that such a position be created on every CDA board.

Human Capital Maintenance

5.50   Human capital is usually the most valuable asset of poor people. It is therefore crucial that human capital formation programs be protected during the transition period of economic reforms despite the planned reductions in government expenditures. This can be achieved through improvements in the pattern of allocation and utilization of available resources. Measures taken to improve the targeting of health and education programs to persons with the greatest need and to increase the efficiency with which services are delivered can lead to the simultaneous improvement of equity and efficiency in these sectors. With this type of measures, the most economically vulnerable members of the population can be sheltered from the social and economic costs of the structural adjustment program without increasing the government's budget for the social sectors, though it should be maintained at its current level in real terms. In addition to exploring structural measures to improve access of the poor to health and education services, this section puts forward proposals on retraining assistance programs for people who would lose their employment as a result of structural adjustment.

Health

5.51 The following options would need to be considered in the health sector:

(i) reorientation of the investment program in favor of primary and community health care;

(ii) rationalization of the existing network of curative facilities on the basis of effective utilization rates and reallocation of recurrent resources to the primary health care facilities and programs;

(iii) introduction of differential user fees to promote cost-recovery in curative services in conjunction with an extension of medical insurance coverage;

(iv) strengthening of the infectious and parasitic diseases control programs; and

(v) complementary measures to improve the quality of care at all levels.

5.52 The investment budget of the Ministry of Health should be revisited with the objective of downscaling the program of construction of new secondary and tertiary curative facilities in urban areas and reallocating resources to the existing primary health care facilities in rural areas. As illustrated by Graph 5.1, the distribution of investment in the current Plan is heavily skewed in favor of curative services facilities.

**Graph 5.1 Functional Distribution of MOH Investment Budget
Five Year Plan 1987-1992**

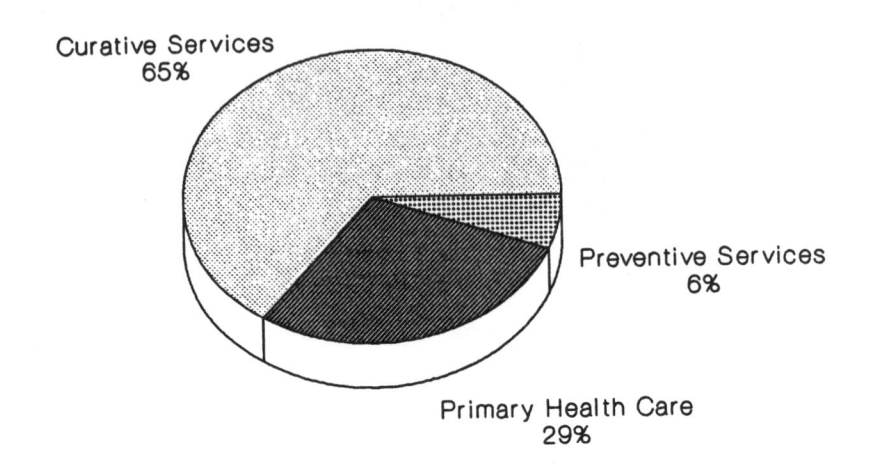

Curative Services 65%
Preventive Services 6%
Primary Health Care 29%

Source: Ministry of Health

The reallocated funds should be used as a matter of priority for the rehabilitation, reequipping and upgrading of rural health facilities in the most remote areas in the poorest Governorates.

5.53   To accompany these measures on the investment side, the Ministry should draw up a medium term plan to rationalize the existing network of curative facilities on the basis of effective utilization rates with a view to reallocating recurrent resources to primary health care facilities and preventive programs.

5.54   To mobilize additional resources and increase equity in the curative health system, the government's program to introduce gradually user fees for both outpatients and inpatients in selected general and central hospitals should be strengthened. For outpatient services, a modest fee should be charged during the regular morning session. Additional clinic sessions could be organized in the afternoon for patients seen by appointment at a higher fee. It would be imperative that patients receive the same quality of professional services in both types of clinics. For inpatient care, hospitals would offer beds in first, second and third class rooms depending on the number of beds in the room and the kind of accessory amenities offered. Patients admitted in third class accommodation would be charged the actual running cost whereas an escalating scale would apply to patients choosing another class of accommodation. A large proportion of third class beds should be reserved for eligible poor families who would be treated free. If well-managed, government hospitals would be able, with this cost-recovery scheme, to offer better quality care at moderate costs and could in the longer run become more competitive in relation to private sector clinics and hospitals. The introduction and extension of the cost recovery scheme should be gradual and the lessons of experience from the Cairo and Alexandria Curative Care Organizations should taken into consideration.

5.55   Medical insurance coverage should be extended in parallel with this reform. All civil servants and private sector workers could be gradually included. Admission policies for widows and dependents should be revised. At the minimum, the General Organization for Insurances and Pensions should take over, for widows, the payments previously made by their deceased husbands' former employers. Extended coverage would require the Health Insurance Organization to establish new contracts with hospitals and polyclinics in order to provide the additional medical care needed.

5.56   In terms of program focus, the infectious and parasitic diseases control programs should be strengthened, notably for bilharzia and leprosy. While the bilharzia control program under way in the Delta is well-structured and follows a well-developed plan, additional financial support is needed to ensure regular supply of drugs for the treatment of cases recently detected and adequate provision of the necessary laboratory equipment and supplies for qualitative and quantitative diagnostic tests. The development of a national leprosy control program, now in the planning stage, should be given high priority. Resources will be needed to staff an evaluation and monitoring unit, involve school and rural health teams in active case-finding, and purchase the quantity of drugs required. The training of traditional midwives and doctors assigned to rural areas in community medicine and the proper management of acute respiratory infectious should be strengthened. Further UNICEF and WHO assistance could be requested for that purpose.

5.57   An integrated program to improve the nutrition situation of vulnerable groups should be designed and implemented. Emphasis should be put on the protection of children in particular, as they have benefited much less from the food subsidies system than the adult population as a result, most likely, of intra-households inequities.

5.58   Although it does not fall under the direct responsibility of the Ministry of Health, the preparation and implementation of an action-plan to increase the production and availability of safe water and adequate sanitation in rural areas would be a determinant component of public health policies to reduce the incidence of many infectious and parasitic diseases in Egypt. The widespread occurrence of waterborne diseases and, in particular, the recent increase in the incidence of infectious hepatitis make the issue of safe water one of great priority.

5.59   Finally, a variety of complementary measures could be envisaged to improve the level of care at all levels. For example, improving the transport facilities at the district level would be important to promote a proper referral system and facilitate a closer supervision of rural health units. Increasing the fringe benefits of health personnel working in rural areas would be important to boost staff motivation and performance. This could be done by granting assignment allowances to compensate for the lack of opportunity for private practice, or by remunerating overtime spent in conducting an appointment clinic outside official working hours, which would make access of the health units easier for households involved in agricultural activities.

Education

5.60   In the education sector, the present level of government expenditures devoted to basic education should be at least maintained in real terms, given the need to achieve universal basic education, particularly for girls, and to improve the qualitative aspects of the educational process. At the same time, it is equally important to rationalize the pattern of allocation and utilization of resources within the education system, considering that the present policy of unlimited expansion at all levels is neither sustainable from an economic viewpoint nor equitable from a social perspective. Greater emphasis should be given to basic education in recognition of the higher social rates of return at that level and the necessity to offer better opportunities to those who are not able to go beyond that level of education.

5.61   The following options could be implemented to increase equity and cost-effectiveness in the delivery of education programs:

- elimination of fees in basic education;

- generalization of cost-recovery measures in higher education;

- improvement in the quality of basic education financed through transfers of budgetary resources from higher education to basic education; and

- introduction of more selective procedures for access to post-secondary education.

5.62   Though modest in amount, the fees which have recently been introduced at the primary and secondary levels have increased the burden of schooling on parents already faced with the high cost of private tutoring. A growing number of parents from poor households are seen to take their children out of school as a result. It is therefore recommended that fees be abolished in basic education to guarantee democratic access at that level.

5.63   In higher education, however, authorities should consider actively ways of extending the cost-recovery measures already introduced in some faculties and institutes, such as user charges and contributions from industry. As seen in Chapter 3, there are strong equity justifications for reducing the degree of subsidization of higher education given the prevailing pattern of misallocation of resources. To protect students of low income groups, scholarships and loans should be made available.

5.64   Improvements in the quality of education offered at the primary and preparatory levels could be financed by reallocating resources from higher education to basic education. The additional resources could be used to finance curriculum reform with the objective of having less exam-driven programs, and improve the quality of textbooks and other instructional material while increasing their availability. Attempts should be made to reduce overcrowding which is an obstacle to better classroom instruction by giving priority to the construction of new schools in those areas where the problem is most acute.

5.65   The consolidation of university education should be achieved through constrained growth of enrollments. Since the financial situation is not likely to improve drastically in higher education as the increase in resources through cost-recovery measures would be partly offset by budgetary transfers to basic education, the only way to be able to devote more resources per student would be to stabilize the number of students. This could be achieved by applying more restrictive access mechanisms on the basis of merit criteria. This has been recently tried on an experimental basis by some faculties of engineering for example. The labor market prospects for graduate employment, or rather the lack of prospects in the present economic context, would also justify such a move.

Retraining Assistance

5.66   Retraining is a costly option for improving employment opportunities and its effectiveness depends on the linkage between the training and employment prospects. Not all displaced workers under structural adjustment will necessarily need retraining. It is therefore important that an assessment of employability needs be made for each displaced worker. This assessment would follow with counselling on the occupations for which training provides a good chance for reemployment. In industrialized countries, this assessment is usually provided by an employment service under a Ministry of Labor, or in the case of Canada, by a special employment service task force that is mobilized once notice of a plant closing is given. The task force offers assessment and referral to a comprehensive set of services. The employment service is equipped to identify job openings in the local labor market for which displaced workers could qualify if retrained. The linking of job information nationally broadens opportunities for reemployment.

5.67   Egypt has no ready mechanism for employability assessment. The upgrading of the Ministry of Labor's employment service would respond to this need in the short run as well as enhance the labor market exchange in the long run. As described in Chapter 3, the MOL's employment service is limited largely to rationing scarce employment opportunities. It does provide some skills assessment and counselling for training, but it does not provide a nationally integrated system of job listings and search assistance. Discussions with a number of employment service managers indicates that there is very little direct contact at the local level with enterprises. Job vacancies are transmitted through the Ministry of Labor to the local office of the employment service. The decentralization of responsibilities and upgrading of services in local MOL employment service offices will be necessary to improve the labor market exchange and assessment of retraining needs.

5.68   The retraining of displaced workers requires training institutions that depart from conventional modes of skills development. These institutions will need to give workers flexibility in the timing of their participation in training (open entry and exit), because workers will not be displaced on a schedule consistent with admission to conventional academic programs. Training will need to be developed in modules to permit flexible entry and exit. Skills development need not follow a fixed time schedule. Instead, it should be competency based. The training must be flexible and able to respond quickly to the needs of displaced workers and enterprises. The emergence of new skills and expanding of old ones will require an institution that is capable of mounting training activities on short notice. This implies flexibility in staffing and curriculum development. The capacity of local training institutions may become a constraint to the retraining of large numbers of displaced workers in short periods of time. A competency based system will help expand capacity by opening positions faster.

5.69   Based on the assessment of employability needs, training grants may be offered to displaced workers as part of the support package to reduce their private cost of adjustment and to increase their productivity and employability. These grants can be transferred to enterprises to encourage the employment and retraining of displaced workers. This would reduce the pressure on local training institutions. The linking of training with employment has been found to improve the cost-effectiveness of the training. Not all enterprises, however, will have the capacity to train. Small enterprises will frequently lack this capacity and will not be able to realize potential economies of scale. New technologies may introduce skills for which enterprises lack the ability to train. This opens a market for training institutions to work closely with enterprises, large and small, to offer training closely linked to employment. The financing of training institutions should include incentives to provide contract training services for enterprises. In countries like Brazil, Jordan, Singapore, and Hong Kong, national training agencies provide these services.

Income Transfers and Price Subsidies

Food Subsidies

5.70   Revamping the ration/food subsidy system is a contentious issue. The government has periodically looked at ways to modify the system but because of concern about public reaction has refrained from any major modifications. Public unrest in countries in the region which have tried to eliminate consumer subsidies has made the Egyptian government cautious.

5.71   Despite the political and social difficulties involved in implementing major changes in the ration/subsidy system, there is an urgent need to take effective measures to reduce the burden on the government budget while at the same time improving the targeting to the nutritionally at-risk segments of the population. While it appears wise to experiment with 3 or 4 new approaches on a pilot basis before recommending adoption on a larger scale, the government should move rapidly on this issue as there is no income or nutritional justification for subsidizing 93% of the population.

5.72   The foods provided through the ration shops (oil, rice and sugar) and the bread/flour subsidy provide a disproportionate share of the food intake of the low income households. In addition, Balady bread has a weakly negative income elasticity (Alderman et al., 1984) and thus consumption decreases in the upper income groups. Given this, it is important to maintain the rationed commodity and the subsidy on bread at its current level while other food security strategies are developed that are targeted to a narrower segment of the population.

5.73   During field visits in November 1989, discussions were held with consumers and shop owners in several low income areas of Cairo. Many people indicated that the primary value of the ration card was that it guaranteed access to basic staples; several consumers indicated that they would be happy to pay a higher price at a cooperative or even an "open market" shop but that sugar, tea and rice typically are not available at these other shops. It would appear therefore important for the government to guarantee easy access to these basic staples as a first step in phasing out a large number of the ration cards.

5.74   Unfortunately the Government Authority for Supply of Commodities (GASC) in the Ministry of Supply is moving at present in a direction which further complicates an already cumbersome system. GASC has proposed issuing a third type of ration card, a "yellow" card, to a segment of the population that does not currently use the ration system. The yellow card would be for diplomats and other types of individuals who are currently excluded from the ration system. The yellow card would entitle the household to buy a rationed quantity of rice, sugar, oil and tea but at the full market price. The purpose of the yellow card is simply to ensure availability of the basic ration. Clearly if these supplies were available through the normal market channels these yellow rations cards would not be needed.

5.75   The government has the opportunity as part of the proposed restructuring of the wage schedule for government and public sector workers to limit the number of ration cards. The participation in the ration system should be limited to the bottom rung of the wage earners, for example the lowest quartile of government and public sector wage earners. The details of this type of targeting would have to be decided in conjunction with the new wage schedules under consideration. Even though this approach would still entail some leakages since the low wage earners often have second or in some cases third jobs, the leakages would be substantially less than in the current system. The phasing out of the rations for the other three quarters of government and public sector workers would be considered in establishing wages for these employees. This approach can only be successful if the supplies of these basic staples can be guaranteed through the normal market channels.

5.76   The ideal way to target the ration/subsidy system is to limit the participation to those who are the nutritionally needy. Most often malnutrition is synonymous with the poor. However the government has no way currently to identify the poor. Therefore it is suggested that the government experiment with some new ways of targeting as a way to learn about some potential methods for making the ration/subsidy system more cost effective. One method which should be considered is geographical targeting. Clearly there are areas with ration shops which are generally recognized as middle and upper income, although this does not mean that there are no poor households in the area. Zamalek in Cairo is such a location. The government could, on a trial basis, experiment in closing ration shops in selected areas. Here again this would only work if the supply of the basic rationed staples - sugar, oil, rice and tea - were ensured through the local market. There would also need to be a system developed for the poor households in these middle/upper income areas to be able to gain access to the rationed commodities from ration shops in other areas. The exact method for this needs to be developed in the context of the current administrative structure of the ration system.

5.77   In discussions about geographic targeting, GASC officials indicated that this approach would not work because some poor people would be hurt. However, it should be noted that the lowest income groups are already getting hurt from the escalating food prices. Rather than giving a small amount of ration to most of the population, it would be more cost-effective to provide larger quantities of the current ration to a more limited segment of the population. This is the basis for the next suggestion on targeting. Again on an experimental basis the government should test the feasibility of providing more food to certain groups of households. One way to do this is to select certain obvious low income areas and test this approach. Not only should the ration be larger but the mix of food should change. Tea should be de-emphasized since this does not make a nutritional contribution to the diet. The government should test the feasibility of a coarse grain flour or a mixed grain flour which would have low appeal to middle or upper income groups but would make a significant contribution to the food intake of the lowest income groups. Years ago, corn flour (a less preferred commodity) was used to make bread. This could be reinstated and a mixture of corn flour and coarse wheat flour could be used to make bread. This in essence might be a self-targeting food.

5.78   This approach was tried in Pakistan where low priced atta (a type of wheat flour) was made available through the ration shop (Rogers, 1978). The poorest households chose atta over the higher priced but generally preferred whole wheat. For each dollar spent a larger quantity of atta than of whole wheat could be purchased and, as a result, household food consumption was increased. A similar experiment was tried in 1978 in Bangladesh (Karim et al., 1984) where sorghum was subsidized to half the price of rice. For each dollar spent, a larger quantity of sorghum than rice could be purchased and the effect on household food consumption was increased. Sorghum sales were low in the urban areas but after three months approximately 70% of the poorest households were purchasing sorghum.

5.79   Not all of these targeting mechanisms will be equally successful. However by testing selected targeting mechanisms on a pilot basis, the government can determine the pros and cons of various approaches before implementing these on a country-wide basis.

5.80   Cooperatives as a distributor of subsidized foods should be phased out over time. The evidence suggests that these are used more by middle and upper income groups than the poor. This would provide a budgetary savings of about 200 million Egyptian pounds to the government without jeopardizing the food security of the lowest income groups.

5.81   The desirability and feasibility of replacing food subsidy with direct income transfers exclusively targeted to the poor should also be considered as a perhaps less costly and more efficient alternative to the existing system of general subsidies.

5.82   The government has no real way currently to monitor the actual impact of price increases on household food security. There is a critical need to have a technical capability within government to evaluate the effects of policy reform on food consumption and nutrition. A system for monitoring the impact of these policies should therefore be put in place by the government. The proposed monitoring and evaluation system should permit the government to identify who are the food insecure and malnourished, where they are located, and what are the causes of their predicament. There also needs to be a mechanism to analyze and evaluate household response to new programs and policies.

Utilities, Transport, Energy and Housing

5.83   *Water*. Because of the high income demand elasticity for water consumption, there is ample room in the present tariff structure for further price discrimination against large users. Some of the additional revenues could be used to subsidize lower income households, specially to lower the cost of connection fees. One mechanism to this end could be to spread the cost of connection and water meters, by charging a rental fee related to the level of household consumption. Lower income households would pay for water connection in more and smaller installments than higher income households. Suppressing water meters is not desirable because of the induced waste and the difficulty of identifying qualifying households.

5.84   Given the heavy losses of water in the system due to leakages, tank overflows, or broken lines, which have been estimated as low as 40 percent and as high as 70 percent of production, the premise of cost recovery pricing is questionable. Certainly, the elimination of wastage should allow to meet the cost recovery objectives with lower tariffs.

5.85   Because of the relatively low coverage of rural and urban low income households, new investments in water supply systems should be targeted to areas where those households reside. In areas where piped water from public utilities is available, the most effective policy will be to increase maintenance expenditures to reduce the high levels of wastage.

5.86   *Electricity*. Changes in the tariff structure should be made in such as way as to protect low-income households at the same time that they eliminate present subsidies to higher income households. One of the options proposed to achieve this goal consist of compressing the sliding quantity brackets in the tariff schedule to smaller increments, say 100 KWH per month, and applying the tariff rate in a proportional way to the entire level of household consumption.

5.87   However, this type of change in the pricing structure has several constraints. First, there is no practical way to identify the income level of consumers except by their level of consumption. Given available data on income demand elasticities for electricity, it may be fair to assume that all households consuming 100 KWH per month or less are low income households. This approximation could be expanded to include all households consuming less than 200 KWH per month. Because of the much larger number of households consuming less than 100 or 200 KWH per month, the policy premise of protecting low income households will have significant budgetary consequences for the Egyptian Electricity Authority. Given the constraint and the objective of full cost recovery, it is recommended that tariffs be set at a substantially higher level than the long run marginal cost of production for high income households and that cross-subsidization of low consumption households by those households consuming larger amounts of electricity can be increased.

5.88   <u>Energy Products</u>. Subsidized prices for gasoline and several other fuel products have not only benefited mostly higher income groups, but have also decreased Egypt's available surpluses for exports, and have led as well to negative externalities in traffic congestion, noise and air pollution. Thus, a pricing policy that would align domestic prices with world oil prices would have multiple social and economic benefits.

5.89   To protect low-income households, it may be desirable to limit price increases for kerosene. Because of the high level of product differentiation, subsidizing kerosene prices is unlikely to benefit other than low-income households. One negative aspect of this policy, however, is that it will tend to slow down conversion to liquified natural gas which is more economical and cleaner than kerosene. Conversion to natural gas may still be induced by limited price increases.

5.90   An alternative approach would consist in allowing kerosene prices align also with World market prices. To protect low income users, the government would introduce a stamp scheme for low income consumers with an entitlement of 5 liters per month for example at a subsidized price. A similar policy was successfully introduced in Sri Lanka in 1979. The advantage of this type of approach is that it protects low income households while, at the same time, inducing conservation or a switch to natural gas since consumers using more than the monthly entitlement would need to purchase it at market prices. The possible disadvantage is the administrative cost involved in the identification of qualifying households and the management of the program.

5.91   <u>Transportation</u>. There appears to be ample room for tariff increases in rail services for luxury and first class services and in luxury buses, both inter- and intra-city. For suburban commuter trains and regular intra-city buses, however, it seems plain that without some sort of subsidization, low income households would be adversely affected. Subsidized tariffs for these services can be justified on other than distributional grounds. Low price public transportation plays a crucial role in urban labor markets for unskilled low wage workers, bringing together locationally mismatched demand and supply for this type of labor services. Encouraging the use of public mass transportation also has beneficial impact of reducing congestion and air and noise pollution. Pricing of general mass transportation services should also take into account the relative subsidies to other modes of transportation (e.g., low price of gasoline or free use of highways).

5.92   Differentiating products and subsidizing only third class rail service and intra-city regular bus services is the most effective way to reduce the leakage of transportation subsidies to higher income households. To keep the transportation subsidy transparent, it would be desirable that the government use an explicit line budget item for passenger subsidies to the Egyptian National Railways and parastatal bus companies.

5.93   Housing. The most effective policy measure that the Government could take to alleviate Egypt's housing shortage would be to remove all rent controls for newly-built units. While it is clear that it would not be politically feasible to suppress rent control for existing housing units, rent ceilings could be raised gradually to encourage landlords to do maintenance work and thus slowdown the deterioration of the housing stock.

5.94   However, free market rental prices would not solve the housing problem of the poorest groups. There is a need for a more ambitious program of construction of low cost units to address their specific needs. In addition, the Government could establish a low cost policy and provide basic public services (water, sewage, street paving and electricity) to open public lands for settlements in an organized way.

Social Welfare

5.95   Many people in the population - the elderly and handicapped and women with young children and no immediate income earner to give them support - are inevitably dependent for subsistence on direct transfer payments. Both state and private organizations are currently active in this area, each with special advantages, and both should continue. Studies suggest that social relief programs do not "crowd out" private family transfers (Tradors, 1984): the demand for assistance is therefore not a limitless one.

5.96   The Ministry of Social Affairs has a widespread delivery system, with many outlets throughout the country. The only sections of the population which may not be well served - as with other types of services - are inhabitants of satellite villages which do not have a "social unit". The truly destitute are certainly least able to travel the often quite considerable distance between satellite and mother villages. The "social units" are well respected in the field and have a non-discriminatory record in making awards. However, the level of awards that are made are extremely low, and staff morale must be affected by the knowledge that the support offered falls far short of the Ministry's own intentions to provide a basic safety net for the poor.

5.97   NGOs seem to play a considerably larger role than the state in providing transfer payments to the poor, though neither the total disbursements nor the composition of their activities is known precisely at the national level. The NGOs' advantage lies in their greater flexibility, their openness to new criteria, and their ability to experiment with new approaches. The most urgent need is to expand their scope by relaxing some of the red tape which surrounds their fund raising operations. Government's desire to monitor NGO activities need not be compromised. The disadvantages of an atomized and hierarchically organized sector for replicability and improvement of operations can perhaps be overcome, without any alteration in the registration arrangements. The arrangements for monitoring program activities could be improved without any fundamental loss of control to the government, whose political imperatives must be respected. By analogy with the requirements for state social assistance programmes themselves, however, the main need is to allow existing NGOs to give support to their particular client groups at a realistic level and to extend coverage among the poorest and most vulnerable groups, such as the elderly and handicapped and widows and divorced women.

5.98   Given the political sensitivities, however, any more innovative programs designed to reach other groups vulnerable to economic changes associated with adjustment, such as retrenched urban workers and unemployed youth, might not be welcomed within the current framework. Such activities could be better handled by the Emergency Social Fund set up to compensate for the impact of adjustment.

5.99   <u>Ministry of Social Affairs</u>. Funding for the Ministry of Social Affairs transfer payments schemes should be greatly increased to allow individual benefits to be increased to a realistic level. There are two part to this:

- first, to increase the level of payments to the current beneficiaries, the fund has to be increased by three times to LE30m annually (if once-off relief payments are left at the present level) or four times to LE40m annually (if once-off payments are also to be increased).

- second, if the coverage of the schemes is to be increased, the amount would have to be increased further. But the fact that NGOs seem likely to significantly increase their funds if fund raising restrictions were lifted suggests that this extra budgetary cost need not be imposed in full. Total transfer payments disbursements by NGOs should, however, be monitored to see how many extra funds they secure, and the total amount of transfer payments made to the poor by public and private organizations should be reviewed periodically and compared with estimates of need.

5.100   The state is preferable to NGOs for providing regular payments on a statutory basis. A study should be made to determine the optimal allocation of beneficiaries of different categories between the two systems, and state funding adjusted accordingly.

5.101   The delivery mechanism for Ministry schemes is sound and well respected. It should perhaps however be extended to cover the population of satellite villages. Extra permanent social units are not called for; rather staff in existing social units should have provision made for them to travel periodically to the satellites to make on-site visits. It is important, given the preponderance of women among the eligible population, that many of these peripatetic staff are themselves women.

5.102   NGOs. The main recommendation rests on the premise that NGOs could greatly increase the scale of their operations if their capacity to raise funds were not so restricted. The legislative framework and administrative practice should be liberalized. It should be possible for NGOs to be set up on the basis of an endowment. The government should ease the restrictions on fund raising from the general public and make it easier for NGOs to receive funds from bona fide international charities and donor agencies. The Ministry should consider introducing a floor level for annual fund raising below which official approval does not need to be sought. The annual auditing which NGOs are required to undergo can provide a check on this.

5.103   The government should cease making subventions to NGOs, which presently take the form of small operational grants and help with recruitment and salary costs (albeit very low). What might be called "semi-voluntary staff" ar provided to NGOs under the social service scheme for unemployed graduates awaiting job placement in government. The amount of support given amounts to 60 percent of the total state social assistance transfer payments budget, which would be better used on the Ministry's own program. Plenty of other support is given to NGOs, particularly in tax exemptions. Subventions of this magnitude (or at all) are not necessary to ensure NGOs' compliance with the regulations.

5.104   In particular, NGOs should be able to pay their own staff out of the expected increase in revenues. The government may still provide a useful service by way of recruitment and placement of unemployed graduates. The financial discipline would be beneficial to NGOs' management capacity. If necessary, NGOs should be given technical assistance to help them through this transition. The government should contract private sector training organizations to provide this assistance.

5.105   NGOs advantages of flexibility and experimentation are not captured for the nation if their successes are not taken up more widely. Means need to be found to encourage replicability in projects and the take-up of best practice projects. The government should thus encourage, for example, exchange of ideas through seminars, production and dissemination of reports, review of best practice projects, and production of training materials. These things should be seen as a desirable and integral part of NGO activities.

5.106   The government should also encourage uptake of best practice methods within the state services themselves, no less than among NGOs. Some cases have already occurred, e.g., use by the public sector of health education packages developed by the ICA (Institute for Cultural Affairs) for use by women health promoters among women in villages in Beni-Suef. The same NGO has also developed an impressive pre-school curriculum based on Montessori methods, modified to local conditions, which could be employed to advantage in Ministry nursery schools.

Unemployment Benefits

5.107   As described in Chapter 3, open unemployment in Egypt is primarily a problem of new entrants. The number of unemployed who have left a job or lost a job is quite small. This is attributable to the labor surplus nature of the economy and restrictions on worker displacement. Labor market adjustments to the level of production are made through real wages rather than expansion and layoffs. This encourages stability in employment levels, but increases the volatility of real wages. As long as cyclical activity remains a risk, it also discourages employment growth. Enterprises are reluctant to expand employment when this employment cannot be easily cut back to reduce costs in a recession. Against this background, Egypt has no experience with unemployment among large numbers of displaced workers. Through the Ministry of Social Insurance it maintains an unemployment insurance fund, but the number of recipients is small. There is reason to believe that the system would be unprepared to handle large numbers of displaced workers.

5.108   Unemployment insurance protects workers from the vagaries of the business cycle. It provides workers who have lost a job through no direct fault of their own with transitional support. It is not designed for structural unemployment which represents a mismatch between jobs and workers. Structural unemployment exists not because the number of job vacancies is less than the number of persons seeking employment, but because the skills these jobs demand, or their location, are significantly different from those of the labor supply. This type of unemployment characterizes the worker displacement of structural adjustment. With the expectation that spells of cyclical unemployment will be of short duration, unemployment insurance in most countries is limited to 26 weeks of eligibility. The solution to structural unemployment, however, may be of longer duration requiring retraining and even relocation, and therefore, countries experiencing structural adjustment have extended the period of eligibility for unemployment insurance up to a year. This insurance typically replaces 60% to 80% of a worker's prior wages up to some maximum.

5.109   Unemployment insurance is generally financed through a payroll levy, but extended benefits may be covered from government revenues as part of the realignment of social costs and benefits of structural adjustment. These extended benefits are an important means for redistributing the social cost of adjustment and protecting the economically vulnerable members of a population. The income support these benefits provide is usually coupled with other services. The determination of eligibility for unemployment insurance in most industrialized countries rests with an employment service which is also assessing the displaced worker's employability. Thus, along with income support, the worker may be provided with a training grant, job search assistance, and in some cases, relocation assistance. A package of income support and services is therefore available to displaced workers.

5.110   This package can be important in reducing worker resistance to structural adjustment. The cost of the unemployment benefits for displaced government workers would be small since instead of paying these workers to sit idle, the government would support their search for productive employment in the private sector. To control the cost of unemployment benefits, a number of industrialized countries have targeted programs to specific economic sectors, geographic areas, or income groups, although this can sometimes lead to certain inequities. These inequities arise where displaced workers may be moved ahead in the job queue in front of other unemployed workers ineligible for benefits. In a weak economy, a displaced worker may find employment by displacing a less skilled worker, trading the employment of one for another. As indicated earlier, some countries have successfully experimented with allowing workers to capitalize some of these benefits, including unemployment insurance, to support and accelerate their transition into the private sector.

5.111   To make Egypt's unemployment insurance system an effective element in the poverty strategy it will need to be linked with an ungraded employment service to ensure a smooth flow of support and services to displaced workers. Not only is there concern for the system's capacity to handle numbers of claimants, there is concern for its financing. It is a system built around a full employment policy. Whether or not its payroll tax rate, two-thirds paid by the enterprise and one-third by the worker, is adequate to meet the needs of structural adjustment is uncertain. The system presently replaces up to 80% of lost earnings based on the earnings of the 2 previous years. Its benefits are partially adjusted for inflation. Like government wages, these benefits are losing value in real terms. The system presently runs a surplus, but with only a small number of claimants. The government needs to study the organization and financial condition of the unemployment insurance system and consider the funding of extended benefits for displaced workers.

Early Retirement Options

5.112   As part of civil service reform in developing countries, options for early retirement have helped accelerate the displacement of redundant labor. Since some who elect early retirement may reenter the labor force, this approach does not assure a reduction in open unemployment. As such, this option is generally considered in situations where alternative employment opportunities for older workers are limited. The available evidence on these programs indicates that they may be a costly form of adjustment assistance, although the costs must be weighed against the unemployment payments that might otherwise have to be made to these workers. Allowing workers to retire voluntarily with an income, moreover, may help achieve a more positive attitude toward change on the part of workers in general. Early retirement can be easily targeted to specific cohorts or agencies with excessive overstaffing as a means to reduce the cost of the program.

5.113   The Ministry of Social Insurance is also responsible for pension programs. The system is not designed to encourage early retirement. Early retirement pensions, for example, are not adjusted for inflation. The concern for the financing of this system is the same as that for unemployment insurance. Both are part of the larger social insurance system covering pensions, disability, health, and unemployment. The government needs to consider changes in the regulations encouraging early retirement for workers in government and public enterprises.

Social Security

5.114   It would be desirable to consider an increase in the statutory maximum salary for contributions to the social security system. The present maximum of LE 625 per month makes the system regressive. Raising the statutory maximum will also make the system more revenue elastic. Without periodic adjustments -- or automatic indexing -- of statutory maximum wages, rates, and benefits, the social security system runs the risk of becoming increasingly irrelevant in periods of high inflation. The Egyptian social security system is presently undergoing this type of erosion. However, adjustments in the statutory maximum salary and/or rates will be difficult to introduce because of the sharp decrease in real wages in recent years.

5.115   An alternative complementary measure would be for the government to increase its contributions for government employees from 1 % of its payroll. This measure would increase the equity of the system's finances because government general revenues are raised, on average, from less regressive sources than the payroll tax. While it is appropriate for the government to implement minimum income maintenance policies such as currently done through the temporary worker social insurance scheme, it is less desirable to finance these policies with funds which have been raised in a regressive fashion, as is the case for contributions to the general scheme by private sector workers. The downside of higher government contributions to the social security system, of course, will be its impact on the overall budget deficit.

5.116   Finally, the social security system should make use of its statutory ability to seek alternative investment vehicles yielding higher rates of return. The trust funds should be able, at the very least, to protect the real value of accumulated surpluses. Making the central government less dependent on social security surpluses may have the added benefits of increasing both national savings and real capital growth in Egypt.

Protecting the Poor during Adjustment: The Emergency Social Fund

5.117   The creation of an Emergency Social Fund (ESF) has the dual objectives of protecting the most vulnerable groups in Egyptian society from the adverse social impacts of economic adjustment and enhancing political support for the government's reform program. The ESF would be a temporary institution with a three to four year lifespan, extendable in the event of success and continuation of adjustment programs, up to ten years.

5.118   The ESF would not be a new implementing agency but rather a coordinating and decision-making institution whose principal functions would be to:

- mobilize international and local financial resources;

- promote the preparation of sub-projects addressing the needs of the most vulnerable households among selected target groups;

- appraise and select sub-projects for funding;

- monitor and supervise the implementation of these sub-projects; and

- strengthen the Government's capacity to design and monitor poverty alleviation policies.

Budgetary Implications of the Poverty Alleviation Strategy

5.119   While it is not possible at this stage to give a detailed quantitative estimate of the budgetary impact of the various poverty alleviation policies and measures recommended, it is however important to outline the broad financial implications of the proposed strategy. Higher payments to re-establish the real value of the Ministry of Social Affairs' welfare programs (Sadat and Social Security pensions) and increased allocations for non-wage expenditures in the other social ministries (Health, Education, Higher Education) would represent an additional burden equivalent to 2.6% of the overall recurrent budget. On the other hand, improvements in the targeting of food subsidies should lead to annual savings of about 1% of the budget, which means a net effect of about 1.6% of the budget.

5.120   The employment transition program to assist displaced workers in restructured public enterprises would involve two types of costs: the payment of compensation benefits and expenditures to support the retraining and job placement interventions of the Social Fund. Compensation benefits would run in the order of 150 million Egyptian Pounds or .7% of the budget while the second category of costs is currently estimated at 85 million Egyptian Pounds or .4% of the budget. Several options exist for funding the compensation benefits. The cost could be absorbed by each public enterprise as part of its restructuring cost. In addition to separation payments, enterprises would continue to pay displaced workers their wages for a specified period of time. Alternatively, while allowing enterprises to pay displaced workers, the cost of this assistance could be redistributed among public enterprises through the introduction of a special tax. It could also be covered through the existing program of unemployment insurance in the Ministry of Social Insurance.

5.121   The poverty alleviation interventions supported by the Social Fund would be financed by additional resources mobilized specifically for this purpose. No extra budgetary cost would result from this operation.

Role of the Bank

5.122   The World Bank could support the proposed poverty alleviation strategy with the following:

- participation in funding the transition costs borne by the most vulnerable members of society during the adjustment period within the framework of the Social Fund;

- assistance to design and implement the restructuring measures associated with the setting up of a new macroeconomic and regulatory framework (labor market reform, retraining programs, food subsidy targeting, reallocation of resources in Ministries of Education and Health, etc); and

- assistance in the establishment of evaluation mechanisms to monitor, on a continuing basis, progress in the social sectors (poverty, income distribution, nutrition, health, literacy, employment, living conditions).

ANNEX A: GENERAL DATA ON EGYPT

TABLE A1 - ECONOMIC AND SOCIAL DEVELOPMENT INDICATORS FOR EGYPT (1973-87)

Year	GDP Growth	Daily Calorie Supply
1973	0.8%	2611
1975	9.1%	2750
1977	13.5%	2760
1979	6.2%	2870
1981	3.8%	2941
1983	7.6%	3163
1985	6.7%	3275
1987	2.5%	3390

Year	Infant Mortality	Life Expectancy
1973	92.4	53
1974	89.8	54
1975	87.2	54
1976	84.6	54
1977	82.0	55
1978	79.6	56
1979	77.2	57
1980	74.8	57
1981	72.4	59
1982	70.0	59
1983	64.9	60
1984	59.9	60
1985	54.8	61
1986	49.7	61
1987	44.7	62

Source: World Development Report, World Bank.

TABLE A2 - INCIDENCE OF POVERTY IN SELECTED COUNTRIES

Countries	RURAL Proportion Below Poverty Line (%)	Ranking	URBAN Proportion Below Poverty Line (%)	Ranking
Afghanistan	36	11	18	4
Algeria	n.a.	-	20	6
Bangladesh	86	30	86	22
Barbados	23	5	23	8
Bolivia	85	29	n.a.	-
Burma	40	13	40	15
EGYPT	25	6	21	7
Burundi	85	29	55	20
Cameroon	40	13	15	3
Chad	56	20	30	12
Colombia	n.a.	-	34	13
Dominican Republic	43	14	45	17
Ecuador	65	24	40	15
El Salvador	32	8	20	6
Ethiopia	65	24	60	21
Fiji	30	7	n.a.	-
The Gambia	40	13	n.a.	-
Guatemala	25	6	21	7
Haiti	78	27	55	20
Honduras	55	19	14	2
Indonesia	51	18	28	11
Iraq	40	13	n.a.	-
Jamaica	80	28	n.a.	-
Kenya	55	19	10	1
Republic of Korea	11	1	18	4
Liberia	75	26	n.a.	-
Madagascar	50	17	50	19
Malawi	85	29	25	9
Malaysia	59	21	21	7
Mali	48	16	27	10
Morocco	45	15	38	14
Nepal	61	23	55	20
Nicaragua	19	3	21	7
Niger	35	10	n.a.	-
Pakistan	43	14	42	16
Panama	30	7	21	7
Papau N. Guinea	n.a.	-	n.a.	-
Paraguay	50	17	19	5
Peru	n.a.	-	49	18
Philippines	n.a.	-	-	n.a.
Rwanda	n.a.	-	30	12
Somalia	70	25	40	15
Sudan	85	29	n.a.	-
Swaziland	50	17	45	17
Tanzania	60	22	10	1
Thailand	34	9	15	3
Togo	n.a.	-	42	16
Trinidad & Tobago	39	12	n.a.	-
Tunisia	15	2	20	6
PDRY	20	4	n.a.	-
Zaire	80	28	n.a.	-
Zambia	n.a.	-	25	9

Source: WDR, World Bank, 1986

ANNEX A
Page 3 of 4

TABLE A3 - DEGREE OF INCOME INEQUALITY IN SELECTED COUNTRIES

Countries	Ratio: 20% richest/20% poorest	Ranking
Low-Income Economy		
Bangladesh	7:1	14
Zambia	18:1	39
India	7:1	14
Kenya	23:1	42
Sri Lanka	9:1	25
Indonesia	8:1	20
Middle-Income Economy		
Philippines	10:1	32
Egypt	7:1	14
Ivory Coast	26:1	43
Thailand	9:1	25
El Salvador	9:1	25
Turkey	16:1	36
Peru	32:1	45
Mauritius	15:1	35
Costa Rica	17:1	38
Malaysia	16:1	36
Mexico	20:1	41
Upper-Middle Income Economy		
Brazil	33:1	46
Hungary	5:1	3
Panama	31:1	44
Argentina	11:1	33
Yugoslavia	6:1	7
Korea	8:1	20
Portugal	9:1	25
Venezuela	18:1	39
Trinidad and Tobago	12:1	34
High-Income Economy		
Spain	6:1	7
Ireland	5:1	3
Israel	7:1	14
New Zealand	9:1	25
Hong Kong	9:1	25
Italy	7:1	14
United Kingdom	6:1	7
Australia	9:1	25
Belgium	5:1	3
Netherlands	4:1	1
France	8:1	20
Germany, Federal Republic	5:1	3
Finland	6:1	7
Denmark	7:1	14
Canada	8:1	20
Sweden	6:1	7
Japan	4:1	1
Norway	6:1	7
United States	8:1	20
Switzerland	6:1	7

Source: World Development Report, World Bank, 1989.

ANNEX A
Page 4 of 4

TABLE A4 - THE NEED FOR ADJUSTMENT IN EGYPT

	1982	1983	1984	1985	1986	1987	1988	1989
GDP Growth	10.1	7.6	6.2	6.7	2.7	2.5	3.2	1.0
Budget Deficit (% of GDP)	19.1	23.1	22.0	22.8	17.1	14.1	16.3	13.8
Current Account Deficit (% of GDP)	-13.5	-8.4	-9.9	-13.6	-15.2	-10.4	-7.7	-10.0
Terms of Trade (1980=100)	93	93	89	88	76	57	56	51
CPI	15.7	22.1	10.3	14.0	23.7	20.0	18.9	20.0

Source: Assad and Commander, 1989
Mission estimates

TABLE A5 - CONSUMER PRICE INDEX IN CAIRO DURING 1989

Family Annual Income	\multicolumn{6}{c}{Category I ≤ LE 500}	\multicolumn{6}{c}{Category II LE 900 - 1300}	\multicolumn{6}{c}{Category III LE 3000 - 6000}
	Jan	May	June	July	Aug	Sep	Jan	May	June	July	Aug	Sep	Jan	May	June	July	Aug	Sep
All Items	100	125.3	130.6	138.1	139.0	142.8	100	112.1	119.4	124.0	124.9	129.4	100	105.7	106.7	107.4	107.6	111.3
I Food, Beverage & Tobacco	100	132.3	137.5	147.2	146.7	151.7	100	115.8	124.4	130.9	131.4	137.2	100	110.7	110.9	111.7	110.0	117.7

Source: Recalculation of data provided by GASC, 1989, Field visits, 1989.

ANNEX B: STATISTICAL TABLES ON POVERTY AND INCOME DISTRIBUTION

ANNEX B
Page 1 of 7

TABLE B1 - EXPENDITURE LEVELS OF THE POOR AND THE NON-POOR
(EGYPTIAN POUNDS PER YEAR)

	Rural	Urban
Poorest 10%	250	380
Poorest 30%	450	517
All Egyptians	1,089	1,441
Wealthiest 10%	2,475	3,676

Source: 1981/82 HBS, CAPMAS

TABLE B2 - AGE STRUCTURE OF THE RURAL POOR IN 1977
(%)

Age Group	Poor	Non-Poor
Youths (Less than 15)	48	40
Adults (15-64)	48	56
Seniors (65 and more)	4	4

Source: Radwan and Lee, 1986

ANNEX B

TABLE B3 - INCOME DIFFERENTIALS BETWEEN RURAL AND URBAN AREAS
(Egyptian Pounds)

Year (1)	Rural (2)	Urban (3)	Ratio (3) / (2)
1966/67	47.6	79.4	1.67
1967/68	45.2	75.1	1.66
1968/69	44.0	72.8	1.65
1969/70	48.1	79.4	1.65
1970/71	47.2	77.7	1.65
1971/72	48.4	81.8	1.69
1972/73	54.3	88.9	1.64
1973/74	72.1	117.6	1.63
1974/75	84.6	137.7	1.63
1975/76	99.7	159.8	1.60
1976/77	123.3	194.8	1.58
1977/78	143.0	222.6	1.56
1978/79	209.4	321.2	1.53
1979/80	235.9	351.0	1.69
1981/82	275.8	403.8	1.66
1982/83	288.1	422.0	1.46
1983/84	344.5	507.3	1.46

Source: Korayem (1987)

TABLE B.4 - INCIDENCE OF POVERTY BY GOVERNORATES

Governorates	Proportion of Rural Households In Poverty (%)	Proportion of Urban Households In Poverty (%)
Cairo	0.0	39.7
Alexandria	0.0	51.8
Port Said	0.0	29.6
Suez	0.0	51.7
Damietta	8.3	23.4
Dakahliya	37.7	50.3
Sharkiya	32.6	61.0
Qalioubiya	53.7	65.1
Kafr El Sheikh	30.4	49.2
Sharkiya	33.6	43.1
Menoufiya	44.0	52.1
Beheira	21.4	30.1
Ismailia	19.4	15.7
Giza	18.7	44.8
Beni Sueif	77.8	56.0
Fayoum	55.1	71.1
Minya	63.9	16.0
Assiut	56.0	6.8
Sohag	50.9	67.4
Qena	37.1	34.5
Aswan	45.7	41.9
M. Sinai	0.0	49.6
Matruh	0.0	72.7
New Valley	0.0	47.4
Red Sea	0.0	18.0
TOTAL	**42.2**	**46.8**

Source: 1981/82, HBS, CAPMAS

TABLE B5 - DISTRIBUTION OF THE POOR BY OCCUPATIONAL ACTIVITY OF HOUSEHOLDS HEADS
(%)

	Urban	Rural
Agriculture	10.5	39.7
Clerical	4.3	0.7
Industry	19.8	6.1
Outside the Labor Force	34.5	36.1
Sales and Services	21.9	7.5
Self-employed	8.9	9.9

Source: 1981/82 HBS, CAPMAS

TABLE B6 - DISTRIBUTION OF THE POOR BY ECONOMIC ACTIVITY

Sector	Rural	Urban
1. Agriculture	39.8	10.4
2. Manufacturing	3.8	12.6
3. Water, Electricity	0.1	0.5
4. Construction	0.9	3.1
5. Services	6.6	17.2
	100.0	100.0

Source: 1981/82 HBS, CAPMAS

TABLE B7 - RELATIVE INCIDENCE OF POVERTY BY ECONOMIC ACTIVITY OF HOUSEHOLD HEAD

Economic Activity	Urban	Rural
Agriculture	1.2	0.8
Mining	0.1	0.4
Manufacturing	0.8	0.6
Electricity, Gas, and Water	0.6	0.5
Building & Construction	0.6	0.4
Trade, Restaurants & Hotels	0.9	0.6
Storage, Transport, & Communications	0.5	0.5
Supply and Insurance	0.3	0.2
Public and Private Social Services	0.8	0.6
Unidentified Activities	2.1	2.5
Other Activities	1.6	2.0

*Economic activity share of total household and poverty divided by economic activity share of total households.

Source: 1981/82 HBS, CAPMAS

TABLE B8 - AVERAGE HOUSEHOLD INCOME BY OCCUPATION OF RURAL HOUSEHOLD HEAD

Occupation	Poor and Marginal Households (LE)	Non-Poor Households (LE)
Housewife	172	340
Farmer	363	594
Farm Laborer	218	339
Craftsman	320	495
Construction	405	345
Service	249	562
Government	400	469
Others	334	200
Disabled	220	346
Regular Army	-	579
National Service	402	407
Student	342	160

Source: Radwan and Fisher, 1988.

TABLE B9 - DISTRIBUTION OF HOUSEHOLD EXPENDITURES (%)

	1958/59 Rural	1958/59 Urban	1964/65 Rural	1964/65 Urban	1974/75 Rural	1974/75 Urban	1981/82 Rural	1981/82 Urban
Lowest 20%	6.7)	) 16.4	7.4)	) 16.5	5.9	8.1	6.0	7.5
20-40%	11.0)		11.6)		11.2	12.7	11.4	13.2
40-60%	16.6	14.5	16.3	14.8	15.8	16.7	16.0	17.2
60-80%	21.9)	) 69.1	22.0)	) 68.8	21.2	22.8	22.6	22.3
Top 20%	43.9)		42.7)		45.9	39.7	44.0	39.8
Gini Coefficient 1/	0.36	0.40	0.29	0.40	0.35	0.37	0.34	0.37
Theil Measures 2/	0.16	n.a.	0.12	n.a.	0.17	n.a.	0.17	n.a.

1/ The Gini Coefficient is an aggregate numerical measure of income inequality calculated on the basis of the variance of the size distribution of income (Lorenz curve) from perfect equality.

2/ The Theil measure of inequality is based on the notion of entropy in information theory. Given a population divided into a number of groups according to certain socioeconomic characteristics, the Theil Index of inequality measures the contribution of inequality of each group to the aggregate inequality.

For mathematical definitions of these measures of inequality, see Kakwani, N., *Income Inequality and Poverty: Methods of Estimation and Policy Applications*, Oxford University Press, 1980.

Source: Hansen and Radwan, 1982

TABLE B10 - DISTRIBUTION OF ASSETS IN RURAL AREAS IN 1977

Income Group	%
Poorest 10%	0.1
Second decile	0.5
Third decile	1.0
Fourth decile	1.6
Fifth decile	4.0
Sixth decile	3.7
Seventh decile	6.3
Eight decile	10.0
Ninth decile	15.9
Richest 10%	56.9

Source: Radwan and Lee, 1986

ANNEX B

TABLE B11 - DISTRIBUTION OF EDUCATION EXPENDITURES BY SOCIOECONOMIC ORIGIN
(%)

	Share of the Population	Share of Education Expenditure
Low Income	25	12
Middle Income	67	74
Upper Income	8	14
TOTAL	100	100

Source: Abdel-Fadil, 1982
Ministry of Education

ANNEX C: DEMOGRAPHIC DATA

ANNEX C
Page 1 of 3

TABLE C1 - SOCIAL COMPOSITION OF HOUSEHOLDS, CAIRO, 1980

Type of Household	Distribution (Percent)	Mean Size
Simple Households		
1 Married couple without children	7	2.0
2 Married couple with children	55	5.2
3 Single parent with children	10	3.8
Subtotal, simple	72	4.7
Complex Households		
4 One couple (with or without children) and additional person(s)	11	5.7
5 Multiple couples with or without children and with or without additional persons	6	7.5
Subtotal, complex	18	6.3
No-couple Households		
6 Person residing alone	7	1.0
7 Multiple persons without any couple	3	2.5
Subtotal, no-couple	10	1.5
All (percent)	100	4.69
Sample N	2103	9863

Source: Shorter, F., 1989

ANNEX C
Page 2 of 3

TABLE C2 - POPULATION AND LABOR FORCE ACTIVITY: 1976-1986

	1976	1986
Population 6+	30,292,119	38,976,690
Labor Force 6+	10,981,435	13,976,690
Employed	10,171,904	12,146,621
Unemployed	809,631	1,232,133
Unemployment Rate	7.4%	9.2%

Source: 1976 and 1986 census.

ANNEX C
Page 3 of 3

TABLE C3 - POPULATION AND LABOR FORCE ACTIVITY BY SEX FOR RURAL AND URBAN AREAS:

EGYPT 1976 - 1986

	Total 1976	Total 1986	Urban 1976	Urban 1986	Rural 1976	Rural 1986
POPULATION 6+						
Men	15,430,960	19,920,095	6,969,900	8,981,419	8,461,060	10,938,676
Women	14,861,159	19,056,595	6,598,107	8,543,374	8,263,052	10,513,221
Total	30,292,119	38,976,690	13,568,007	17,524,793	16,724,112	21,451,897
LABOR FORCE 6+						
Men	9,996,537	11,817,291	4,142,146	5,211,642	5,854,391	6,605,649
Women	984,998	1,561,463	628,079	1,089,376	356,919	472,087
Total	10,981,435	13,378,754	4,770,225	6,301,018	6,211,210	7,077,736
EMPLOYED 6+						
Men	9,473,800	10,949,447	3,867,042	4,775,966	5,606,758	6,173,481
Women	698,104	1,197,174	474,421	849,027	223,683	348,147
Total	10,171,904	12,146,621	4,341,463	5,624,993	5,830,441	6,521,628
UNEMPLOYED						
Men	522,737	867,844	275,104	435,676	247,633	432,168
Women	286,894	364,289	153,658	240,349	133,236	123,940
Total	809,631	1,232,133	428,762	676,025	380,869	556,108
UNEMPLOYMENT RATE						
Men	5.2%	7.3%	6.6%	8.4%	4.2%	6.5%
Women	29.1%	23.3%	24.5%	22.1%	37.3%	26.3%
Total	7.4%	9.2%	9.0%	10.7%	6.1%	7.9%
EMPLOY-POP:RATIO						
Men	61.4%	55.0%	55.5%	53.2%	66.3%	56.4%
Women	4.7%	6.3%	7.2%	9.9%	2.7%	3.3%
Total	33.6%	31.2%	32.0%	32.1%	34.9%	30.4%
LABOR PART.RATE						
Men	64.8%	59.3%	59.4%	58.0%	69.2%	60.4%
Women	6.6%	8.2%	9.5%	12.8%	4.3%	4.5%
Total	36.3%	34.3%	35.2%	36.0%	37.1%	33.0%

Source: 1976 and 1986 Census

ANNEX D: DATA ON EMPLOYMENT AND WAGES

ANNEX D

TABLE D1 - DISTRIBUTION OF THE LABOR FORCE BY OCCUPATION OF HOUSEHOLD HEAD

Occupation	Poor and Marginal Households	Non-Poor Households
Farmer	39.5	42.2
Farm Laborer	19.7	7.1
Craftsman	7.4	7.7
Construction	1.5	2.3
Service	4.5	6.7
Government	5.2	15.6
Others	5.1	3.2
Army and	0.3	2.1
National Service	5.6	6.6
Looking for work	2.1	1.6
TOTAL	100.0	100.0

Source: Radwan and Lee, 1986

TABLE D2 - SIZE OF THE TOTAL LABOR FORCE AGE 6 AND OLDER

	1976	1986
Labor Force 6+	10,981,435	13,378,754
Youths 15-24	2,434,898	3,376,651
Women	984,998	1,561,463

Source: Census, 1976 and 1986

ANNEX D
Page 2 of 5

TABLE D3 - EMPLOYMENT BY SECTOR OF ECONOMIC ACTIVITY: 1976 and 1986

	1976	%	1986	%
Agriculture, Fishing, and Hunting	4,881,009	47.58%	4,566,945	37.60%
Mining	33,831	0.33%	52,769	0.43%
Industry	1,369,482	13.35%	1,475,608	12.15%
Electricity	61,761	0.60%	91,077	0.275%
Construction	425,084	4.14%	817,644	6.73%
Trade, Hotel, Restaurant	861,286	8.40%	852,124	7.02%
Trans, Comm, Stor.	482,253	4.70%	640,827	5.28%
Fin. and Insurance	88,392	0.86%	224,061	1.84%
Social Services	1,868,289	18.21%	2,614,477	21.52%
Other not elsewhere Classified	186,438	1.82%	811,089	6.68%
TOTAL	10,257,825	100.00%	12,146,621	100.00%

Source: 1976 and 1986 Census

TABLE D4 - EMPLOYMENT BY TYPE OF EMPLOYER: 1976 AND 1986

Type of Employer	1976	%	1986	%
Government	1,786,064	17.5	2,567,219	21.9
Public Enterprise	964,583	9.4	1,201,008	10.2
Private Enterprise	7,355,770	71.9	7,930,492	67.6
Agriculture	4,881,009	47.7	4,566,945	39.0
Non-Agriculture	2,474,761	24.2	3,363,547	28.7
Cooperative	18,471	0.2	n/a	
Foreign	4,959	0.0	12,042	0.1
Not Declared	100,102	1.0	14,244	0.1
TOTAL	10,229,949	100.0	11,725,005	100.0

Source: 1976 and 1986 Census

TABLE D5 - REAL WAGE TRENDS BY SECTOR (1973-100)

Category	1973	1974	1975	1976	1977	1978	1979	1980	1981	1982	1983	1984	1985	1986	1987
Agriculture															
Public	100	105	67	84	114	82	79	77	81	85	84	88	118	94	77
Private	100	110	130	155	173	180	200	207	239	268	288	324	328	290	240
Manufacturing															
Public	100	97	89	93	98	100	109	108	116	123	117	120	108	101	95
Private	100	111	108	116	136	134	136	136	145	153	161	179	168	149	135
Construction															
Public	100	111	100	104	109	118	139	125	120	115	130	150	134	120	110
Private	100	127	148	162	171	168	174	156	151	145	132	132	140	132	116
Services															
Public	100	117	99	89	95	118	101	96	99	100	94	96	93	82	74
Private	100	100	96	103	106	140	134	125	126	126	124	130	157	126	107
Blue Collar (all sectors)															
Public	100	101	94	97	108	104	114	113	121	127	123	128	121	108	99
Private	100	92	90	102	115	114	129	123	127	129	134	147	141	126	115
White Collar (all sectors)															
Public	100	104	88	86	91	106	97	91	92	92	88	92	84	74	66
Private	100	92	88	87	94	98	115	108	108	108	108	115	123	103	89
Public Enterprises	100	103	92	94	102	107	110	107	112	116	111	116	108	98	90
Private Sector*	100	103	82	89	103	100	117	112	115	117	121	132	134	115	102
Government	100	87	83	84	87	83	82	80	86	87	78	77	71	60	55

Source: Assaad and Commander, 1989, Appendix Table 1, p.26

* Enterprises of 10 workers or more

TABLE D6 - REAL WAGE TRENDS BY ECONOMIC SECTOR

Year	Government	Public Enterprise	Private Sector
1973	100	100	100
1974	87	103	103
1975	83	92	82
1976	84	94	89
1977	87	102	103
1978	83	107	100
1979	82	110	117
1980	80	107	112
1981	86	112	115
1982	87	116	117
1983	78	111	121
1984	77	116	132
1985	71	108	134
1986	60	98	115
1987	55	90	102

Source: Assad and Commander, 1989

TABLE D7 - UNEMPLOYMENT BY EDUCATION LEVEL (1986)

Education Level	No. of Unemployed
Illiterate	38,248
Read and Write	32,448
Primary	15,701
Less than Secondary	30,259
Secondary	785,954
Upper Secondary	73,872
University	236,530
Non Declared	321
TOTAL	1,230,133

Source: Ministry of Labor

ANNEX D
Page 5 of 5

TABLE D8 - OPEN UNEMPLOYMENT RATES FOR MEN AND WOMEN IN URBAN AND RURAL AREAS: 1976 - 1986

	Urban		Rural	
	Men	Women	Men	Women
1976	6.6	24.5	4.2	37.3
1986	8.4	22.1	6.5	26.3

Source: 1976 and 1986 Census

ANNEX E: NUTRITION DATA

ANNEX E
Page 1 of 6

TABLE E1 - AVERAGE PER CAPITA FOOD SUPPLY OF EGYPT (G/DA)

Country	Cereals	Pulses	Starches	Veg. & Fruits	Meat	Eggs	Fish	Milk	Sugars	Oil	Protein Total	Animal	Calories
Developed (74)	326	16	312	364	151	30	190	570	88	49	90	44	3050
Developing (74)	386	49	195	184	30	2.7	11	79	30	11	58	9	2150
Egypt (70-71)	618	27	35	385	25	3.8	6.1	133.7	50.8	23.3	85.4	10.1	3050
Egypt (74)	633	26	35	386	26	3.6	8.8	138	63	23	86.6	10.7	3122
Egypt (77)	662	26	46	406	28	4.1	12	162	71	29	91.8	12.2	3362
Egypt (80)	668	21	53	473	34	5	12	163	74	23	96	15	3390

Source: Galal and Amine, 1984.

TABLE E2 - DAILY CALORIE SUPPLY PER CAPITA FOR SELECTED COUNTRIES OF THE REGION

Country	Calories	% of Requirement
Morocco	2544	105
Egypt	3163	126
Turkey	3100	123
Tunisia	2889	121

Source: World Development Report, 1986.

ANNEX E
Page 2 of 6

TABLE E3 - MEAN HB VALUES AND PREVALENCE OF ANAEMIA AMONG MOTHERS OF DIFFERENT PHYSIOLOGICAL STATUS

Physiological Status	Mean Hb ± S.D. g%	% Anaemic	Total No. examined
Non-pregnant	13.5 ± 1.6	17.0 %	402
Lactating	12.8 ± 1.6	25.3 %	823
Pregnant	11.8 ± 1.5	22.1 %	253
Total	12.7 ± 1.7	22.4 %	1478

Source: CAPMAS and UNICEF, 1988

ANNEX E

TABLE E4 - THE QUANTITY AND VALUE FOR THE RATIONED SUPPLIES FOR INDIVIDUAL IN RATION CARD
(1984-1989)

Commodity	1984 Monthly Ration in Kg.	1984 Value in P Full / Partial	1985 Monthly Ration in Kg.	1985 Value in P Full / Partial	1986 Monthly Ration in Kg.	1986 Value in P Full / Partial	1987 Monthly Ration in Kg.	1987 Value in P Full / Partial	1988 Monthly Ration in Kg.	1988 Value in P Full / Partial	1989* Monthly Ration in Kg.	1989* Value in P Full / Partial
Sugar												
Subsidized ration	.750 g.	7.5 P / 22.5 P	.750 g.	7.5 P / 22.5 P	.750 g.	7.5 P / 22.5 P	.750 g.	7.5 P / 22.5 P	.750 g.	7.5 P / 22.5 P	.750 g.	7.5 P / 22.5 P
Market price ration	.750 g.	22.5 P / 22.5 P	.750 g.	22.5 P / 22.5 P	.750 g.	22.5 P / 22.5 P	.750 g.	22.5 P / 22.5 P	.750 g.	22.5 P / 22.5 P	.750 g.	22.5 P / 22.5 P
Tea												
Subsidized ration	.040 g.	5.5 P / 10.0 P	.040 g.	5.5 P / 10.0 P	.040 g.	5.5 P / 10.0 P	.040 g.	5.5 P / 10.0 P				
Market price ration	.040 g.	10.5 P / 10.5 P	.040 g.	10.5 P / 10.5 P	.040 g.	10.5 P / 10.5 P	.040 g.	10.5 P / 10.5 P	.040 g.	10.5 P / 10.5 P	.040 g.	10.5 P / 10.5 P
Oil												
Metro Cairo	.450 g.	4.5 P / 13.5									.450 g.	4.5 P / 13.5 P
Coastal city	.600 g.	6.0 P / 18.0									.600 g.	6.0 P / 18.0
Coastal city	.300 g.	3.0 P / 9.0									.300 g.	3.0 P / 9.0
Villages	.150 g.	1.5 / 4.5									.150 g.	1.5 / 4.5
Mkt value rates in cities	.100 g.	3.0 / 3.0									.100 g.	3.0 / 3.0
Mkt value rates in villages	.150 g.	4.5 / 4.5									.150 g.	4.5 / 4.5
Rice												
Cities												
1-2 indiv per card	3.0 kg	28			2.0 kg	.30 P / 30.0 P			2.0	.80	2.0	.80
3-4 indiv per card	4.0 kg	56			4.0 kg	.60 / 60.0			4.0	1.20	4.0	1.20
5 & over per card	6.0 kg	84			6.0 kg	.90 / 90.0			6.0	2.40	6.0	2.40
Villages												
1 card	2.0 kg	28			2.0 kg.	.30 / 30.0			2.0	.80	2.0	.80
Detergent												
Soap	4.0				2pcs=.225g	4.0 / 4.0			1 pc=.225g	4.0 / 4.0	1 pc m. wt	4.0
Detergent					1 pc=.135g	8.0 / 8.0			2pc=.135g	12.0 / 12.0		

* = Ration supplies has been cancelled beginning 11/29/87

** = Used to be 10 pcs per card whatever the number of individuals until 4/1/88 when it was reduced to 5 pcs maximum on each card

*** = Used to be 5 pcs per card until 4/1/87 when it was reduced to 3 pcs. maximum per card until 5/1/88 when it was cancelled

TABLE E5 - INCOME TRANSFERS FROM FOOD SUBSIDIES AND DISTORTED PRICES, BY EMPLOYMENT GROUPS

	Rural Households							Urban Households		
	Farm Households			Land-less Farm Labor	Non-farm Wage Labor	Non-farm Self-Employed	Others	Self-Employed	Wage Labor	Others
Source of Transfer	Small Farms	Medium-Size Farms	Large Farms							
	(LE/capita/year)									
Cereal production	-1.35	-9.41	-30.89	0.00	-1.46	-2.44	-2.97	...	...	...
Wheat	-0.39	-1.65	-8.86	0.00	-0.40	-0.40	-0.31	...	...	...
Rice	-0.69	-6.75	-17.75	0.00	-0.81	-1.83	-2.55	...	...	...
Maize, sorghum, and barley	-0.19	-0.59	-2.47	0.00	-0.23	-0.15	-0.04	...	...	...
Beans and lentils	-0.06	-0.41	-1.79	0.00	-0.01	-0.04	-0.07	...	...	...
Animal production	6.77	17.34	15.61	0.78	4.98	4.69	4.60	...	...	...
Livestock	6.80	16.71	17.18	1.34	5.43	5.31	5.51	...	...	...
Dairy	0.42	1.14	1.08	0.12	0.24	0.04	0.73	...	...	...
Poultry	-0.44	-0.51	-2.65	-0.69	-0.69	-0.66	-1.64	...	...	...
Sugar production	-0.36	-1.26	-7.84	0.00	-0.40	-0.04	-0.09	...	...	...
Cotton production	-5.66	-28.45	-88.09	0.00	-5.87	-3.26	-9.21	...	...	...
Inputs	6.73	12.85	30.57	1.61	4.14	4.14	5.55	...	...	...
Total transfer from production	6.13	-8.93	-80.65	2.38	1.37	3.08	-2.11	...	...	...
Government channels	21.20	15.60	13.68	19.57	21.48	19.98	23.03	27.14	29.52	32.13
Basic ration	5.83	5.51	4.90	5.10	5.68	5.81	6.01	6.61	7.23	7.70
Additional ration	1.19	0.85	0.79	0.84	1.01	0.90	1.34	1.18	1.47	1.99
Purchases from co-operatives	0.24	0.33	0.27	0.15	0.75	0.42	0.36	1.49	1.91	2.38
Frozen meat	0.23	0.21	0.16	0.03	0.87	0.21	0.48	1.20	2.22	2.21
Flour and bread	13.69	8.68	7.54	13.44	13.15	12.61	14.82	16.64	16.66	17.84
Open market	2.66	2.37	-6.20	4.59	-0.12	0.62	5.69	-20.93	-13.93	-16.58
Cereals	12.12	11.18	8.33	13.01	10.92	12.14	16.00	-0.04	2.35	2.58
Sugar, oil, and tea	-0.38	-0.32	-0.35	-0.58	-0.29	-0.27	-0.28	-0.17	-0.04	-0.05
Meat, fish, and poultry	-8.74	-8.06	-13.53	-7.48	-10.29	-10.89	-9.51	-20.60	-16.14	-19.01
Beans and lentils	-0.32	-0.43	-0.64	-0.35	-0.45	-0.35	-0.51	-0.10	-0.10	-0.09
Share of survey households (percent)	8.0	14.5	1.6	5.4	12.2	6.8	10.0	10.0	21.2	10.3

Sources: Data from the household survey made by the International Food Policy Research Institute and Institute of National Planning, Cairo, 1981/82. Alderman and von Braun, 1984.

Notes: Households are classified by the main employment of the head of the household. Small farms have less than 1 feddan; medium size farms have between 1 and 5 feddan; large farms have more than 5 feddan.

The subtotals for cereal production, government channels; and so forth do not always equal the sum of their parts because of rounding.

Inputs include fertilizers, insecticides, machinery, feed mix, cotton cake, maize, and berseem sales. Basic rations include sugar, oil, tea, and rice. Additional rations include these commodities, at higher prices, plus beans and lentils. Purchases from cooperatives include the same commodities included in additional rations. The category "flour and bread" includes only the flour and bread distributed through government channels. Flour sold on the open market is included in cereals.

ANNEX E
Page 5 of 6

TABLE E6 - RATIO OF AREA PLANTED BY CROP TO TOTAL AREA (BY FARM SIZE, 1976)

Commodity	< 1	1-3	3-5	5-10	> 10	All
Wheat	.20	.22	.24	.18	.17	.21
Maize	.08	.22	.18	.14	.09	.17
Rice	.53	.40	.41	.36	.46	.42
Cotton	.24	.33	.27	.40	.32	.32
SS berseem	.24	.31	.22	.38	.29	.29
LS berseem	.41	.37	.31	.31	.23	.33
Others*	.15	.11	.28	.14	.26	.17

Farm size (in feddans)

Notes: *Others = potatoes, tomatoes, onions, and fruits.
SS = short season; LS = long season.

Source: Dethier, 1989.

ANNEX E
Page 6 of 6

TABLE E7 - SOURCE OF CEREALS FOR HOUSEHOLDS OF VARYING FARM SIZES

Components	0 - 1 Feddan	1 - 3 Feddan	3 - 5 Feddan	More than 5 Feddan
	\multicolumn{4}{c}{(kilograms/capita/year/of wheat grain equivalent)}			
Cereal production	97.7	268.1	360.9	606.5
Wheat	30.1	87.5	96.4	210.6
Rice (milled)	10.9	70.9	144.0	214.0
Maize	41.2	78.1	63.4	84.4
Sorghum	13.1	13.6	20.8	25.6
Barley	0.0	1.6	3.2	21.7
Subsidized cereals	131.1	78.4	59.2	55.0
Balady flour[a]	80.2	44.5	34.4	29.7
Fino flour[a]	20.0	10.8	12.1	5.7
Balady bread[a]	17.3	10.0	4.4	3.5
Afrangi bread[a]	2.0	1.1	0.3	0.4
Shami bread[a]	0.6	0.6	0.1	1.2
Rice (milled)				
Rationed	6.5	5.8	4.8	4.3
From cooperatives	0.7	0.8	0.2	0.8
Maize (yellow)	2.5	3.3	1.8	8.2
Sales of cereals	15.0	84.0	149.6	293.1
Wheat	3.7	18.9	21.7	86.5
Rice (milled)	6.5	48.3	93.8	136.5
Maize	3.0	3.8	6.0	18.2
Sorghum	0.4	1.0	5.1	6.8
Human consumption[b]	329.2	327.6	314.5	332.3
Wheat and wheat products[b]	232.3	203.0	184.4	183.0
Rice (milled)	24.9	37.4	52.3	63.7
Maize and maize flour	53.1	71.5	57.2	55.4
Sorghum	13.3	7.1	8.0	14.2

Source: Alderman and von Braun, 1984.

ANNEX F: DATA ON HEALTH

ANNEX F

TABLE F1 - EVOLUTION OF INFANT AND CHILD MORTALITY (NO. OF DEATHS PER THOUSAND)

Year	Infant Mortality	Child Mortality
1970	116	42.8
1975	89	32.2
1980	76	22.6
1982	70	22.8
1987	45	7.5

Source: CAPMAS and UNICEF, 1988
Ministry of Health

TABLE F2 - INFANT AND CHILD MORTALITY RATES BY GOVERNORATES

Country	I.M.R. Registration	I.M.R. Adjustment for Under reporting	C.M.R. Rates
Cairo	47	47	3.8
Alexandria	38	41	3.3
Port Said	27	36	2.5
Suez Canal	36	50	2.4
Damietta	26	34	3.3
Daqahlia	26	36	4.3
Sharqiya	34	47	6.6
Qalyoubia	49	56	6.7
Kafr Elsheikh	25	43	4.6
Gharbia	33	35	4.4
Menoufia	47	47	7.9
Beheira	36	50	5.7
Ismailia	33	39	4.4
Giza	71	85	9.3
Benisuef	55	98	12.7
Fayoum	50	84	10.9
Minya	55	95	12.5
Assiut	58	93	9.1
Sohag	51	88	12.5
Qena	48	104	12.8
Aswan	76	89	10.5
Red Sea	73	x	4.8
New Valley	46	x	4.1
Matrouh	29	x	4.2
Sinai Nth	35	x	4.5
Sinai Sth	15	x	
EGYPT	45	60	7.4

Source: Ministry of Health
x Adjustment factors not available for frontier governorates.

TABLE F3 - BILHARZIA CONTROL PROGRAM

I. **Middle Egypt** - Prevalence Rates**(S. Haematodium) (based on annual sample surveys).

	1977	80	81	82	83	84	85	86	87	88
Benisuef	27.7	14.8	15.5	15.2	9.3	6.8	6.1	4.9	4.8	4.2
Minya	33.6	17.3	14.7	4.0	11.6	9.1	7.3	6.2	4.9	4.6
Assiut (N)	19.3	9.9	10.4	7.6	8.9	10.4	7.3	7.2	5.0	9.0
TOTAL		15.3	14.1	13.2	10.5	9.2	7.0	5.9	4.9	4.6

* 1977 Rates : Baseline data (at the beginning of control).
** Prevalence Rates: Proportion of population infected. Expressed in percentage of total population.

I. **Upper Egypt** Prevalence Rates (S. Haematodium)

	1980*	81	82	83	84	85	86	87	88
Assiut	15.9	15.7	15.1	14.1	11.4	13.4	7.8	7.7	9.6
Sohag	20.9	20.2	16.0	12.1	11.4	9.3	8.4	8.9	8.2
Qena	31.9	30.8	26.0	18.5	16.0	12.5	11.6	10.1	10.3
Aswan	17.0	17.1	4.6	3.2	1.9	1.7	1.7	0.9	0.4
TOTAL		21.1	20.4	16.0	15.5	11.4	7.8	8.5	7.3

* Baseline data, July 1980

1983 Delta Prevalence Survey

GOVERNOR	Exam	Stool * + Positive	%	Urine ** + Positive	%
Gharbia	1804	774	42.9	185	10.2
Qalyoubia	1734	493	28.4	96	5.6
El Beheira	2763	1466	53.1	236	8.5
Sharkia	2578	653	25.3	139	5.4
kafr Elshiekia	1419	714	50.3	59	4.1
Domietta	926	437	47.2	12	1.2
Minofia	1570	314	20.0	84	5.3
Dakhalia	2568	1089	42.4	154	6.0

* Stool + = Infection with Mansoni.
** Urine + = Infection with Haematobium
Source: Ministry of Health, Department of Endemic Diseases.

TABLE F4 - THE RURAL PRIMARY HEALTH CARE NETWORK (1989)

GOVERNORATES	Rural Population in 1000	Rural Units	Rural Centers	Rural Hospitals	Total Units	Rural Average Population Per Unit
Cairo		4			4	
Alexandria		19	2		21	
Port Said		5			5	
Suez Canal		7			7	
Damietta	670	43	5	6	54	12,400
Dakhalia	2,790	214	56	5	275	10,100
Sharkya	2,907	189	45	4	238	12,200
Kalyubia	1,511	82	22	8	112	13,500
Kuer ElShiekh	1,482	131	18	5	154	9,600
Gharbia	2,064	123	34	9	166	12,400
El Menuf	1,918	124	39	4	167	11,500
Behera	2,674	193	42	4	239	11,200
Ismailia	291	26	-	1	27	10,800
Giza	1,686	101	18	7	126	13,400
Beni Suef	1,163	89	24	4	117	9,900
Fayoum	1,279	74	22	5	101	12,700
Menya	2,267	153	37	9	199	11,400
Assiut	1,715	106	30	5	141	12,200
Souhag	2,064	135	41	2	178	11,600
Qena	1,860	127	38	1	166	11,200
Aswan	523	72	15	3	90	5,800
Sinai (N)	58	32	-	-	32	1,800
Sinai (S)	29	5	2	2	9	3,200
Matrua	87	15	-	-	15	5,800
New Valley	58	17	2	2	21	2,800
Red Sea	29	9	-	-	9	3,200
T O T A L	29,065	2,095	492	86	2,673	10,800

Source: Ministry of Health

TABLE F5 - THE URBAN PRIMARY HEALTH CARE NETWORK (1989)

GOVERNORATES	Urban Population in 1000	Urban Centers*	MCH Visits	School Health	Health Offices	Urban Average Population Per Unit
Cairo	6,528	31	31	23	52	
Alexandria	3,139	5	14	12	29	
Port Said	432	2	3	-	4	
Suez Canal		2	5	6	4	
Damietta	205	6	7	1	6	12,400
Dakhalia	978	2	12	22	30	10,100
Sharbia	773	8	12	9	16	12,200
Kalyubia	1,183	13	9	11	16	13,500
Kuer ElShiekh	432	4	10	8	11	9,600
Gharbia	1,024	2	12	8	14	12,400
El Menuf	1,918	3	11	11	12	11,500
Behera	819	3	19	15	20	11,200
Ismailia	296	4	2	5	5	10,800
Giza	2,274	5	8	11	19	13,400
Beni Suef	387	3	11	23	11	9,900
Fayoum	386	3	8	4	9	12,700
Menya	591	6	10	10	13	11,400
Assiut	660	5	15	19	17	12,200
Souhag	502	2	12	21	15	11,600
Qena	569	7	11	9	11	11,200
Aswan	341	2	6	6	6	5,800
Sinai (N)	114	-	2	1	8	1,800
Sinai (S)	23	-	1	-	9	3,200
Matrua	91	1	1	3	7	5,800
New Valley	45	1	2	-	1	2,800
Red Sea	68	1	3	1	3	3,200
TOTAL	22,759	171	237	238	349	10,800

* Urban Centers offer only OPD services and are complemented in their task by the outpatient Department of Urban hospitals.

Source: Ministry of Health

F6 - EXPANDED PROGRAM OF IMMUNIZATION

I. **Immunization coverage by Antigen (in percent) 1984 and Nov. 1987 surveys**

	1984	1987
BCG	53	72
Polio(3)*	67	88
DPT (3)*	57	82
Measles	41	76

(Children age 12-23 mons)

* Having received the third injection (complete immunization)
DPT - Immunization against diptheria pertusis and tetanus

II. **Reported Numbers of cases of diseases covered by the expanded program of immunization.**

YEAR	DIPTH.	MEASLES	PERTUSIS	POLIO	TETANUS	NEONATAL TETANUS	TBC (ALL FORMS)
1985	663	5554	18	416	9286	6632	1183
1986	630	1176	9	339	9995	7256	1133
1987	368	1805	14	492	9287	6910	1281
1988	184	3672	22	416	8624	6554	1378
1989*	46	3484	7	121	790	1154	679

* First 6 months only.

III. **Neonatal Tetanus decline in 1989 (6 first months**

Month	No. of Cases
January	468
February	223
March	164

Month	No. of Cases
April	132
May	93
June	74

Source: National Survey for vaccination coverage (Dec. 1987) MOH and UNICEF and Communicable Disease Report (MOH).

TABLE F7 - THE HOSPITAL NETWORK

I. CENTRAL AND GENERAL HOSPITALS (1950- 1989)

YEAR	NO. OF UNITS	NO. OF BEDS	RATIO BED PER 10000
1950	90	5089	2.49
1960	123	8526	3.27
1970	162	19785	5.99
1980	165	21562	5.10
1985	183	24275	5.03
1987	191	25468	4.97
1989	197	27699	5.35

II. SPECIALIZED HOSPITALS (1986)

TYPE	NO. OF UNITS	NO. OF BEDS	OUTPATIENT	INPATIENT
Chest	34	7,254	590,344	19,740
Psychiat.	8	8,594	71,278	11,451
Eyes	32	1,545	2,305,632	24,042
Fever	75	7,129	1,814,201	169,253
Skin	1	86	695,611	342
TOTAL	150	24,608	5,477,066	224,828

Source: Ministry of Health Statistics

F8 - OTHER PROVIDERS OF SECONDARY LEVEL MEDICAL CARE

1989	SOURCE	TYPE	UNITS	BEDS
Government *	MOH	Cent. & Gener.	197	27,699
		Specialized	150	24,608
	Railways	For employed	4	420
	MOE	For students	2	181
	MOI	Police & Jails	18	978
Public Sector	Big companies	For employed	N/A	1,066
	Cairo CCO	General public	12	3,593
	Alex CCO	General public	5	867
Social Sector	Health Ins. O.	For beneficiary	26	3,841
Private Sector	Private Hosp.	General public	245	N/A

* Information on military hospitals is not available.

Source: Third World Forum Report, March 1989.

TABLE F9 - DEGREE OF UTILIZATION OF HEALTH SERVICES

Hospitalization

Level of of Care	Types	Total Pop. Served	No. of Beds	Cases Admitted	Length of Stay	Occupancy Rate
Primary	Rural H	13,778	7,500	13,360	5 days	2%
Secondary	Gen.+Central	10,877	25468	893,405	6 days	58%
	Spec. Hosp.	10,877	24608	224,829	?	?
	Cairo CCO	6,528	2315	63,595	9 days	71%
	H. Inqur.H.	4.1	4041	117,997	8 days	64%
Tertiary	Teaching Hosp.	11.817	3358	76,259	8 days	51%
	Cairo Univ.	10421	2839	94,358	7 days	64%

Note: Data for rural, general, central and specialized hospitals pertained to a 1986 survey -- Cairo University Hospital 1985. Data for health insurance Cairo curative care organization and teaching refer to 1988-89 financial year.

Outpatient Services

Level of care	Sources	Population Served	OPD Visits In Thousand	Annual Attendance Ratio per per Benef.
Primary	Rural Units	13,778	21,827	1.6
Secondary	Gen. Center	10,877	20,386	1.9
	Spec. Hosp.	10,877	5,477	0.5
	Cairo CCO	6,528	785	0.12
	Health Ins.	4,141	1,510	2.1
	Health Ins. Policy Clinic	4,141	1,209	1.2
Tertiary	C. Univ. Hosp.	5,980	993	0.16
	Teaching Hosp.	6,528	768	0.016

Source: Ministry of Health

ANNEX F
Page 10 of 11

TABLE F10 - FUNCTIONAL DISTRIBUTION OF MOH PERSONNEL
(%)

Subsector	Physicians	Nurses
Hospital Services	55	52
Primary Care	24	30
Preventive Services	18	15
Administration	2	3
Total	100	100

Source: Ministry of Health

ANNEX F
Page 11 of 11

TABLE F11 - INFANT AND CHILD MORTALITY BY CAUSE OF DEATH (1982) (%)

Causes of Death	Neonatal Deaths	Infant Deaths	Child Deaths
Communicable Diseases	0.03	0.4	2.5
Acute Bronchitis Pneumonia and other Respiratory System Diseases	12.0	29.5	35.4
Diarrhea and Other Intestinal Diseases	11.6	47.2	45.8
Complications mainly due to pregnancy	49.6	12.2	6.5
Congenital Anomalies	7.6	1.9	2.4
Others	19.1	8.8	7.4
Total	100.0	100.0	100.0

Source: CAPMAS

ANNEX G: DATA ON HOUSING AND WATER SUPPLY

ANNEX G
Page 1 of 2

TABLE G1 - DWELLINGS BY SOURCE OF WATER IN 1986
(Percentages)

	Piped Public System	Pump	Well	Other	Total
URBAN	92.4	5.1	0.2	2.3	100
RURAL	55.9	31.6	1.1	11.4	100
TOTAL	73.1	19.1	0.7	7.1	100

Source: Population, Housing, and Establishment Census, CAPMAS, 1986.

TABLE G2 - DISTRIBUTION OF HOUSING UNITS BY TYPE

	Urban Areas		Rural Areas	
Apartment	4,612,324	78.7%	1,079,431	19.8%
Villa	19,837	0.3%	9,377	0.3%
Rural House	491,561	8.4%	4,148,255	76.0%
Separate Rooms	673,517	11.5%	170,013	3.1%
Marginal, Residential Places	61,732	1.1%	48,491	0.8%
Total	5,858,971	100.0%	5,455,567	100.0%

Source: 1986 Census, CAPMAS.

TABLE G3 - DISTRIBUTION OF HOUSING UNITS BY TYPE (%)

	Urban Areas	Rural Areas
Apartments	78.7	19.8
Marginal Residence	0.8	1.1
Separate Rooms	11.5	3.0
Rural Houses	8.4	76.0
Villas	0.3	0.3
Total	100.0	100.0

Source: 1986 Census, CAPMAS

TABLE G4 - HOUSING DEFICIT

Period	New Units Built	Additional Households
1960-1979	700,000	2,700,000
1981-86	812,000	844,000

Source: Ministry of Planning

ANNEX H: STATISTICS ON EDUCATION

ANNEX H
Page 1 of 3

TABLE H1 - GROWTH OF EDUCATION ENROLLMENTS

	Primary Education	Secondary Education	Higher Education
1951/52	1,092,816	154,341	37,668
1987/88	6,955,455	3,867,760	484,976
Average Annual Growth Rate	5.1%	9.1%	7.1%

Source: MOE and MOHE Statistics

TABLE H2 - ILLITERACY IN EGYPT
(% OF POPULATION AGE 10 AND ABOVE)

YEAR	MALE	FEMALE	TOTAL
1907	87.0	98.6	92.7
1917	86.8	97.7	91.2
1927	76.1	95.6	85.9
1937	76.6	93.9	85.2
1960	56.9	86.0	70.5
1976	42.6	72.5	57.2
1986	37.8	61.8	49.6

Sources: Population Census, CAPMAS
Hansen, 1989

ANNEX H

TABLE H3 - SEX DISPARITIES IN PRIMARY SCHOOLING
(%)

Year	Enrollment Rate (at age 6) Boys	Girls	Total	Participation Rate (6 - 11) Boys	Girls	Total	Proportion of Girls
1966/67	82.2	60.8	72.0	81.9	36.7	69.8	45.2
1970/71	88.9	63.0	77.5	81.6	54.3	68.5	39.9
1975/76	80.1	58.3	69.6	79.9	54.2	67.6	40.3
1980/81	87.0	69.5	78.6	77.8	57.5	68.1	40.5
1985/86	92.7	79.0	86.0	85.8	70.8	78.6	44.0
1986/87	98.0	82.6	90.4	88.1	74.1	81.6	45.6

Source: Ministry of Education

ANNEX H
Page 3 of 3

TABLE H4 - EVOLUTION OF THE NON-SCHOOLED POPULATION
(AGE 6-11)

Year	Reference Population Boys	Reference Population Girls	Out of School Boys	Out of School Girls	In School Boys	In School Girls
1966	2577	2428	466	1051	2111	1377
1967	2625	2460	499	1100	2126	1360
1968	2666	2487	501	1127	2165	1360
1969	2701	2511	513	1173	2188	1338
1970	2732	2533	503	1158	2229	1375
1971	2761	2555	478	1150	2283	1405
1972	2788	2578	466	1057	2322	1521
1973	2816	2604	569	1211	2247	1393
1974	2846	2632	538	1200	2308	1432
1975	2879	2665	579	1221	2300	1444
1976	2916	2703	548	1187	2368	1516
1977	2959	2748	586	1198	2373	1550
1978	3008	2800	635	1221	2373	1579
1979	3066	2859	650	1227	2416	1632
1980	3134	2928	696	1537	2438	1391
1981	3213	3006	681	1238	2532	1768
1982	3303	3094	641	1194	2662	1900
1983	3404	3193	603	1130	2801	2063
1984	3518	3303	559	1064	2959	2239
1985	3645	3424	518	1000	3127	2424
1986	3784	3558	450	922	3334	2636

Source: Ministry of Education and CAPMAS

# ANNEX I: DATA ON SOCIAL SECURITY AND TAXATION

TABLE I1 – ORGANIZATION OF THE EGYPTIAN SOCIAL SECURITY SYSTEM

ANNEX I

Dates of Basic Laws and Types of Programs	Coverage	Source of Funds	Qualifying Conditions
Old Age, Invalidity, Death First laws: 1950 (social assistance) and 1955 (provident and insurance fund). Current law: 1975 (basic pension), 1984 (supplementary pension). Social insurance system (1 pound equals 73.5 U.S. cents) Note: A 1984 amendment to the current law introduced supplementary, earnings-related benefits into the old-age, invalidity, and survivor pension program. Contributions are now paid on 100% of salary up to 250 pounds a month in the first tier, and on 30% of salary between 250 pounds and 625 pounds a month in the second. Any changes caused by the amendment are not reflected here due to a lack of details of the program.	Employed persons aged 18 and over (16 and over if government employees). Special systems for casual agricultural workers, domestic servants, and self-employed persons with modest income.	Insured person: 10% of earnings; self-employed, 15%. Employer: 15% of payroll. Government: 1% of payroll plus any deficit. Maximum earnings for contribution and benefit purposes: 625 pounds a month.	Old-age pension: Age 60 and 120 months of contribution (or age 55 with 240 months or employed under arduous conditions); reduced pension from any age if 240 months of contribution (contribution periods under prior public and private programs credited). Retirement from insured employment. Invalidity pension: Total and permanent incapacity for any gainful employment. Contributions during 3 consecutive months, or for total of 6 months. Survivor pension: Deceased met contribution conditions for invalidity pension or was pensioner at death. Lump sum compensation (if not qualified for pension): Age 60; leaving country; totally disabled; widow age 51.
Sickness and Maternity First law: 1959 (enabling provisions only) and 1964 (workers in public and private sectors). Current law: 1975. Social insurance system (cash and medical benefits)	Employed persons aged 18 and over (16 and over if government employees). Exclusions: Casual agricultural workers, domestic servants, and self-employed.	Insured person: 1% of earnings. Pensioner pays 1% of pension. Widow, 2% of survivor pension (optional). Employer: 4% of payroll (may be reduced to 3% for employers that provide cash and medical benefits to own employees). Government: None.	Cash sickness and medical benefits: Contributions throughout last 3 months, or for 6 months including last 2 months. Cash maternity benefits: Contributions throughout last 10 months.
Work Injury First law: 1936. Current law: 1975. Social insurance system	Employed persons aged 18 and over (16 and over if government employees). Exclusions: Casual agricultural workers, domestic servants, and self-employed.	Insured person: None. Employer: 3% of payroll (may be reduced to 2% or less if employer provides temporary disability benefits to own employees). Government: None.	Work-injury benefits: No minimum qualifying period.
Unemployment First law: 1959 (enabling provisions only). Current law: 1975. Compulsory insurance system	Employed persons. Exclusions: Casual agricultural workers, domestic servants, family labor, public employees, and employees over age 60.	Insured person: None. Employer: 2% of payroll. Government: Any deficit.	Unemployment benefits: 6 months of contribution, including 3 consecutive months. Able and willing to work; registration and regular reporting at manpower office. Unemployment not due to voluntary leaving, discharge for misconduct, refusal of suitable job offer, or refusal of training.
Family Allowances			

TABLE I1 (cont'd)

Cash Benefits for Insured Workers (except permanent disability)	Permanent Disability and Medical Benefits for Insured Workers	Survivor Benefits and Medical Benefits for Dependents	Administrative Organization
Old-age pension: 2.22% (up to 2.78% for periods of arduous work) of average monthly earnings during last 2 years times number of years of contribution (contribution periods under earlier public and private programs credited toward latter), plus lump-sum benefit equal to 15% of average annual wage for each year of contribution in excess of period required to qualify for maximum pension. Minimum pension: 20 pounds a month; maximum, 80% of average earnings (100% if average 30 pounds or less), or 200 pounds a month. Lump-sum compensation (if not qualified for pension): 15% of average annual wage during last 2 years times years of contribution. Special pension payable to all persons not covered under compulsory program.	*Invalidity pension:* 2.22% of average monthly earnings during the last year for each year of contribution plus 3 extra years, or 50% of average monthly earnings, whichever is greater. To the resulting percentage is added half the difference between it and 80% (maximum pension). Constant-attendance allowance: 20% of pension. Partial invalidity: Lump sum of 4 years' pension proportionate to degree of disability, if less than 30% disability. Minimum pension: 20 pounds a month; maximum, 80% of average earnings (100% if average 30 pounds or less) or 200 pounds a month. Special pension payable to all persons not covered under compulsory program. Lump-sum compensation (if not qualified for pension): 15% of average annual wage during last 2 years times years of contribution.	*Survivor pension:* 2.22% of average monthly earnings during the last year for each year of contribution plus 3 extra years, or 50% of average monthly earnings, whichever is greater. To the resulting percentage is added half the difference between it and 80% (maximum pension); minimum, 65% of average earnings. Minimum pension: 20 pounds a month; maximum, 80% of average earnings (100% if average 30 pounds or less) or 200 pounds a month. Pension divided among survivors, according to schedule in law: Dependent widow or widower; divorcee without other source of income and married at least 20 years; dependent sons and brothers under age 21 (26 if student, no limit if invalid); unmarried daughters and sisters; and dependent parents. Also payable to invalid widower. Death grant: 3 times the wage or pension in month death occurred. Funeral grant: 2 month's pension; minimum, 50 pounds. Lump-sum compensation (if not qualified for pension): 15% of average annual wage during last 2 years times years of contribution.	Ministry of Social Insurance, general supervision. Social Insurance Organization, administration of program through regional and district offices; managed by tripartite board. Insurance and Pensions Organization, administration of program for government employees through regional offices.
Sickness benefit: 75% of daily wage during 1st 90 days of sickness; 85% of earnings thereafter. 100% of earnings payable in case of specified chronic diseases. Minimum benefit: 12 pounds a month. Payable for up to 180 days in a calendar year, or without limit on duration for specified chronic diseases. *Maternity benefit:* 75% of daily wage. Payable for up to 50 days before and after confinement, 3 months for government employees.	*Medical benefits:* Service benefits provided by employer, public, or other facilities under contract with and paid directly by the Organization. Includes general and specialist care, surgery, hospitalization, maternity care, dental care, laboratory services, medicines, appliances, and transportation. Patients required to pay small fees for some services. Maximum duration: No limit.	*Medical benefits for dependents:* Medical care and treatment provided widow of the insured.	Ministry of Health, general supervision. Social Insurance Organization and Insurance and Pensions Organization, administration of contributions and cash benefits. Health Insurance Organization, administration of medical benefits through its own hospitals. Managed by tripartite board.
Temporary disability benefit (work injury): 100% of earnings. Payable from 1st day after injury until recovery or certification of permanent disability.	*Permanent disability pension* (work injury): 80% of average monthly earnings during last year (up to 100% when coupled with OASDI pension benefits), if totally disabled. Minimum pension: 20 pounds a month; maximum, 200 pounds a month. Partial disability: Percent of full pension proportionate to degree of disability, if latter 35% or over. Lump sum of 4 years' pension proportionate to degree of incapacity, if less than 35% disabled. Both pensions increased by 5% each 5 years disability continues, up to age 60. *Medical benefits* (work injury): General and specialist care, surgery, hospitalization, medicines, X-rays, appliances, and rehabilitation.	*Survivor pension* (work injury): 80% of average monthly earnings of deceased during last year (up to 100% when coupled with OASDI pension benefits). Minimum pension: 20 pounds a month; maximum, 200 pounds a month. Pension divided among following survivors, according to schedule in law: Widow of any age, dependent sons and brothers under age 21 (26 if student, no limit if invalid); unmarried daughters and sisters; and dependent parents. Any pension may be commuted to lump sum. Also payable to invalid widower. Funeral grant: 2 months' pension; minimum, 50 pounds.	Ministry of Social Insurance, general supervision. Social Insurance Organization and Insurance and Pensions Organization, administration of contributions and cash benefits. Health Insurance Organization, administration of medical benefits.
Unemployment benefit: 60% of last monthly wage. Payable after 7-day waiting period for up to 16 weeks (may be extended to 28 weeks if contributions paid throughout last 24 months).			Ministry of Social Insurance, general supervision. Social Insurance Organization, administration of program, in collaboration with local manpower offices.

TABLE I2 - NUMBERS OF HEALTH INSURANCE BENEFICIARIES
1977 - 1987
(In Thousands)

Year	No. of Beneficiaries
1977	1,081
1978	1,255
1979	1,427
1980	1,651
1981	2,516
1982	2,720
1983	2,950
1984	3,073
1985	3,225
1986	3,630
1987	3,750

Source: Health Insurance Organization 1987.

TABLE I3 - TOTAL NUMBER OF INSURED IN SOCIAL INSURANCE SCHEMES
(IN THOUSANDS)

Year	General Scheme	Self-Employed	Migrant Workers	Temporary and Domestic Workers	Total
1980-81	5,781	578	10	3,934	10,303
1981-82	6,025	626	12	4,007	10,668
1982-83	6,162	798	15	3,969	10,944
1983-84	6,339	908	19	3,953	11,219
1984-85	6,639	960	21	3,963	11,583
1985-86	6,877	1,023	27	4,092	12,019
1986-87	7,158	1,080	29	4,265	12,532
1987-88	7,474	1,146	31	4,399	13,050
1988-89	7,691	1,199	33	4,526	13,449

Source: Ministry of Social Insurance

TABLE I4 - **TOTAL SOCIAL INSURANCE EARNINGS AND EXPENDITURES (1984-1989)**
(IN LE MILLIONS)

Year	Earnings	Expenditures	Surplus
1980-81	685.3	535.3	150.0
1981-82	1,016.9	753.2	263.7
1982-83	1,131.2	858.2	273.0
1983-84	1,357.0	1,042.9	314.10
1984-85	1,828.0	1,194.7	633.3
1985-86	2,151.0	1,410.8	740.2
1986-87	2,284.2	1,529.9	754.3
1987-88	2,635.7	1,837.0	798.7
1988-89	3,033.2	2,020.5	1,012.7

Source: Ministry of Social Insurance

TABLE I5 - EARNINGS BY SOCIAL INSURANCE SYSTEM
(IN LE MILLIONS)

Year	General System	Self-Employed	Migrant Workers	Temporary and Domestic Workers	Total
1980-81	671.9	23.6	4.6	35.2	685.3
1981-82	939.9	31.4	4.9	40.7	1,016.9
1982-83	1,056.1	35.7	6.1	33.3	1,131.2
1983-84	1,263.0	49.1	7.8	37.1	1,357.0
1984-85	1,714.8	65.3	10.0	37.9	1,838.0
1985-86	2,022.2	69.0	15.2	45.2	2,151.6
1986-87	2,151.4	73.5	14.0	45.3	2,284.2
1987-88	2,501.4	77.2	10.5	46.6	2,635.7
1988-89	2,915.0	85.6	14.4	18.2	3,033.2

Source: Ministry of Social Insurance

TABLE I6 - EXPENDITURES BY SOCIAL INSURANCE SYSTEM
(IN LE MILLIONS)

Year	Temporary and Domestic Workers	All Other Systems	Total
1980-81	74.7	460.6	535.3
1981-82	181.0	572.2	753.2
1982-83	188.3	669.9	858.2
1983-84	189.0	853.9	1,042.9
1984-85	192.4	1,002.3	1,194.7
1985-86	208.3	1,202.5	1,410.8
1986-87	194.2	1,335.7	1,529.9
1987-88	196.5	1,640.5	1,837.0
1988-89	206.7	1,813.8	2,020.5

Source: Ministry of Social Insurance

TABLE I7 - COMPOSITION OF EGYPTIAN TAX REVENUE
(1980/81 TO 1986/87)

	Total Direct Taxes*	**Total Indirect Taxes****
1980/81		
LE Millions	1,622.4	2,354.9
Percent	40.8	59.2
1981/82		
LE Millions	1,701.4	2,821.0
Percent	37.6	62.4
1982/83		
LE Millions	1,929.0	3,271.4
Percent	37.1	62.9
1983/84		
LE Millions	1.649.2	3,713.9
Percent	30.8	69.2
1984/85		
LE Millions	1,994.2	3,928.7
Percent	33.7	66.3
1985/86		
LE Millions	2,452.0	4,066.8
Percent	37.7	62.3
1986/87		
LE Millions	2,390.9	4,445.7
Percent	35.0	65.0

*   Direct taxes are corporate profit tax, income tax, estate duties and taxes on Immovable property.

** Indirect taxes are consumption tax, import duties, stamp tax and other.

Sources: Ministry of Finance.

ND
ANNEX J: SOCIAL SECTORS BUDGET DATA

ANNEX J
Page 1 of 11

TABLE J1 - FUNCTIONAL DISTRIBUTION

Subsector	Resources (LE Million)	Percentage
Hospital Services	320	61
Primary Care	116	22
Preventive Services	79	15
Administration	10	2
TOTAL	525	100

Source: Ministry of Health

TABLE J2 - DISTRIBUTION OF EXPENDITURES BY LEVEL OF EDUCATION (%)

	Share of the Population	Share of Education Expenditure
No Schooling	30	0
Primary Schooling Only	40	20
Preparatory Schooling Only	12	13
Secondary Schooling Only	8	17
University	10	50
TOTAL	100	100

Source: Abdel-Fadil, 1982, Ministry of Education data

TABLE J3 - PROPORTIONAL DISTRIBUTION OF RESOURCES BETWEEN LEVEL AND TYPES OF EDUCATION
(1987/88)

(Million Pounds)

	Investment	Recurrent	Students
Primary	87.6	758.8	6,631,265
Preparatory	32.8	359.6	2,447,065
General Secondary	6.2	104.3	564,678
Technical Secondary	29.9	247.4	901,271
Higher Institutes	4.3	25.9	190,961
Universities	117.2	666.6	502,532
TOTAL	278.0	2162.6	11,237,772

* Including USAID grant.

Source: Ministy of Education/Ministry of Higher Education statistics

(Percentage)

	Investment	Recurrent	Students
Primary	31.5	35.5	59.0
Preparatory	11.8	16.6	21.8
General Secondary	2.2	16.2	5.0
Technical Secondary	10.8	11.4	8.0
Higher Institutes	1.5	32.1	1.7
Universities	42.2	30.8	4.5
TOTAL	100.0	100.0	100.0

Source: Ministy of Education/Ministry of Higher Education

TABLE J4 - EXPENDITURES ON SUBSIDIES & SUPPLIES: PER CAPITA/PER STUDENT (IN 1980 LE)

	Health	Social Affairs	Education	Higher Education
1980/81	1.26	1.74	7.14	146.67
1981/82	1.42	1.06	7.43	159.71
1982/83	1.47	0.97	6.69	154.18
1983/84	1.47	0.69	5.92	156.31
1984/85	1.08	0.70	5.47	168.65
1985/86	0.95	0.61	4.73	158.86
1986/87	0.76	0.46	3.67	132.91
1987/88	0.92	0.41	3.43	142.09
1988/89	0.59	0.37	2.77	112.31
1989/90	0.55	0.33	2.37	123.90

TABLE J5 - SHARE OF EXPENDITURES IN GDP (%)

	Health	Social Affairs	Education	Higher Education	Total
1980/81	0.9	0.6	2.2	1.1	4.8
1981/82	1.1	0.5	2.7	1.3	5.6
1982/83	1.1	0.5	2.7	1.4	5.7
1983/84	1.0	0.4	2.7	1.5	5.6
1984/85	1.0	0.4	2.8	1.7	5.9
1985/86	0.9	0.4	2.8	1.6	5.7
1986/87	0.8	0.3	2.7	1.4	5.2
1987/88	0.8	0.3	2.5	1.4	5.0
1988/89	0.7	0.3	2.3	1.2	4.5
1989/90	0.6	0.3	2.0	1.1	4.0

Source: Ministry of Finance statistics

TABLE J6 - SOCIAL EXPENDITURES IN GOVERNMENT BUDGET (%)

Year	Education	Higher Education	Health	Social Affairs	TOTAL
1980/81	5.1	2.5	2.0	1.4	11.0
1981/82	7.1	3.2	2.8	1.2	14.3
1982/83	7.5	3.8	3.0	1.3	15.6
1983/84	7.2	3.9	2.8	1.1	15.0
1984/85	7.7	4.6	2.8	1.2	16.3
1985/86	7.9	4.4	2.6	1.1	16.0
1986/87	8.6	4.6	2.7	1.1	17.0
1987/88	8.7	4.9	2.9	1.1	17.6
1988/89	8.7	4.8	2.6	1.1	17.2
1989/90	8.8	5.1	2.8	1.1	17.8

Source: Ministry of Finance

TABLE J7 - TOTAL EXPENDITURES PER CAPITA/PER STUDENT (IN 1980 LE)

	Health	Social Affairs	Education	Higher Education
1980/81	3.52	2.37	51.48	331.06
1981/82	4.77	2.004	69.10	405.34
1982/83	5.11	2.10	73.57	467.87
1983/84	5.86	2.17	88.98	573.45
1984/85	6.42	2.43	100.53	735.63
1985/86	6.88	2.59	119.71	834.23
1986/87	8.04	2.98	146.13	1038.16
1987/88	10.27	3.67	184.62	1436.04
1988/89	11.14	4.24	205.96	1684.98
1989/90	13.02	4.81	230.66	1951.36

Source: MOF, MOE, MOH, MOSA, MOHE

TABLE J8 - SOCIAL EXPENDITURES: HEALTH
(MILLIONS LE)

	CPI	GSI/SSE	Expenditures in Nominal Terms	Expenditures in Real Terms Salaries	Subsidies & Supplies	Total
1980/81	100	100	148.4	95.5	52.9	148.4
1981/82	114.7	107.5	226.5	144.9	61.6	206.5
1982/83	132.7	108.8	263.3	162.0	65.6	227.6
1983/84	162.0	97.5	298.4	211.1	57.2	268.3
1984/85	178.7	96.2	333.3	252.1	50.8	302.9
1985/86	203.7	88.8	349.2	287.9	45.9	333.8
1986/87	252.0	75.0	366.5	361.1	38.0	399.1
1987/88	302.4	28.8	467.3	474.3	46.6	520.9
1988/89	359.6	67.0	477.3	547.6	30.7	578.3
1989/90	431.5	66.0	565.6	666.2	29.2	691.4

TABLE J9 - SOCIAL EXPENDITURES: SOCIAL AFFAIRS
(MILLIONS LE)

	CPI	GSI/SSE	Expenditures in Nominal Terms	Expenditures in Real Terms Salaries	Subsidies & Supplies	Total
1980/81	100	100	99.8	26.6	73.2	99.8
1981/82	114.7	107.5	98.2	42.3	45.9	88.2
1982/83	132.7	108.8	111.7	50.3	43.0	93.3
1983/84	162.0	97.5	117.1	67.8	31.5	99.3
1984/85	178.7	96.2	137.5	81.5	33.1	114.6
1985/86	203.7	88.8	145.6	96.0	29.8	125.8
1986/87	252.0	75.0	151.2	124.7	22.9	147.6
1987/88	302.4	28.8	177.2	165.7	20.9	186.6
1988/89	359.6	67.0	203.6	201.2	19.2	220.4
1989/90	431.5	66.0	232.9	238.0	17.6	255.6

GSI = Government Salary Index
SSE = Share of Salaries in Expenditures
Source: Ministry of Finance

TABLE J10 - SOCIAL EXPENDITURES: EDUCATION
(MILLIONS LE)

	CPI	GSI/SSE	Expenditures in Nominal Terms	Expenditures in Real Terms		
				Salaries	Subsidies & Supplies	Total
1980/81	100	100	372.2	320.6	51.6	372.2
1981/82	114.7	107.5	569.3	469.3	56.5	525.8
1982/83	132.7	108.8	657.9	539.0	53.9	592.9
1983/84	162.0	97.5	774.0	709.8	50.6	760.4
1984/85	178.7	96.2	915.8	860.0	49.5	909.5
1985/86	203.7	88.8	1071.0	1102.1	45.32	1147.4
1986/87	252.0	75.0	1172.4	1444.9	35.2	1480.1
1987/88	302.4	28.8	1423.8	1910.5	36.2	1946.7
1988/89	359.6	67.0	1581.5	2199.2	30.0	2229.2
1989/90	431.5	66.0	1788.8	2538.5	26.3	2564.8

TABLE J11 - SOCIAL EXPENDITURES: HIGHER EDUCATION
(MILLIONS LE)

	CPI	GSI/SSE	Expenditures in Nominal Terms	Expenditures in Real Terms		
				Salaries	Subsidies & Supplies	Total
1980/81	100	100	180.8	100.7	80.1	180.8
1981/82	114.7	107.5	569.3	143.5	93.3	236.8
1982/83	132.7	108.8	337.8	194.1	95.4	289.5
1983/84	162.0	97.5	418.0	264.2	99.0	363.2
1984/85	178.7	96.2	550.9	368.8	109.7	478.5
1985/86	203.7	88.8	599.3	438.3	103.1	541.4
1986/87	252.0	75.0	625.5	558.5	82.0	640.5
1987/88	302.4	28.8	791.5	775.9	85.2	861.1
1988/89	359.6	67.0	860.3	928.4	66.3	994.7
1989/90	431.5	66.0	1026.9	1078.2	73.1	1151.3

GSI = Government Salary Index
SSE = Share of Salaries in Expenditures

Source: Ministry of Finance

TABLE J12 - RECURRENT BUDGET EXPENDITURES
(IN MILLION EGYPTIAN POUNDS)

(EDUCATION)

Year	Salaries	Subsidies & Supplies	Total
1980/81	320.60	49.10	372.20
1981/82	504.50	63.50	569.30
1982/83	586.40	70.20	657.90
1983/84	692.00	80.30	774.00
1984/85	827.30	86.70	915.80
1985/86	978.70	90.50	1071.00
1986/87	1083.70	86.10	1172.40
1987/88	1314.40	106.00	1423.80
1988/89	1473.50	106.20	15?1.50
1989/90	1675.40	110.90	1788.80

FUNCTIONAL DISTRIBUTION OF RECURRENT EDUCATION EXPENDITURES

Year	Salaries	Subsidies & Supplies
1980/81	86.14%	13.19%
1981/82	88.62%	11.15%
1982/83	89.13%	10.67%
1983/84	89.41%	10.37%
1984/85	90.34%	9.47%
1985/86	91.38%	8.45%
1986/87	92.43%	7.34%
1987/88	92.32%	7.44%
1988/89	93.17%	6.72%
1989/90	93.66%	6.20%

Source: Ministry of Finance

ANNEX J
Page 8 of 11

TABLE J13 - RECURRENT BUDGET EXPENDITURES IN MILLION EGYPTIAN POUNDS)

(HEALTH)

Year	Salaries	Subsidies & Supplies	Total
1980/81	95.50	52.40	148.40
1981/82	155.80	70.40	226.50
1982/83	176.30	86.70	263.30
1983/84	205.80	92.30	298.40
1984/85	242.50	90.40	333.30
1985/86	255.70	92.20	349.20
1986/87	270.80	92.10	366.50
1987/88	326.30	123.40	467.30
1988/89	366.90	90.10	477.30
1989/90	439.70	102.00	565.60

FUNCTIONAL DISTRIBUTION OF RECURRENT HEALTH EXPENDITURES

Year	Salaries	Subsidies & Supplies
1980/81	64.35%	35.31%
1981/82	68.79%	31.08%
1982/83	66.96%	32.93%
1983/84	68.97%	30.93%
1984/85	72.76%	27.12%
1985/86	73.22%	26.40%
1986/87	73.89%	25.13%
1987/88	69.83%	26.41%
1988/89	76.87%	18.88%
1989/90	77.74%	18.03%

Source: Ministry of Finance

TABLE J14 - RECURRENT BUDGET EXPENDITURES
(IN MILLION EGYPTIAN POUNDS)

(HIGHER EDUCATION AND SCIENCE)

Year	Salaries	Subsidies & Supplies	Total
1980/81	100.70	73.30	180.80
1981/82	154.20	97.40	261.20
1982/83	211.20	114.00	337.80
1983/84	257.60	147.90	418.00
1984/85	354.80	177.50	550.90
1985/86	389.20	175.70	599.30
1986/87	418.90	154.90	625.50
1987/88	533.80	194.50	791.50
1988/89	622.00	197.10	860.30
1989/90	711.60	228.90	1026.90

FUNCTIONAL DISTRIBUTION OF RECURRENT HIGHER EDUCATION AND SCIENCE EXPENDITURES

Year	Salaries	Subsidies & Supplies
1980/81	55.70%	40.54%
1981/82	59.04%	37.29%
1982/83	62.52%	33.75%
1983/84	61.63%	35.38%
1984/85	64.40%	32.22%
1985/86	64.94%	29.32%
1986/87	66.97%	24.76%
1987/88	67.44%	24.57%
1988/89	72.30%	22.91%
1989/90	69.30%	22.29%

Source: Ministry of Finance

ANNEX J
Page 10 of 11

TABLE J15 - RECURRENT BUDGET EXPENDITURES
(IN MILLION EGYPTIAN POUNDS)

(SOCIAL AFFAIRS AND INSURANCE)

Year	Salaries	Subsidies & Supplies	Total
1980/81	26.60	72.60	99.80
1981/82	45.50	52.50	98.20
1982/83	54.70	55.70	111.70
1983/84	66.10	50.90	117.10
1984/85	78.40	58.90	137.50
1985/86	85.20	59.90	145.60
1986/87	93.50	57.30	151.20
1987/88	114.00	62.50	177.20
1988/89	134.60	39.50	203.60
1989/90	157.10	42.10	232.90

FUNCTIONAL DISTRIBUTION OF RECURRENT SOCIAL AFFAIRS AND INSURANCE EXPENDITURES

Year	Salaries	Subsidies & Supplies
1980/81	26.65%	72.75%
1981/82	46.33%	53.46%
1982/83	48.97%	49.87%
1983/84	56.45%	43.47%
1984/85	57.02%	42.84%
1985/86	58.52%	41.14%
1986/87	61.84%	37.90%
1987/88	64.33%	35.27%
1988/89	66.11%	19.40%
1989/90	67.45%	18.08%

Source: Ministry of Finance

ANNEX J
Page 11 of 11

TABLE J16 - FUNCTIONAL DISTRIBUTION OF MOH INVESTMENT BUDGET (FIVE-YEAR PLAN 1987-92)

Subsector	Resources (LE Million)	Percentage
Curative Services	245	65
Primary Health Care	109	29
Preventive Services	22	6
TOTAL	376	100

Source: Ministry of Health

ANNEX K: CALCULATION OF AN ULTRA-POVERTY LINE

ANNEX K
Page 1 of 1

CALCULATION OF AN ULTRA-POVERTY LINE

Lipton (1988) defines the ultrapoor as those households whose food consumption is equal to less than 85% of the minimum level of food expenditures calculated to estimate the poverty line. Based on this definition and using Ghattas' estimate of the poverty line (World Bank, 1989), the thresholds for ultrapoverty in rural and urban Egypt were estimated as follows:

Urban Areas:

Poverty Line:	LE 831.9
Food Expenditure (80% of minimum basket):	LE 394.7
Food Expenditure as percentage of total income:	64.3%
Ultrapoverty line:	LE 394.7/.643 = 613.8

Rural Areas:

Poverty Line:	LE 680.1
Food Expenditure (80% of minimum basket):	LE 351.5
Food Expenditure as percentage of total income:	69.6%
Ultrapoverty line:	LE 351.5/.696 = 505.28

ANNEX L: METHODOLOGICAL NOTE ON THE CALCULATION OF EDUCATIONAL EXPENDITURES AMONG VARIOUS GROUPS

ANNEX L
Page 1 of 2

METHODOLOGICAL NOTE ON THE CALCULATION OF EDUCATIONAL EXPENDITURES AMONG VARIOUS GROUPS

The following formula is used to compute the share (Si) of total educational expenditures received by a given population group i:

$$Si = \frac{(X^i_B \times B) + (X^i_P \times P) + (X^i_S \times S) + (X^i_H \times H)}{B + P + S + H} \times 100$$

Where:

B = budget for primary education
P = budget for preparatory level
S = budget for secondary education
H = budget for higher education

and the X^i_s represent the proportion of youths from group i attending basic, preparatory, secondary and tertiary education.

In 1987/88, the education budget (investment and recurrent) was distributed as follows:

- primary education   : 846.4 million LE
- preparatory education : 392.4 million LE
- secondary education   : 387.8 million LE
- higher education   : 814.0 million LE

To measure for instance the share of educational resources received by girls, one needs to consider the preparation of girls in basic, preparatory, secondary and tertiary education which were respectively on the basis,

$$S \text{ girls} = \frac{.441 \times 846.4 + .403 \times 392.4 + .376 \times 387.8 + .350 \times 814.0 \times 100}{2440.6}$$

= 39.5%

To calculate the distribution of education expenditures by socioeconomic origin, two operations were necessary. First, the evolution of an education cohort was simulated to measure the percentage of students reaching the various levels of the education ladder. Using observed promotion, repetition and dropout rates for children entering primary school in 1970-71, the following results were computed.

1970 cohort	10,000
access to primary education:	7,000
access to preparatory level:	3,000
access to secondary level :	1,800
access to university :	1,500
graduating from University :	1,200

ANNEX L
Page 2 of 2

The second step consisted of making assumptions on the socioeconomic distribution of students by education level, using data presented in Abdel-Fadil's pages (1982) and 1976 census statistics on the socioeconomic distribution of the male labor force.

SOCIOECONOMIC ORIGIN OF STUDENTS BY EDUCATION LEVEL
(%)

	Low Income	Middle Income	Upper Income
Never Schooled	25	67	8
Primary Level	15	75	10
Preparatory Level	13	75	12
Secondary Level	10	72	18
Tertiary Level	8	72	20

The distribution of education expenditures by socioeconomic group was then calculated on the basis of the formula presented at the beginning of the Annex.

For example, for the low-income group (Group L),

$$S_L = \frac{.15 \times 846.4 + .13 \times 392.4 + .10 \times 387.8 + .08 \times 814.0}{2440.6}$$

$$= 11.5\%$$

Bibliographical References

Background Documents on Poverty Alleviation and Other Dimensions of Social Development

Addison, T., and Demery, L., "The Economics of Poverty Alleviation under Adjustment", Overseas Development Institute, London, March 1988.

Altimir, O., and Sourrouille, J., "Measuring Levels of Living in Latin America: an Overview of Main Problems", World Bank, Living Standards Measurement Study, working paper number No 3, 1980.

Fallon, P. and Riveros, L., "Adjustment and the Labor Market," PPR Working Papers WPS 214, Washington, D.C.: World Bank, June 1989.

Foster, J., Greer, J., and Thorbecke, E., "A class of decomposable poverty measures", Econometrica, vol. 52 No 3 (May), pp 761-766.

Friedman, M., Capitalism and Freedom, University of Chicago Press, 1962.

Glewwe, P., and de Tray, D., "The Poor in Latin America during Adjustment": a Case Study of Peru", World Bank, Living Standards Measurement Study, working paper No 56, 1989.

Glewwe, P., and van der Gaag, J., "Confronting Poverty in Developing Countries: Definitions, Information, and Policies", World Bank, Living Standards Measurement Study, working paper No 48, 1988.

Kanbur, R., "The Principles of Targeting", University of Warwick, UK, mimeo, March 1988

Karim, R.M. and Levinson, F.J. The Bangladesh Sorghum Experiment. Food Policy, Feb. 1980.

Mayer, S.E., and Jencks, C., "Poverty and the Distribution of Material Hardship", The Journal of Human Resources, volume XXIV, 1, 1989, pp. 88-114.

Psacharopoulos, G., " The perverse effects of public subsidization of education or how equitable is free education?", Comparative Education Review, vol 21, 1977.

Rogers, B., et al., 1981. Nutrition Intervention in Developing Countries, Study V: Consumer Food Subsidies. Oelgeschlager, Gunn and Hain, Cambridge, Massachusetts.

Sen, A.K., *Poverty and Famines*, Oxford, 1981.

Temali, M. and Campbell, C., "Business Incubator Profiles: A National Survey," Minneapolis, MN: Hubert H. Humphrey Institute, 1984. (mimeo)

Selected Documents on Egypt

Alderman, Harold and Joachim von Braun, "The Effects of the Egyptian Food Ration and Subsidy System on Income Distribution and Consumption". International Food Policy Research Institute, Research Report Number 45, Washington, D.C., July 1984.

Abdel-Fadil, M., "Educational Expansion and Income Distribution in Egypt, 1952-1977", in Abdel-Khalek, G., and Tignor, R., ed., *The Political Economy of Income Distribution in Egypt*, Holmes and Meier Publishers, London, 1982.

Adams, R. H. Jr., "Worker Remittances and Inequality in Rural Egypt," *Economic Development and Cultural Change*, October 1989, pp. 45-71.

Assad, R., "The Employment Crisis in Egypt: Trends and Issues," Cairo: American University in Cairo, 1989. (mimeo)

Assad, R. and Commander, S., "Egypt: The Labour Market Through Boom and Recession," July 1989 (mimeo)

Bol, D., "The Economics of the Productive Families Programme in Egypt", CDP, Utrecht, 1986.

Capmas and Unicef, *The State of Egyptian Children*, Cairo, June 1988.

Catholic Relief Service, "The Effect of Food Costs on Family Behavior". CRS, Cairo, 1989.

Dethier, Jean-Jacques. 1989. Trade, Exchange Rate, and Agricultural Pricing Policies in Egypt. Volume I: The Country Study. World Bank Comparative Studies. World Bank, Washington, D.C.

Eckaus, R.S., McCarthy, F.D., and Mohie-Eldin, A., "A Social Accounting Matrix for Egypt", *Journal of Development Economics*, 9 (1981), pp. 183-203.

El Safy, M., "Cairo: The Urban Scene", Mimeo, American University of Cairo, 1987.

El Salmi, A., *Public Sector Management: An Analysis of Decision-Making and Employment Policies and Practices in Egypt*, Geneva: ILO, 1983, p. 30.

Euroconsult, "Evaluation of socio-economic impact of the Productive Families Programme in Sohag Province, Egypt", Arnhem, the Netherlands, 1987.

Galal, O. and Ezzat A., "Nutrition: Proceedings of a Workshop on Identification and Prioritization of Nutritional Problems in Egypt". Ministry of Health, Nutrition Institute and United Nation Children's Fund. Cairo, Egypt, October 1984.

Hailey, J., "The Productive Families Programme Export Strategies", for the British Council, Cairo, April 1988.

Handoussa, H., Public Sector Employment and Productivity in the Egyptian Economy, Geneva: ILO, 1983

Handoussa, H. "The Burden of Public Service Employment and Remuneration: A Case Study of Egypt," prepared for the ILO, Cairo: The American University in Cairo, 1988. (mimeo)

Handoussa, H., "Small and Medium Scale Industries and Economic Development in Egypt," Cairo: The American University in Cairo, 1989. (mimeo)

Hansen, B. and Radwan, S., Employment Opportunities and Equity in Egypt, Geneva: ILO, 1982.

Hansen, B., "The Egyptian Labor Market An Overview," Report No. DRD169, Development Research Department, Economics and Research Staff, Washington, D.C.: World Bank, 1985, p.30.

Hansen, B., "A Full Employment Economy and its Responses to External Shocks: The Labor Market in Egypt from World War II," Report No. DRD253, Development Research Department, Economics and Research Staff, Washington, D.C.: World Bank, 1986.

Hansen, B., The Political Economy of Poverty, Equity and Growth in Egypt, World Bank publication, forthcoming, 1990.

Hopkins, N., Agrarian Transformation in Egypt, Westview Special Studies, Westview Press, U.K., 1987.

Hussein, M.A., Gazi, C. Bassiuny, N.M., Fayad, I and Nelson C., "Influence of Cultural and Traditional Beliefs of Mothers in an Egyptian Village upon their Nutrition Habits and Child Feeding," 1978.

Ibrahim, S., "Social Mobility and Income Distribution in Egypt, 1952-1977", in Abdel-Khalek, G., and Tignor, R., ed., The Political Economy of Income Distribution in Egypt, Holmes and Meier Publishers, London, 1982.

International Labor Organization, Employment Strategy: Egypt in the 1990's, an issues paper prepared for the National Conference on Employment Strategy, Geneva: ILO, 1988.

Ismail, A.F., Casterline, J.B., and Cooksey, E., "Household Income and Child Survival", in Hallouda, A., Farid, S., and Cochrane, S., ed., Demographic Responses to Modernization, CAPMAS, Cairo, 1988.

Joint Egyptian-American Team, "Basic Education in Egypt", Washington D.C., 1979.

Jones, R. M., "Small Scale Industry in Egypt: An Examination of Channels Available to Donors for Activities in Small Scale Industry Sector in Egypt," prepared for the Development and Co-operation Division of the Netherlands Embassy, Cairo: 1988.

Korayem, K., "The Impact of Economic Adjustment Policies on the Vulnerable Families and Children in Egypt," The Third World Forum and UNICEF, Cairo, 1987.

Latowfsky, R., "Evaluation of Project Support for the Productive Families Credit Program", prepared by the Royal Netherlands Embassy, Cairo, mimeo, July 1987.

Makinson, C., "Sex Differentials in Infant and Child Mortality in Egypt", Unpublished Ph.D. dissertation, Princeton University, 1986.

National Bank of Egypt, "The Taxation System in Egypt", Economic Bulletin, vol. 37, No. 1, 1984.

Radwan, S., and Lee, E., Agrarian Change in Egypt: an Anatomy of Rural Poverty, Croom Helm, London, 1986.

Rashad, H., "Measuring the Demographic Impact of Oral Rehydration TherapyL Learning from Experience", Population Council Regional Paper, 1988.

Richards, A., "Rural Migration and Its Impact on Agricultural Production and Rural Development in the Near East," prepared for the Food and Agriculture Organization of the United Nations, Rome, May 1989 (mimeo)

Richards, A., "Agricultural Employment, Wages, and Government Policy in Egypt During and After the Oil Boom," prepared for the International Labor Organization, Cairo: The American University in Cairo, 1989b.

Rizk, K., "Structure et Fonctionnement du Secteur Informel en Egypte," Faculte d'Economie et de Sciences Politiques, Universite du Caire, September 1988 (mimeo), p. 16.

Shorter, F., "Cairo's Leap Forward: People, Households and Dwelling Space," Papers in Social Science, Vol. 12, No. 1, Spring 1989, The American University in Cairo Press.

Springborg, R., "Rolling Back Agrarian Reform in Egypt," Macquarie University, Australia, September 1989, Mimeo.

von Braun, and de Haen, H., "The Effects of Food Price and Subsidy Policies on Egyptian Agriculture". International Food Policy Research Institute Research Report Number 42. Washington, D.C., November 1983.

Waterbury, J., "Patterns of Urban Growth and Income Distribution in Egypt", in

Abdel-Khalek, G. and Tignor, R., ed., <u>The Political Economy of Income Distribution in Egypt</u>, Holmes and Meier Publishers, London, 1982.

World Bank, "Egypt Industrial Sector Memorandum", Report 7491-EGT, 2 volumes, Washington, D.C.: World Bank, November 1988.

World Bank (a), "Arab Republic of Egypt: A Study on Poverty and the Distribution of Income", a draft report of the Country Operations Division, CDIII, EMENA, January 5, 1989.

World Bank (b), "Arab Republic of Egypt Country Economic Memorandum: Economic Readjustment with Growth", Report No. 7447-EGT, 2 volumes, Washington, D.C.: World Bank, January 1989.

Zurayk, H., and Shorter, F., "The Social Composition of Households in Arab Cities and Settlements: Cairo, Beirut and Amman", The Population Council Regional Papers, West Asia and North Africa, Giza, Egypt, 1988.

Distributors of World Bank Publications

ARGENTINA
Carlos Hirsch, SRL
Galería Guemes
Florida 165, 4th Floor-Ofc. 453/465
1333 Buenos Aires

AUSTRALIA, PAPUA NEW GUINEA, FIJI, SOLOMON ISLANDS, VANUATU, AND WESTERN SAMOA
D.A. Books & Journals
648 Whitehorse Road
Mitcham 3132
Victoria

AUSTRIA
Gerold and Co.
Graben 31
A-1011 Wien

BAHRAIN
Bahrain Research and Consultancy
Associates Ltd.
P.O. Box 22103
Manama Town 317

BANGLADESH
Micro Industries Development
Assistance Society (MIDAS)
House 5, Road 16
Dhanmondi R/Area
Dhaka 1209

Branch offices:
Main Road
Maijdee Court
Noakhali - 3800

76, K.D.A. Avenue
Kulna

BELGIUM
Jean De Lannoy
Av. du Roi 202
1060 Brussels

CANADA
Le Diffuseur
C.P. 85, 1501B rue Ampère
Boucherville, Québec
J4B 5E6

CHINA
China Financial & Economic
Publishing House
8, Da Fo Si Dong Jie
Beijing

COLOMBIA
Infoenlace Ltda.
Apartado Aereo 34270
Bogota D.E.

COTE D'IVOIRE
Centre d'Edition et de Diffusion
Africaines (CEDA)
04 B.P. 541
Abidjan 04 Plateau

CYPRUS
MEMRB Information Services
P.O. Box 2098
Nicosia

DENMARK
SamfundsLitteratur
Rosenoerns Allé 11
DK-1970 Frederiksberg C

DOMINICAN REPUBLIC
Editora Taller, C. por A.
Restauración e Isabel la Católica 309
Apartado Postal 2190
Santo Domingo

EL SALVADOR
Fusades
Avenida Manuel Enrique Araujo #3530
Edificio SISA, ler. Piso
San Salvador

EGYPT, ARAB REPUBLIC OF
Al Ahram
Al Galaa Street
Cairo

The Middle East Observer
8 Chawarbi Street
Cairo

FINLAND
Akateeminen Kirjakauppa
P.O. Box 128
SF-00101
Helsinki 10

FRANCE
World Bank Publications
66, avenue d'Iéna
75116 Paris

GERMANY
UNO-Verlag
Poppelsdorfer Allee 55
D-5300 Bonn 1

GREECE
KEME
24, Ippodamou Street Platia Plastiras
Athens-11635

GUATEMALA
Librerias Piedra Santa
5a. Calle 7-55
Zona 1
Guatemala City

HONG KONG, MACAO
Asia 2000 Ltd.
6 Fl., 146 Prince Edward
Road, W.
Kowloon
Hong Kong

INDIA
Allied Publishers Private Ltd.
751 Mount Road
Madras - 600 002

Branch offices:
15 J.N. Heredia Marg
Ballard Estate
Bombay - 400 038

13/14 Asaf Ali Road
New Delhi - 110 002

17 Chittaranjan Avenue
Calcutta - 700 072

Jayadeva Hostel Building
5th Main Road Gandhinagar
Bangalore - 560 009

3-5-1129 Kachiguda Cross Road
Hyderabad - 500 027

Prarthana Flats, 2nd Floor
Near Thakore Baug, Navrangpura
Ahmedabad - 380 009

Patiala House
16-A Ashok Marg
Lucknow - 226 001

INDONESIA
Pt. Indira Limited
Jl. Sam Ratulangi 37
P.O. Box 181
Jakarta Pusat

ITALY
Licosa Commissionaria Sansoni SPA
Via Benedetto Fortini, 120/10
Casella Postale 552
50125 Florence

JAPAN
Eastern Book Service
37-3, Hongo 3-Chome, Bunkyo-ku 113
Tokyo

KENYA
Africa Book Service (E.A.) Ltd.
P.O. Box 45245
Nairobi

KOREA, REPUBLIC OF
Pan Korea Book Corporation
P.O. Box 101, Kwangwhamun
Seoul

KUWAIT
MEMRB Information Services
P.O. Box 5465

MALAYSIA
University of Malaya Cooperative
Bookshop, Limited
P.O. Box 1127, Jalan Pantai Baru
Kuala Lumpur

MEXICO
INFOTEC
Apartado Postal 22-860
14060 Tlalpan, Mexico D.F.

MOROCCO
Société d'Etudes Marketing Marocaine
12 rue Mozart, Bd. d'Anfa
Casablanca

NETHERLANDS
InOr-Publikaties b.v.
P.O. Box 14
7240 BA Lochem

NEW ZEALAND
Hills Library and Information Service
Private Bag
New Market
Auckland

NIGERIA
University Press Limited
Three Crowns Building Jericho
Private Mail Bag 5095
Ibadan

NORWAY
Narvesen Information Center
Book Department
P.O. Box 6125 Etterstad
N-0602 Oslo 6

OMAN
MEMRB Information Services
P.O. Box 1613, Seeb Airport
Muscat

PAKISTAN
Mirza Book Agency
65, Shahrah-e-Quaid-e-Azam
P.O. Box No. 729
Lahore 3

PERU
Editorial Desarrollo SA
Apartado 3824
Lima

PHILIPPINES
International Book Center
Fifth Floor, Filipinas Life Building
Ayala Avenue, Makati
Metro Manila

POLAND
ORPAN
Palac Kultury i Nauki
00-901 Warszawa

PORTUGAL
Livraria Portugal
Rua Do Carmo 70-74
1200 Lisbon

SAUDI ARABIA, QATAR
Jarir Book Store
P.O. Box 3196
Riyadh 11471

MEMRB Information Services
Branch offices:
Al Alsa Street
Al Dahna Center
First Floor
P.O. Box 7188
Riyadh

Haji Abdullah Alireza Building
King Khaled Street
P.O. Box 3969
Dammam

33, Mohammed Hassan Awad Street
P.O. Box 5978
Jeddah

SINGAPORE, TAIWAN, MYANMAR, BRUNEI
Information Publications
Private, Ltd.
02-06 1st Fl., Pei-Fu Industrial
Bldg.
24 New Industrial Road
Singapore 1953

SOUTH AFRICA, BOTSWANA
For single titles:
Oxford University Press
Southern Africa
P.O. Box 1141
Cape Town 8000

For subscription orders:
International Subscription Service
P.O. Box 41095
Craighall
Johannesburg 2024

SPAIN
Mundi-Prensa Libros, S.A.
Castello 37
28001 Madrid

Libreria Internacional AEDOS
Consell de Cent, 391
08009 Barcelona

SRI LANKA AND THE MALDIVES
Lake House Bookshop
P.O. Box 244
100, Sir Chittampalam A.
Gardiner Mawatha
Colombo 2

SWEDEN
For single titles:
Fritzes Fackboksforetaget
Regeringsgatan 12, Box 16356
S-103 27 Stockholm

For subscription orders:
Wennergren-Williams AB
Box 30004
S-104 25 Stockholm

SWITZERLAND
For single titles:
Librairie Payot
6, rue Grenus
Case postale 381
CH 1211 Geneva 11

For subscription orders:
Librairie Payot
Service des Abonnements
Case postale 3312
CH 1002 Lausanne

TANZANIA
Oxford University Press
P.O. Box 5299
Dar es Salaam

THAILAND
Central Department Store
306 Silom Road
Bangkok

TRINIDAD & TOBAGO, ANTIGUA BARBUDA, BARBADOS, DOMINICA, GRENADA, GUYANA, JAMAICA, MONTSERRAT, ST. KITTS & NEVIS, ST. LUCIA, ST. VINCENT & GRENADINES
Systematics Studies Unit
#9 Watts Street
Curepe
Trinidad, West Indies

UNITED ARAB EMIRATES
MEMRB Gulf Co.
P.O. Box 6097
Sharjah

UNITED KINGDOM
Microinfo Ltd.
P.O. Box 3
Alton, Hampshire GU34 2PG
England

VENEZUELA
Libreria del Este
Aptdo. 60.337
Caracas 1060-A

YUGOSLAVIA
Jugoslovenska Knjiga
P.O. Box 36
Trg Republike
YU-11000 Belgrade